European Social Work Educati

CW00419296

Series Editors

Nino Žganec, Department of Social Work, University of Zagreb, Zagreb, Croatia
Marion Laging, Faculty of Social Work, Health Care, Esslingen University of
Applied Sciences, Esslingen am Neckar, Baden-Württemberg, Germany

E A S S W European Association
of Schools of Social Work

European Social Work Education and Practice is a Series developed within the frame of the contributions of the European Association of Schools of Social Work (EASSW) on the current developments of social work education and its links to the practice of social work in a European context. The Series supports the international dialogue among social work academics, practitioners, service users, and decision-makers. The aim of the Series is to provide a platform for identification and discussion of various challenges and developments within European social work. Similar to other professions, social work also is constantly contending with new demands regarding changing fields of work, new financial models, rising competition among the institutions, new groups and types of service users, and many other challenges. All of these circumstances require professionals to be well prepared and to provide new responses on how to work in the context of globalization and neoliberalism while adhering to the principles of solidarity, social justice, and humanity.

More information about this series at http://www.springer.com/series/16359

Marion Laging • Nino Žganec

Editors

Social Work Education in Europe

Traditions and Transformations

 Springer

Editors
Marion Laging
Faculty of Social Work, Health Care, and
Nursing Sciences
Esslingen University of Applied Sciences
Esslingen, Germany

Nino Žganec
Faculty of Law, Department of Social Work
University of Zagreb
Zagreb, Croatia

ISSN 2662-2440 ISSN 2662-2459 (electronic)
European Social Work Education and Practice
ISBN 978-3-030-69703-7 ISBN 978-3-030-69701-3 (eBook)
https://doi.org/10.1007/978-3-030-69701-3

This Springer imprint is published by the registered company Springer Nature Switzerland AG
The registered company address is: Gewerbestrasse 11, 6330 Cham, Switzerland

Preface

The idea for this book grew out of the efforts by the European Association of Schools of Social Work (EASSW) to enhance social work education through numerous activities in the course of the last two decades. The main focus of the EASSW is to promote the development of social work education throughout Europe, to develop standards for enhancing the quality of social work education, to encourage international exchange and to provide forums for sharing social work research and scholarship. The EASSW says the following about its mission and vision: "EASSW's mission is to promote social justice and develop high quality education, training and knowledge for social work practice, social services, and social welfare policies in Europe. The EASSW's vision is Europe as a socially just region with the highest quality of social work education that promotes unity and nurtures diversity." Aware of the need to make a kind of inventory of education traditions and models throughout European countries, we wondered what the best way was to go about it, keeping in mind that it is impossible to cover all European countries. That is to say, as also prescribed by the EASSW's bylaws, "The membership of the association shall be composed of those engaged in social work education within the Council of Europe membership. Members of EASSW can be outside of the countries listed as members by the Council of Europe, where there are historical and cultural links with Europe." Such a definition of the rather broad membership did not allow us to include all countries, so we decided on an alternative path. Specifically, in the conception of this book, we aimed at selecting countries that could provide quality insight into typical examples of various traditions of educational models for social work in different parts of Europe. Aware of the many limitations of such an approach, we believe that readers will still have the opportunity to gain solid insights into what we can roughly call the "European model of education for social work". As can be seen from the various contributions in the book, it would probably be better to talk about different models, but if we accept this difference as a common feature, then this is a certain backbone of the "common model". The book represents ten countries from northern to southern Europe – Finland, Latvia, Germany, United Kingdom, the Netherlands, France, Italy, Croatia, Romania and Cyprus. Unfortunately, despite our efforts, we were unable to provide an overview of two other countries that would significantly complement the overall picture, namely Poland and Spain. We believe that in some future edition these countries (as well as some others) will certainly be represented. We asked the contributors, who are all social work academics, to look at some of the key determinants that affect social work education in their countries. These determinants included, among other things, the following items:

- description and analysis of significant moments in the process of professional social work development in their respective countries
- description of the main areas of activity of social work in the respective country
- description of the current model of education for social work in their respective countries, including a description of levels of academization which social work education has achieved
- critical analysis of whether or to what extent the educational system is able to reflect on and respond to the current challenges faced by social work as well as providing several types of answers, for example: What features should an educational programme have to prepare students for sustainable and responsible social work that is based on human rights and social justice? Are there discrepancies between what educational institutions aim for and what the practice field demands? What importance do social policy analysis and awareness have for the development of critical practice competences of social workers? What meaning/importance/potential has academic social work achieved in this context? What role does or could a European perspective or European organizations and exchanges play in this process? What specifically could students from other countries learn from a study period in social work in this country?

The aim of this book is to provide an in-depth overview of current social and socio-political transformations in Europe and their effects on social work and its educational structures. It elucidates these transformations and structures on the individual level of selected countries and goes on to elaborate a European perspective in this field. Readers are offered insight into the variety of activities in social work and its educational structures in Europe and at the same time understanding starting points for the exchange of ideas, collaboration and further development in individual countries and in Europe.

The authors' contributions point to very interesting national traditions in social work education that are influenced by various factors such as socioeconomic conditions, historical development, key challenges residents face and many more. All these factors influence the development of specific models of education, along with professional, educational and scientific assistance that some countries receive from abroad. With this book, EASSW, in collaboration with Springer, is launching a book series entitled *European Social Work Education and Practice* with the aim of gathering a wide range of knowledge, opinions and expertise, ultimately creating a focal point for the exchange of best practices, theories and empirical data in European social work. We truly hope that the different titles planned for publication within the framework of the aforementioned series will provide comprehensive insight into the state of the art of European social work.

Plans to prepare and publish this book were in the works long before the COVID-19 pandemic. Although a number of changes have taken place in the interim regarding the way education is conducted and in the priority topics dealt with by educators and students (and, of course, social work practitioners), the contributions in this book are not specifically focused on the new normal. Nevertheless, we believe that their relevance is beyond question. The introductory chapter, written by Professor Walter Lorenz at a time when COVID-19 was already widespread, partially resolves this issue and temporally contextualizes the topics addressed in the book. Because the impacts of the pandemic on education and social work practice will certainly be manifold, impact analyses will have to be conducted. Some of the future titles in the book series *European Social Work Education and Practice* will, in our view, focus on the analysis of these impacts.

The editors would like to take the opportunity to thank all the authors for their very valuable and useful contributions, as well as EASSW and Springer for the opportunity to collaborate on this important project.

Esslingen, Germany   Marion Laging
Zagreb, Croatia   Nino Žganec

Contents

Editors and Contributors

About the Editors

Marion Laging, PhD, is a qualified social worker with a specialization in education and many years of experience in several social work fields like care for the elderly and persons with disabilities, adult education and addiction care. After completing her PhD in 2005, she obtained the post of professor for social work at Esslingen University of Applied Sciences in Germany. Since 2008, she has been director of the Bachelor's degree programme in social work and is especially committed to the internationalization of the degree. Since 2019, she has been Vice President for Education and Advanced Studies at Esslingen University of Applied Sciences. As a board member of the German Association of Schools of Social Work and of the Executive Committee of the European Association of Schools of Social Work (EASSW), she is engaged in the further development of social work qualifications at the national and European levels.

Nino Žganec, PhD, was born in Croatia, where he completed the Study of Social Work at the Faculty of Law, University of Zagreb. Since the beginning of his career he has worked as faculty teacher in various positions – assistant professor, associate professor and full professor. The fields of his practical and scientific interest include community social work, ethics and human rights, organization of social services and international social work. He has published in various domestic and international journals and books, participated in domestic and international scientific research projects in his fields of interest, and delivered many keynote speeches at domestic and international social work conferences. He has experience in political engagement as assistant minister and state secretary in the Croatian Ministry of Labour and Social Welfare. During his term in office, comprehensive reform of the social care sector was launched. Since 2011 he has served on the executive committee of the European Association of Schools of Social Work (EASSW), and in 2015 he was elected president of this association for the 2015–2019 mandate. In the same period he served as vice president of the International Association of Schools of Social Work (IASSW). He was also elected member of the executive committee of the European Anti-Poverty Network and president of the Croatian Anti-Poverty Network for the 2014–2020 mandate. His teaching activities include graduate and postgraduate programmes, including PhD programmes in several European countries.

Contributors

Hakan Acar, **PhD,** is a lecturer in social work at Liverpool Hope University in the United Kingdom. In 1996, Acar trained as a social worker at Hacettepe University in Ankara, Turkey, where he completed his PhD in 2006. In 2014, he was appointed professor of social work at Kocaeli University in Turkey. His research interests include street children, child labour, child protection systems, social work values and ethics, and social work education. Acar served as executive member of International Federation of Social Workers, European Region (IFSW Europe e.V.) for a three-year period (2012–2015). He was then elected executive board member of the European Association of Schools of Social Work (EASSW) in 2015 for a four-year term.

Robert Bergougnan, **MA,** is Director of ERASME – Institut du Travail Social (Social Work Institute) in Toulouse, France. He has worked for 20 years as a qualified social worker. His fields of activity are international social work and ecosocial transition. He is a member of the executive committee of the European Association of Schools of Social Work (EASSW) and Vice President of the Conference of International NGOs of the Council of Europe. In his research and teaching he focuses on social networks and interactions of living systems and their effects on organizations, management and collective training in social work.

Teresa Bertotti, **PhD,** is Associate Professor of Social Work at the University of Trento in Italy and previously was at the University of Milan – Bicocca. Before starting her academic career, she worked for more than 20 years in the field of child protection as a professional social worker and manager. Her current research interests focus on professional ethics, quality of social work in the field of child welfare, relations between professionals and organizations, and social work education. She has published across a range of issues related to these subjects. She is a co-founder of the Social Work Ethics Research Group Special Interest Group (SWERG SIG) and a member of the Decision Assessment and Risk Interest Group (DARSIG) within the European Social Work Research Association (ESWRA). She is currently President of the European Association of Schools of Social Work (EASSW).

Florence Fondeville, PhD, is the training and research director of the school of social work at ERASME – Institut du Travail Social (Social Work Institute) in Toulouse, France. She has a PhD in social and occupational psychology. She worked for 10 years as a research trainer. Her research and teaching focus on groups, professionalization and the evolution of social work.

Peter Hendriks, PhD, is senior lecturer in social work and researcher at the Research Centre for Social Innovation at HU University of Applied Sciences Utrecht in the Netherlands. His research focuses on the impact of increasing diversity on social work education and practice. In his PhD research he explored the experiences of newly started Turkish-Dutch and Moroccan-Dutch female professionals in social work. As far as his current research projects are concerned, his interest lies mainly in methods of participatory research, such as with refugee students.

Raymond Kloppenburg, PhD, is associate professor at the Knowledge Centre Social Innovation of HU University of Applied Sciences Utrecht in the Netherlands. His research focuses on educational issues within the domain of social work. The subject of his PhD research concerns a comparison of assessments of social work students in school and in practice. For more than 15 years he was involved in curriculum development, in particular, a generic bachelor of social work. In 2015, he chaired the project 'Common knowledge base of social work education in the Netherlands'. Currently his research focuses on the development of learning networks in the triangle of education, practice and research. In addition to his research work, he is a board member of European and global associations for social work education.

Sanna Lähteinen, MSS (Social Work), MA (Education), has worked as a coordinator for the National Finnish University Network for Social Work, Sosnet, in Finland since 2004. She works at the University of Lapland in close cooperation with all six of the country's universities with social work degree programmes and specialization programmes in social work. As a coordinator for Sosnet Lähteinen she works to foster national and international cooperation at all levels of social work education and is closely connected with national stakeholders in relation to social work in Finland. She has published six peer-reviewed scientific articles and 18 other professional or scientific articles, mainly on the topics of social work education, expertise and client safety in social welfare.

Florin Lazăr, PhD, is a Professor Habilitated at the Department of Social Work, Faculty of Sociology and Social Work, University of Bucharest, Romania. He teaches social policy, social work with at-risk groups, social work research methods and advanced social research at both the BA and MA level. He carried out more than 25 research projects using mixed research methods financed by the government of Ireland, EU, UNFPA, UNICEF and the Ministry of Education. He worked for 12 years as a social worker with people living with HIV and vulnerable children and youth, advised the Romanian government on social assistance reform (2011) and on a strategy for the promotion of children's rights (2013). He is a member of the editorial board of the *European Journal of Social Work* (Routledge), executive editor of *Revista de Asistenţă Socială* (*Social Work Review*), a member of the executive committee of the European Association of Schools of Social Work (EASSW), a board member of the European Social Work Research Association (ESWRA), and President of the Social Work Research Commission of the National College of Social Workers of Romania (the national professional organization). Recently he carried out research on HIV stigma, the rights of children in residential care and the social work profession.

Miriam Lorenz, MA, is a qualified social worker (Master of Arts) with experience in the care of children and adolescents, international youth work and social work with immigrant families. She studied in Stuttgart and Esslingen, Germany, and is currently working as research assistant at Esslingen University of Applied Sciences on a participatory research project with refugees while doing her PhD.

Walter Lorenz, PhD, MSc, was professor of social work at University College Cork in Ireland (1978–2001) and at the Free University of Bozen-Bolzano in Italy (2001–2017), where he also served two terms as rector. He is currently contract professor at Charles University Prague, Czech Republic. A native of Germany, he qualified as Social Worker at the London School of Economics and practised for 8 years in East London, UK. His research interests cover current and historical aspects of European social work and social policy. He was awarded honorary doctorates from the Universities of Ghent and Aalborg in Belgium and Denmark respectively.

Marika Lotko, MSW, holds a master's degree in social work and is currently studying in a PhD programme. Since 2008 she has worked at the Department of Welfare and Social Work, Rīga Stradiņš University, Latvia, as lecturer and since 2018 has been head of a bachelor's degree programme in social work. She teaches several courses in areas such as social work, outreach work, social work theories and methods, social work with community and macro social work. She is an executive committee member of the European Association of Schools of Social Work (EASSW). Parallel to her work at the university she participates in various research and practical projects: her current participation in research on social service provision in times of the crisis caused by COVID-19, recent research in the United States on positive outcomes of animal-assisted therapy with children, and international projects about contemporary families and youth employability. During her professional practice she has worked with victims of human trafficking and different target groups in social services in municipalities.

Steven Lucas, PhD, is a Lecturer in Social Work at Liverpool Hope University in the United Kingdom. His research interests are in multi-agency arrangements for child and family social work and international fieldwork placements and experiential learning in social work education. He has published in *Child and Family Social Work, Journal of Children's Services* and the *Mental Health Review Journal*. Dr Lucas trained as a social worker in Aberdeen, Scotland, in 1987 and worked as a social worker in local area teams in Scotland and in England before completing a PhD at the University of Nottingham in 2016.

Aila-Leena Matthies, PhD, has been a Professor of Social Work at the University of Jyväskylä, Finland, since 2007. She leads the unit of social sciences at the Kokkola University Consortium Chydenius, including bachelor-, master- and doctoral-level education in social work as well as research and development projects. She is significantly involved in advancing the research, teaching and practice of environmental sustainability and ecosocial approaches in the field of social work. She has also been profiled in the research of participation and role of civil society in welfare services. Currently she serves as coordinator of a H2020-funded European doctoral training project, 'Applying Sustainability Transition Research in Social Work Tackling Major Societal Challenges of Social Inclusion'. She has published 74 peer-reviewed scientific articles and co-edited 14 books or special issues. From 2013 to 2021 she was member of the executive committee of the European Association of Schools of Social Work (EASSW).

Ana Opačić, PhD, is an assistant professor at the Faculty of Law, Department of Social Work at the University of Zagreb, Croatia. She is an experienced researcher and lecturer. Her major fields of teaching and research interests are community development, theory of social work and international social work. Dr Opačić is specifically engaged in research on disadvantaged communities, poverty and social services. Alongside research and teaching projects, she is actively involved in developing community-based projects, evaluating projects and providing training in action research for field practitioners. She holds lectures on undergraduate, graduate and postgraduate studies in social work and social policy.

Christos Panagiotopoulos, PhD, received his PhD from the University of Manchester, School of Psychiatry and Behavioural Sciences, in the United Kingdom in 2002. He is currently coordinator of the bachelor and master programmes in social work at the University of Nicosia, Cyprus, and member of the school council. His research and teaching interests lie in the fields of mental health, school interventions and interdisciplinary practice in social welfare and health care. He publishes in international peer-reviewed journals and is the editor of two books, one in Greek and one in English. He is a member of the editorial board of the *European Journal of Social Work* and secretary of the European Association of Schools of Social Work (EASSW). He has served in the position of Vice Dean at the School of Humanities, Social Sciences and Law and has been a member of the senate.

Peter Schäfer, PhD, is a qualified lawyer, criminologist and mediator with many years of experience in several social work fields as in-house lawyer, managing director and consultant, and also as lawyer and assistant professor at the Institute of

Social Pedagogy at the University of Lüneburg, Germany. After completing his PhD, he was appointed Professor for Family Law and Youth Welfare Law at the University of Applied Sciences Lower Rhine in Mönchengladbach. For many years he was Dean of the Faculty of Applied Social Sciences, Speaker for the North Rhine-Westphalian Conference of Deans and Chairman of the German Association of Schools of Social Work. Furthermore, he is head of a public arbitration board on conflicts in the child and youth welfare system for North Rhine-Westphalia in Cologne and also speaker of the German Conference of Heads of the Arbitration Boards and permanent member of an accreditation agency (AHPGS) for the accreditation and evaluation of study programmes in social work, law, mediation, criminology and police science in national and international contexts, as well as member of the executive committee of the World Society of Victimology. His main fields of interest are alternative dispute regulation in social work and criminology and victimology, the effects of law and especially European law on social work and social management, and the development and conception of study programmes and competences in social work and affine studies and their further development.

Lolita Vilka, PhD, holds an associate professor position at the Rīga Stradiņš University in Latvia. Currently she heads the Department of Welfare and Social Work at the university. Dr Vilka is a member of the Council of Cooperation of Social Work Specialists (under the Welfare Ministry of Latvia). Her areas of expertise include social welfare issues and social work education. She has more than 60 publications on social welfare and social work issues in the international and local editions.

Agamemnonas Zachariades, MSW, is an adjunct faculty member in the Social Work Programme at the University of Nicosia, Cyprus. He holds a Master's Degree in Social Work from the University of Nicosia. Currently he is a PhD candidate at the Department of Social Sciences at the University of Nicosia. He has extensive research as well as professional experience in the areas of social policy, bi-communal approaches, migration and social cohesion of socially excluded groups, social welfare and management. His research interests lie in the provision of social services, social policy planning and social work education. In this connection he has participated in various research projects at local and European levels. He has participated in various projects related to migration, education, social inclusion, social orientation and civic education funded by national and European Union funds. He has also published papers in journals and a book chapter on these subjects.

Introduction: Current Developments and Challenges Facing Social Work Education in Europe

Walter Lorenz

1 Europe Under the Impact of the Corona Crisis

This introduction sets out to reflect on the chapters of this volume, a task which suddenly takes on an entirely new dimension, unexpected at the start of this project. The other chapters were all written before the COVID-19 pandemic shook the global society, and now the questions being asked are the following: Are we facing a completely new scenario of future developments in social work education in view of a crisis that has become the hardest test for economic, social and indeed political recovery since World War II? What will social work's contribution be, how can this be furthered through appropriate social work education programmes, and, above all, will this be a task for the individual nations of Europe or does a European orientation count specifically in this unprecedented situation? With respect to the overview presented in this volume, it is interesting to note that significant international surveys on social work education were also conducted in the face of impending or after immediately experienced profound world crises. Alice Salomon published the first international survey of social work education, funded by the Russell Sage Foundation, in 1937, the year she had to flee Nazi Germany, having been well aware the threat nationalism posed to the social work profession, which had asserted its international orientation so spectacularly and successfully at the 1928 International Conference of Social Work in Paris (Kuhlmann 2008). In addition, in the aftermath of World War II, the newly founded United Nations commissioned Katherine Kendall in 1950 to survey social work education internationally, an exercise which was repeated in 1955 and again in 1958 by Eileen Younghusband in recognition of the cross-national importance of social work education in the democratic

W. Lorenz (✉)
Department of Management and Supervision in Social and Health Care Organisations,
Faculty of Humanities, Charles University, Prague, Czech Republic
e-mail: wlorenz@unibz.it

© Springer Nature Switzerland AG 2021
M. Laging, N. Žganec (eds.), *Social Work Education in Europe*,
European Social Work Education and Practice,
https://doi.org/10.1007/978-3-030-69701-3_1

1

reconstruction of war-torn societies (Healy 2008). Hence it is entirely appropriate that this European survey also speaks to the current crisis, which forces us to re-examine thoroughly the principles that guide our social work education programmes. Not only is this exercise of importance for social work educators, but it holds up a mirror to society at large in which social tensions and unresolved issues become apparent, issues which social work must address.

The contributions of this volume focus on selected countries in Europe, and whilst they were never conceived from a purely descriptive perspective but with a view to drawing lessons from the experiences of those countries for future develop-ments in social work education, the current crisis lets us recognize much more sharply the salience of these features of social work and the impending challenges for social work education. Furthermore, the corona crisis has underlined the urgency for social work educators to examine their fundamental understanding of social work, the profession's role in society, its methodology, its theoretical grounding and its political mandate in order to then confront the acute question how to equip future practitioners with knowledge and skills that will allow them to make an impact on the reconstruction of societies. For nothing less is facing Europe and the interna-tional society but the necessity to re-examine its social, economic and political order fundamentally in the face of a crisis whose nature has never before confronted the global community.

References to wars and past pandemics are at least partly valid comparative ref-erence points, not so much because of the vast scale of the disruption caused by the virus but on account of the enormous vulnerability which it revealed in a global, intricately interconnected world. To use war analogy: many societies lacked appro-priate defences against the onslaught of the virus in terms of the lack of medical equipment but above all with regard to weaknesses in their organizational structure and capacity. Something went wrong in the nation states' balanced handling of this dense web of potentially contradictory, economy-driven promises of globalization and of personal liberation. A social work perspective makes the failures that brought about and accentuated the crisis quite evident: it was the blatant neglect of the social dimension of human interrelations and the prioritizing instead of "mechanisms" that were partly determined by economic (i.e. profit) and partly by political (i.e. power) interests, mostly in combination (Lorenz 2016). The central tenet of social work, itself a product and "invention" of modernity, is that "the social" is never to be treated as a (quasi-automatic) by-product either of genetic or of psychological or economic self-regulating processes. Instead, the quality of human social relations can only be established and assured by paying explicit attention to the factors that make possible living in constructive and productive communities. The "capabili-ties" of which Amartya Sen and Martha Nussbaum speak as the essence of a "life worth living" are not innate personal capacities but consist of an array of rights, freedoms and opportunities that enable citizens to "function" fully in society and hence also take on responsibilities (Nussbaum 2011; Sen 2005). The utter depen-dence on others, which humans show from birth, is not organized and secured by any instinctual, innate psychological processes any more than the cohesion of a community or a society is secured by blood relations or by territorial boundaries, no matter how much nationalists operate with this fiction. The capacity to become "social beings" develops through being accepted in one's individuality by a social community is a matter of socializing through education, a matter of providing adequate material resources and of experiencing the "right to belong" in a legal, political and cultural sense. Around this realization and with the aspiration to secure this requirement in legal terms the notion of social justice and citizenship developed in Western modern societies (Lorenz 2014).

An emblematic term that made the rounds during the crisis, both as a safety device and as an unwelcome restriction on personal liberties was "social distancing". Through the ambiguity contained in this (highly inappropriate) term, a pronounced polarization of reactions ensued which demonstrated how deeply the notion had already penetrated the sensitivity of the population before the crisis. On the one hand, compliance with isolation was widespread, but on the other hand, various forms of discontent surfaced, sometimes violently in demonstrations against restrictions of liberty and indeed in riots and attacks on state authorities in the form of the police. Evident at the economic level in the form of the accelerating distancing of wealth and poverty and at the political level in that of the rise of populist nationalism and racism, social distancing surreptitiously had already infiltrated social and political processes under the pretext that "there was no alternative" and that its results were ultimately "in the common interest" (Aluffi Pentini and Lorenz 2020). If the concept and method of distancing become "normalized" after the crisis or in the light of recurring epidemics, the isolation of particular groups of society like elderly people, people living in residential institutions, at-risk buildings or neighbourhoods may enter the repertoire of accepted social and health measures without much debate. Alternatively, the reliance on "herd immunity" (a term with a clear racist history) will deliver the "selecting" and segregating effects quasi-automatically. Without fundamental political revisions the continuation of current policies, which divide further the winners and losers of globalization, will deepen this divide. Despite pronouncements that "we were all in the same boat", life during lockdown brought into sharp relief the plight of unemployed people living in cramped conditions with few outside connections against the quasi-holiday conditions enjoyed by those protected by continued secure incomes, ample living space and unrestricted access to resources.

The Europe that forms the background to this volume is showing its fragility during the crisis very openly. The closure of borders and the prioritizing of national interests, for instance by prohibiting the export of medical crisis equipment to neighbouring countries, were revealing spontaneous political reflexes. It seemed that already in the period before the corona crisis Europe was on the verge of being driven apart not by Brexit alone or by the measures of "distancing" through material and ideological fences which countries like Hungary and Poland were erecting against "external threats", but also by the economic politics which lately prevailed in the EU. The fading of a European social policy agenda which had once been promoted under the Delors EU Council presidency and the subsequent focus on enforcing market principles and fiscal control caused widespread scepticism concerning the state of European solidarity and painful internal divisions in countries like Greece and others bordering the Mediterranean on account of their total blindness to the social dimension necessary for European integration (Streeck 2019). The future of Europe as a unification project and as a sociocultural model of unity in full recognition of cultural diversity will depend on a radical reversal of these policies that prevailed right into the heart of the crisis and which then had to be hastily and provisionally revamped. It is the voice of social workers and others who are charged with low-paid but now glorified caring tasks that needs to count in a more permanent and sustainable reversal of these misguided policies and overall in the reconstruction of the social fabric of Europe. This volume serves to focus on those voices and to chart a way forward for social work education based on the lessons the social professionals are entitled to derive from the experience of this crisis.

2   Educating for What Version of Social Work?

The reports on social work education in the countries of this volume at first glance give a picture of an academic discipline still struggling to find an identity. This manifests in various ways. Firstly, there is considerable variety in the areas of need for which education is meant to prepare future practitioners. In some countries social workers are responsible for assessing people's eligibility for welfare payments and therefore need to be taught corresponding legal and procedural details, while in others this is not considered the task of social workers at all and the focus is much more on counselling, bordering even on or overlapping with therapeutic responsibilities. It seems sometimes as if the area of social responsibilities were defined by so-called gaps in the system, when other services, for instance the medical, the educational or the judicial system, reach the limits of their mandate and people are in danger of "falling through the gaps in the system". This can give social work the appearance of "rescue work" for which, in order to be performed competently, knowledge of selected elements of all these systems is required to make up the curriculum with no clear core subject other than something like "social work principles". Secondly, this is reflected in the wide range of methods of intervention taught in social work courses. Here it is of significance that the methodological "schools" that used to characterize training models and institutions in the pioneering phase of the profession, such as psychodynamic, psychosocial, behavioural or systemic approaches, no longer prevail in these countries, and pragmatic considerations determine the choice of methods presented, with the recent emphasis on evidence-based practice (EBP) making a strong and ominous appearance everywhere in these accounts, signalling some kind of convergence. However, the role of EBP as a guide to appropriate methods has also attracted widespread criticism in terms of the implied narrowing of the whole purpose of methodology to a "what works best" pragmatism (Ziegler 2020). This debate has at least spurred a growing emphasis on research as the basis for a clearer methodological orientation, but this trend again is characterized by a great deal of dependency on research traditions of other, "bordering" disciplines such as sociology, psychology, political science and anthropology. A clear definition of what constitutes specific social work research approaches and social work research fields is only occasionally discernible (Lorenz and Shaw 2017).

This lack of specificity is partly due to a tension that characterized academic programmes for social workers right from the beginning, the tension between the need to maintain an orientation towards national requirements in terms of legal frameworks, social policies, service structures and, not least, cultural factors, on the one hand, and the requirement, if social work were to justify its claim to "proper" scientific status, to focus on universal aspects of human behaviour and of social, economic and historical processes. In this lingering tension, not only is social work's academic status at stake, but the autonomy of the profession from national political and legal conditions is as well, a neutrality which some earlier international programmes in social work education sought to promote according to the motto "people are people". This tension is particularly visible in countries where the impetus for the development of academic social work training came from outside the country, as was the case in most parts of Western Europe after World War II when US, UK and UN "social reconstruction" programmes promoted a kind of standard model of social work, in the form of casework, group work and community work, with the aid of predominantly English-language literature (Harrikari and Rauhala 2018). Similar influences and pressures are reported on more recent developments in Cyprus and in former Communist countries after 1989. In all these cases the attraction of scientific universalism rubs against the need to "indigenize" social work education, as shall be discussed subsequently. Yet the overall impression of the countries under review here is that there is no sign of convergence to a "standard model of social work" in Europe, and the meaning and the implications of this diverse state of affairs need to be considered very comprehensively (Lorenz 2017).

3   Social Work, Welfare Politics and Political Conflict

Therefore, these country reports rightly include very explicit references not only to the national histories of social work education but also to the history of the development of very distinct welfare traditions. The epochal change from traditional agricultural to modern industrial types of societies, which occurred obviously at different points in the history of these countries, had brought with it the necessity to organize and ensure social cohesion and indeed national unity by way of devoting explicit political attention to the organization of social solidarity provisions and, hence, of welfare measures. In this process the three key players that could be entrusted with the primary responsibility for ensuring welfare, i.e. the autonomous individual, the organizations of civil society and the state itself, gave rise to the defining political panorama of major political parties with their correspondingly ensuing "welfare regimes" (Esping-Andersen 1990): Liberalism with its preference for ensuring liberty, and hence also the responsibility of the individual, produced residual public welfare structures in which the state is only allowed to function as a last resort so as not to "pamper" individual citizens and make them less motivated to look after themselves; Bismarckian conservatism stressed the importance of civil society as the primary provider of integrative impulses, emphasizing the principle of subsidiarity according to which the state must always give preference to but also subsidize the efforts of traditional or community-grounded organizations like churches or philanthropic societies like the Red Cross, and indeed the core social unit in conservative thinking, the family; social democracy as the third option declared the provision of comprehensive welfare support to be a public and, hence, a state responsibility in order to ensure the equity of welfare coverage through universal entitlements.

Social workers came to play very distinct roles in the different emergent political systems, whilst at the same time they promoted their international orientation and, hence, the desire for autonomy from political influences. Evidence of this were the lively worldwide exchanges of the prevalently female pioneers of social work for whom this international orientation was particularly important (Hering and Waaldijk 2003; Kniephoff-Knebel 2006). Even as these political constellations seemed to converge recently towards neoliberal principles, which have left a definitive mark on all the countries described in this volume, the traces of these political traditions are still noticeable. References to these established but submerged preferences in political culture serve social workers, for instance, in Finland as points of critique and resistance against the pressure to conform to neoliberal principles that seek to promote "activation" among welfare recipients instead of defending their welfare rights.

Relating current politics and virulent internal conflicts back to corresponding national histories is by no means only an academic exercise for social work educators but is essential for the development of specific competences to deal effectively with the psychological and social implications of these conflicts and their aftermath. This volume contains vivid illustrations of the unavoidable need by social workers to understand acute political conflicts critically because history has an impact on the entire social fabric of a nation in the cases of Cyprus, Croatia and Northern Ireland. The experience of these countries teaches that preparing social work students for situations of acute or latent conflict is not a matter of specialization for those few who might be seeking work in foreign conflict zones or deal with refugees as victims of political violence, but it needs to form a "standard" element of professional competence. Only by learning to confront this necessity were social work courses positioned to effectively address situations like sectarianism and civil war in the case of Northern Ireland. For most social workers in Europe, political conflict has – so far – thankfully been a marginal issue, but this is no reason to marginalize the required skills. The accounts of social workers in Northern Ireland show the consequences of not being able to address explicitly the political implications of those situations. For a long time they were left to cope only by avoiding being drawn into the political conflict and withdrawing into an assumed position of neutrality, until it was realized that this neutrality made them incapable of really reaching clients and their specific combination of needs, which were invariably affected by the conflict (Campbell et al. 2019). War situations are indeed not a hypothetical scenario for social workers in Europe but form part of the lived reality of many, either in open political conflict, as is still the case in Northern Ireland, or in dealing with the consequences of war, as in Croatia and Cyprus and all countries through encounters with refugees. And when we analyse those experiences and the way they were taken up in the various social work curricula at a more general level, we realize that they contain insights and messages for mainstream social workers because traces of political conflict, to varying degrees of visibility, are to be found everywhere in European societies, whether in the form of racism or in that of other forms of hostile exclusion and discrimination, right down to situations of domestic violence, which ultimately also have political implications. These skills will again become particularly acute in the aftermath of the COVID-19 crisis, which has already brought about a rise in domestic violence and will lead to increased social tensions at all levels, for instance in the severity with which racism has resurfaced as an acute issue right in the middle of what cannot be limited to being considered just a health crisis. Social workers operate on the boundary between latent and open conflict because they have to negotiate constantly between conflicting interests. Therefore, an understanding of the wider structural background of conflicts in history and in politics is an essential part of social work education in all countries that allows students to recognize the connection with the immediate helping situation.

4   Addressing Diversity as a Core Strength of Social Work

With these reflections on the tensions and indeed conflicts in which social work is enmeshed, the seeming lack of focus in the contributions concerning the orientation of social work education takes on a completely different significance. Rather than portraying the discipline as "incomplete" and the profession as being in disarray, the reports bear witness to the necessary but difficult engagement with different historical and political processes that is the distinguishing mark of social work. What appears to be a weakness when compared to other disciplines like psychology or medicine, which can be taught more or less according to the same international format and the same scientific paradigms across countries, social work teaching finds its particular strength in taking into account the specific context in which it is being practised and for which it is preparing students. Therefore, efforts to harmonize the appearance of the discipline internationally are not only futile but miss and weaken this distinguishing element of social work. Harmonization was indeed on the agenda of the European Union when it issued a mandate to establish a consortium consisting of the European Association of Schools of Social Work (EASSW), the Formation d'Educateurs Sociaux Européens (FESET) and the European Centre for Community Education (ECCE) for forming the First Thematic Network in the Social Profession in the 1990s (Chytil and Seibel 1999). But the exchanges and discussions over the profiles of social work and social work education across countries conducted by this consortium focused much more fruitfully on such questions as to what can be learned from the apparent different "versions" of social work

operating in different countries and how a comparative European analysis can contribute to national social work courses examining their specificities more critically.
The tensions and apparent inconsistencies one notices when looking over the chapters are indicators of an essential ongoing process of development. External inputs
from other countries prevent this process from exhausting itself in the minutiae of
regulatory alternatives instead of confronting fundamental questions.

In this way, several dimensions concerning unresolved dilemmas for social work
education that span across most of the presentations in this volume can be identified
and questioned as to their deeper significance:

1. There are considerable discrepancies concerning the academic level and status of
   social work education. While there is a universal drive for full "academization",
   meaning access to universities at all three levels of B.A., M.A. and Ph.D., a pronounced dualism persists between "classical" universities and other higher education institutions with a more vocational orientation offering social work
   education in parallel. It is nevertheless remarkable that more and more Ph.D. programmes are springing up, even, slowly, at German "universities of applied sciences". Potentially, this renders visible the specificity of social work as an
   academic discipline, but in most countries that have instituted a Ph.D. in social
   work there is still a dependence on so-called neighbouring disciplines like sociology, psychology or pedagogy. The same applies to the qualifications of staff
   themselves who teach social work courses. The requirement that they should
   have at least a Ph.D. if they take up academic positions, and not remain employ-
   able only as contract staff, is gradually gaining ground, but this does not mean
   that those candidates necessarily have a Ph.D. in social work, even when they are
   called to teach core social work courses. This is particularly apparent in Italy,
   where 30 years ago the professional association had campaigned very strongly
   for social work education to be exclusively located at universities, a demand
   which was conceded but at the price of most of the professors, who had led and
   taught courses on non-university schools of social work, not gaining access to
   academic university positions (Facchini and Tonon Giraldo 2013). There, social
   work education is struggling to assert its identity against the prevalence of professors who represent other fields and disciplines. The question of social work's
   place in academia generally hinges very much on the role practice elements play
   on social work courses, and this concerns not just the quantity of placement time
   included in the curricula but how they can be planned, supervised and evaluated
   to professional social work standards. Giving practice this prominence and linking it so strongly with theoretical curriculum contents, as is necessary for a pro-
   fessionalizing degree, often jars with academic expectations, even though other
   disciplines like medicine or economics make the same claims. Placements that
   are structured and designed properly so that they help students to reach standards
   of professional accountability are very labour intensive and, hence, costly to the
   university as they require extra staff for supervision in addition to the tutors
   appointed in the respective agencies and extensive written reports. Furthermore,

the results of placements are not easy to quantify and to put in relation to academic subjects concerning the award of credit points within the Bologna Process.

Nevertheless, for a number of countries where social work was in the process of being established as an academic discipline, the Bologna Process was a useful vehicle for achieving full integration into academic structures, for meeting formal requirements and for justifying the minimum length of social work education. This helped social work education, for instance, in the UK to finally achieve the minimum of a three-year B.A. programme in 2003. However, the rigid adherence to the rule of 3 + 2-year cycles also meant that, for instance, Finland had to split its integrated 5-year programme into two phases, and there was resistance also in countries like Romania and Germany against this standardization. Overall, the idea that all university courses should conform to a three-year cycle with the pre-defined levels of competence laid down in the Dublin Descriptors became accepted, but uncertainty remained as to whether the qualifying level for social work should be the B.A. or the M.A. In view of the growing demands on the social work profession arising from ever more complex situations of need, it is really not possible to cover all fields of practice and all methods at the undergraduate level. Yet without adequate funding and support from employers, students enrol for specialized M.A. courses and indeed Ph.D. programmes more or less only at their own expense, which means that most students seek work already after the B.A. and employers correspondingly do not generally recognize a higher qualification in terms of higher salary levels.

2. This relates to the question, which features in all the reports, whether there is scope for specialization in undergraduate courses. Some countries have always emphasized the generic nature of social work training that would allow graduates to find employment in a variety of fields and learn the required specialized skills "on the job". Others, however, maintained separate avenues of specialization right from the beginning. The Netherlands is an interesting example in this regard because it went through phases of merging the separate training strands and then more recently differentiating them again in the latter stages of undergraduate courses into "Social Work and Community Development and Inclusive Society", "Social Work and Health Care" and "Social Work and Youth Professionals". But despite these attempts at grouping training around such pre-defined areas, the various fields of social work practice are differentiating more and more, if one considers the impact of legislation alone in areas like psychiatry or child protection. Yet there simply is not enough space in undergraduate courses to accommodate more than an overview of fields like family work, medical or psychiatric social work, disability, probation, and work in educational settings, to say nothing of community work or community action or work in crisis situations such as with refugees or in the current pandemic. Furthermore, it appears to be a paradoxical consequence of the trend towards EBP that the idea of an organically structured build-up of knowledge and skills, starting with a generic core and branching out into ever more specialized fields of practice and methods, is disappearing – which is paradoxical because natural sciences organize epistemologies exactly in such an hierarchical way. At the academic level in human

sciences, this departure from a pattern of core and specialized methodology fields can be attributed to the impact of postmodernism and its critique of "dominant narratives". At the practice level, agency policies swing towards demanding a "what works best" pragmatism for which evidence-based models, grounded in empirical research, form the foundation in parallel with such developments in medicine. It appears, however, that there is widespread scepticism among social work educators, for instance in Germany and the UK, that this trend could enforce "technocratization" and force social workers to focus too much on individual cases and human behaviour as the sole cause of social problems. There are also concerns that a full critical debate on what constitutes "evidence" and how it actually needs to be derived from specific social work forms of practice research (Uggerhøj 2011) cannot be included in B.A. programmes so that students become more dependent on following rules and regulations when they start working in the various types of agencies. Course developments in the UK are telling in this regard because training for the Probation Service in England and Wales was completely separated out from mainstream social work education in the 1990s for political motives that sought to promote a more punitive approach to offenders. Social work courses contained too much critical content for UK governments intent on providing quick and "cost-effective" solutions to social problems, for which purpose also "fast-track" postgraduate qualifying programmes were implemented in England for child and family and for mental health social workers.

3. This in turn points to another fundamental ambiguity of social work and social work education that comes out in the current overview, namely the tension between academic and professional autonomy on the one hand and state influence or agency pressure on the other. "Traditionally" professional training should closely relate to practice in the form of agency placements, but the performance level of students was always to be assessed by a representative of the academic institution independently of the fieldwork provider. This principle applied also to "in-service" training routes where students attended university while being employed part-time and where placements and skills assessments outside the employing agency were mandatory. There are indications that employers (supported by governments, particularly in the UK and the Netherlands) have recently pushed for more influence over placement and indeed academic curriculum contents with the argument that employers require a focus on technical-instrumental qualifications. The Land Baden-Württemberg in Germany operated for quite some time with the vocational model of "*Berufsakademien*", where students remained in employment throughout their studies and were assessed on their agency performance (Wendt 1981). In conjunction with this, England is challenging the autonomy of university courses further by promoting competition through private training providers with all the subsequent problems for students of gaining recognition for their qualifications outside England and even by the regulatory "Care Councils" of the other nations of the UK, Wales, Scotland and Northern Ireland.

4. Much of this hinges on the issue of the accreditation of academic courses. In countries where this is a matter for an organ of the state, the effects of political prioritizing and lobbying are substantial. Where this responsibility is delegated to a body of the relevant professional association, more autonomy or practice orientation can result. Where it is left to academic organs entirely there is a danger of academic and professional or agency interests clashing, with the result that when curricula become too "academic", employers gain more power over what graduates they want to recruit for particular services. The professional quality of training is, however, not so much a matter of the procedural organization of accreditation but of contents, which have been formulated, for instance, in the form of a "qualifications framework" agreed between the academies and representatives of the profession, as was recently negotiated in Germany. Where this has not been achieved, there is a tendency, particularly in the wake of privatization in both the service delivery and the education arenas, whereby differences in titles and qualifications grow wildly. This seems to be the case, for instance, in Latvia, where, in parallel with social workers, professions like "social rehabilitators", "organizers of social benefits", "social carers" and even "charity (Caritas) social workers" have sprung up. But progress can be made only when all the stakeholders in professional social work education are brought together rather than leaving quality control to one of the institutions alone.

5. A separate but related issue is the professional registration of social work graduates as a pre-condition for employment in designated social work positions. Here again a tension remains largely unresolved between the following positions: professional interests, often arising from the example of other professions like psychology or medicine, which through their "guilds" had managed to establish a high degree of autonomy and control over access to their professions with corresponding political clout; academic interests that may regard registration as a restriction on research-based innovation, with the risk, however, that completing a university degree does not guarantee automatic admission to the professional register; wider political interests that seek to either abolish registration and leave the question of employability to the free labour market and its changing demands or exercise influence over the profession by imposing ideological registration conditions. Keeping a professional register is certainly a means of ensuring quality of service and of holding licensed professionals to account for their practice, but this very much depends, for instance, on the continued updating of skills and how cases of malpractice are handled. The risk of "de-professionalization" of social work, mentioned in several of the reports, seems to arise not so much from the absence or weakness of registration provisions but from the tendency towards the privatization of public services, which can by-pass registration restrictions by simply re-designating service tasks to other professional groups.

6. Tensions and insecurity therefore characterize questions concerning the professional boundaries of social work very directly and consistently. Accreditation, registration and regulation are all measures aimed at ensuring the identity and cohesion of social work, and many country reports indicate that the "Global Definition of Social Work", devised in the course of intensive exchanges between

the International Association of Schools of Social Work (IASSW) and the International Federation of Social Workers (IFSW) (IFSW 2014), has been used as an important reference point in many countries. At the same time, by comparison with, for instance, psychology, the reach and visibility of social work in society remain vague and its contribution to interprofessional collaboration in areas like counselling, psychotherapy and education is at times contested. Identity confusion is furthermore reflected in the variety of titles under which "social work" is being practised across Europe, and this is not so much on account of linguistic issues when, for instance, the Nordic term "*socionom*" counts easily as the equivalent of "social worker". Critical boundary issues exist, rather, with professional titles like "youth worker", "animateur" and indeed the various versions of "educator", where the case of the boundary with "social pedagogues" is perhaps the best known and least understood. Germany, as the country often credited with having originally produced the notion of social pedagogy and this professional entity well before international influences established the parallel training of *Sozialarbeiter* in that country, has in recent decades made strenuous efforts to reduce the difference between both professions and academic disciplines to the point of using both professional titles interchangeably. Yet other countries in this range of contributions, like Finland, Italy and Latvia, maintain a clear distinction. Interestingly, the concept and title of social pedagogy as a vehicle for providing a professional identity have recently found a foothold in the UK, after years of incomprehension of the nature of "pedagogy" as distinct from "education". Social pedagogical approaches are beginning to function as a means of training the vast group of "care workers" whose training requirements had been largely left unattended and unregulated (Cameron 2016). But this case shows also that establishing a professional identity relates not just to the nature and clarity of a training programme but to the entire cultural and political context of a country in which it develops, and this means that such models cannot be simply "transplanted" across countries. Boundary tensions emerge inevitably for social work as indicators of conflicting professional, academic and indeed political interests and, hence, of the strong links of the social professions, under whatever label they can be grouped, to specific historical contexts, which is not the case to the same extent for professions like psychology or medicine.

5   Social Work Education – Preparing for a Critical and Constructive Engagement with Politics

It is apparent that the tensions contained in the issues listed here (and there would be a whole range of other unresolved items concerning the identity and role of contemporary social work) are not the sign of a profession "still in the making", although in most countries of central and eastern Europe the re-start of social work education is of a more recent date. Communist ideology had either totally suppressed the pre-existing forms of social work and of training institutions or, when tolerating them to an extent as in Hungary or particularly in the former Yugoslavia, had subjected social work to its own ideological ends. After 1989 the question arose in these countries as to the model at which to orient the emergent social work courses, the need for which was immediately apparent owing to the enormous social costs of the radical change in political direction. In many cases, Western educational institutions and initiatives, often promoted by civil society welfare institutions like the Catholic Caritas, offered "development aid" to partner universities in the form of a "standard model of social work" in repetition of the international "reconstruction programmes" for Western Europe after World War II. But it was soon realized that the particular historical and social situation these countries found themselves in not only required considerable adjustments of training programmes to these circumstances, but that this orientation would also benefit from re-connections with pre-existing approaches to social work education. Furthermore, there were initiatives under communism that in fact practised social work but not under this title, in neighbourhood or trade union contexts, whose experience was very valuable for understanding the complex needs of people in this phase of transition (Lorenz et al. 2020). This means that by addressing these particular circumstances, tensions inevitably arose concerning a clear professional identity and a corresponding recognizable presence in the academic context.

But this engagement with political processes can have very different effects for social work. It has been widely reported that there is a risk that the profession is coming ever more directly under political influence. The dilemma is particularly acute for social work practitioners because while social work courses can articulate and teach wider political processes to equip students with a critical understanding of this fundamental dimension of social work, on entering employment graduates soon come under pressure to relinquish their learned critical stance and adjust to regulations and bureaucratic procedures. As a consequence, the report from the Netherlands speaks of how social work courses have reacted by reducing the attention paid to the political dimension of social work, which a few decades ago was a strong feature of courses there.

Taking the political dimension seriously on social work courses means, for instance, preparing students for the extent and the effects of racism and other forms of oppression and discrimination they will certainly encounter and to equip them with the necessary competences to deal with these effectively. Graduates of social work must accompany the most vulnerable people of society in finding their ways of coping with and resistance to this phenomenon. The worldwide response to the racist killing of George Floyd, a black citizen, in the US by a white police officer in the middle of the corona crisis has demonstrated that racism is not a phenomenon confined to the US or to countries with a high diversity of ethnicities. The global crisis has in many countries exposed glaring and systemic injustices which require addressing at the level of both personal relationships and, above all, legal and material entitlements. This divisive social and political issue shows that social work skills and academic training cannot be divided into disciplinary compartments so that professional attention would be more clearly directed to the personal or the political level. Instead, it requires sophisticated political and sociological analysis combined with a clear vocational orientation to make practical use of such knowledge in complex situations. According to its professional mandate, social work needs to be prepared to be directly exposed to the contradictory developments of a society rather than isolating itself in elitist notions of professional autonomy, and this social mandate demands that social workers have a wide range of skills, which in turn need to be kept in constant dynamic development. Social work education cannot but be interdisciplinary, and in acknowledging this, academics find themselves as part of a broader movement for transformative, transdisciplinary knowledge creation by which leading academics in other disciplines respond to the intensifying requirements of complex modern societies for sustainable knowledge production (e.g. Evans 2015; Lawrence 2010; Mittelstrass 2011; Nowotny et al. 2001). Progressive researchers call for a "knowledge alliance" not only between representatives of different academic disciplines but above all between academics and practitioners in order to face up to the current challenges of society (Stigendal and Novy 2018). All this coincides with current trends in social work education when these are seen in a positive light.

The COVID-19 pandemic, under whose immediate impact this is being written, contains the clearest appeal for such readiness to look critically at existing forms of knowledge production and practice frameworks and demands openness towards a transformation of perspectives. It is simply unacceptable that as the pressure on socially and materially disadvantaged families and individuals increased under the demands for "social distancing", social workers and other carers were either ordered to maintain a distance with clients or minimize personal contact with them out of consideration of the high risk to themselves since insufficient personal protective equipment was available. The crisis not only hit the health services in a state of inadequate preparation but also affected social and care services equally. Educational services were more directly compelled to adjust to digital teaching methods that enabled most (though by no means all) pupils to continue with some form of schooling, and universities mobilized similar resources. But patients dying in hospitals or frail elderly people confined to total isolation in care homes in most cases were not even furnished with cell phones that would have allowed them to contact close relatives, let alone being allowed to receive them in person with the necessary protective precautions. In this regard, little imagination concerning of how to address social isolation according to reports from several countries. For instance, these services should have developed new ways of seeking and maintaining contacts with clients in the crisis or of mobilizing extra resources for homeless people other than by the provision of empty low-cost hotels in which they were often confined. The pandemic created circumstances which threaten the social cohesion of society massively and for some time to come, and the social professions and their educators urgently need to prepare new approaches to achieve social justice and equality.

The same applies to the teaching social work courses under lockdown conditions. The teaching of academic subjects generally transitioned to online, like other subject areas, but regarding the arrangement of practice placements in some countries, an extensive discussion ensued as to how to complete and evaluate them. On the one hand, this debate vividly highlighted once more the importance of place-ments for the professionalization of courses and, on the other hand, rarely led to imaginative ways of adjusting practice to prevailing special conditions. The prom-ises and limits of digitalizing social work courses became apparent, but the overall learning opportunities were not used fully, for instance in terms of assessing stu-dents' abilities to deal with crises, to overcome communication difficulties or to reflect systematically on practice situations, perhaps using the old-fashioned "pro-cess recording" method. Courses could emphasise more reflection on how the crisis affected students as people and as practitioners themselves. Facing emergency con-ditions of such magnitude would offer ample opportunities to re-think how to make social services more widely available to citizens and to experiment with new types of interventions in crisis situations. Where this happened, as in the case of Croatia, it became possible through close collaboration between students and lecturers in the form of webinars and of taking shared responsibility for continuing the learning process. Yet in view of all those protective emergency measures the fact remains that social work service delivery depends on face-to-face contact and communica-tion, no matter how much of the work can be done over distance via digital media.

The fundamental agenda of this volume, and the larger publication series, is to demonstrate how detailed knowledge concerning the way social work is being taught and practised in different European countries today constitutes a valuable resource which educators and practitioners in their respective national contexts can use to critically interrogate their own current state of practice. This is not meant as a kind of marketplace where particular elements of social work models can be exchanged or borrowed to be inserted casually and inconsistently into national cur-ricula. Instead, these insights, systematically analysed, build up to what could be called a "European model of social work", and not as a new standard, but as a shared commitment by social work educators to realize what it means to work within a wider European tradition and by practitioners to question critically the national con-straints on their practice from the wider European perspective (Kessl et al. 2020).

Europe urgently needs a social agenda and social policies in order to transcend the divisions which have caused so much war and suffering in its common history. However, transcending divisions and promoting social solidarity, particularly in the times after the corona crisis and in view of the crisis of the European unification project, does not mean levelling the cultural and political differences between coun-tries but rather understanding and recognizing differences in national and indeed regional and local cultures from a critical perspective that upholds the principles of justice and equality. Secure national, just as much as secure personal, identities are never the result of the hostile rejection of all that is "foreign" but, on the contrary, spring from the openness towards diversity in the process of a critical examination of what constitutes one's uniqueness. Social work is concerned with fostering these processes as its core competence and therefore has an important role to play in over-coming the divisions that currently threaten to divide Europe and to render European citizens ever more insecure. The concern for stable, confident social relations requires the kind of highly sophisticated, research-based education effort that is going on in all parts of Europe, as evidenced by these contributions.

References

Aluffi Pentini, A., & Lorenz, W. (2020). The Corona crisis and the erosion of 'the social' – Giving a decisive voice to the social professions. *European Journal of Social Work*. https://doi.org/1 0.1080/13691457.2020.1783215.

Cameron, C. (2016). Social pedagogy in the UK today: Findings from evaluations of training and development initiatives. *Pedagogía Social/Journal of Research in Social Pedagogy, 27*. Retrieved from https://recyt.fecyt.es/index.php/PSRI/article/view/44163.

Campbell, J., Ioakimidis, V., & Maglajlic, R. A. (2019). Social work for critical peace: A comparative approach to understanding social work and political conflict. *European Journal of Social Work, 22*(6), 1073–1084.

Chytil, O., & Seibel, F. W. (Eds.). (1999). *European dimensions in training and practice of social profession*. Boskovice: ECSPRESS-Edition.

Esping-Andersen, G. (1990). *The three worlds of welfare capitalism*. Princeton: Princeton University Press.

Evans, T. L. (2015). Transdisciplinary collaborations for sustainability education: Institutional and intragroup challenges and opportunities. *Policy Futures in Education, 15*(1), 70–97.

Facchini, C., & Tonon Giraldo, S. (2013). The university training of social workers: Elements of innovation, positive and critical aspects in the case of Italy. *The British Journal of Social Work, 43*(4), 667–684.

Harrikari, T., & Rauhala, P.-L. (2018). *Towards glocal social work in the era of compressed modernity: Towards an era of distorted modernity*. London: Routledge.

Healy, L. M. (2008). *International social work: Professional action in an interdependent world*. Oxford: Oxford University Press.

Hering, S., & Waaldijk, B. (Eds.). (2003). *History of social work in Europe (1900–1960): Female pioneers and their influence on the development of international social organisations*. Opladen: Leske Budrich.

IFSW, I. (2014). *Global definition of the social work profession*. http://ifsw.org/get-involved/ global-definition-of-social-work. Accessed 6 May 2020.

Kessl, F., Lorenz, W., Otto, H.-U., & White, S. (Eds.). (2020). European social work – An introduction to the compendium. In F. Kessl, W. Lorenz, H.-U. Otto, & S. White (Eds.), *European social work – A compendium* (pp. 9–20). Opladen/Berlin/Toronto: Barbara Budrich Publishers.

Kniephoff-Knebel, A. (2006). *Internationalisierung in der Sozialen Arbeit* [Internationalisation in social work]. Wiesbaden: Wochenschau Verlag.

Kuhlmann, C. (2008). Alice Salomon. *Social Work & Society, 6*(1), 128–141. Retrieved from http://www.socwork.net/sws/article/view/99/388.

Lawrence, R. J. (2010). Beyond disciplinary confinement to imaginative transdisciplinarity. In V. A. Brown, J. A. Harris, & J. Y. Russell (Eds.), *Tackling wicked problems: Through the transdisciplinary imagination* (pp. 16–30). Oxon: Abingdon/Earthscan.

Lorenz, W. (2014). The emergence of social justice in the West. In M. Reisch (Ed.), *Routledge international handbook of social justice* (pp. 14–26). London/New York: Routledge.

Lorenz, W. (2016). Rediscovering the social question. *European Journal of Social Work, 19*(1). https://doi.org/10.1080/13691457.2015.1082984.

Lorenz, W. (2017). Social work education in Europe: Towards 2025. *European Journal of Social Work*. https://doi.org/10.1080/13691457.2017.1314938.

Lorenz, W., & Shaw, I. (Eds.). (2017). *Private troubles or public issues? Challenges for social work research*. Abingdon: Routledge.

Lorenz, W., Havrdová, Z., & Matoušek, O. (Eds.). (2020). *European social work after 1989. East-West exchanges between universal principles and cultural sensitivity*. Cham: Springer.

Mittelstrass, J. (2011). On transdisciplinarity. *Trames, 15*(4), 329–338.

Nowotny, H., Scott, P., & Gibbons, M. (2001). *Rethinking science: Knowledge and the public in an age of uncertainty*. Cambridge: Polity.

Nussbaum, M. (2011). *Creating capabilities*. Cambridge, MA: Harvard University Press.

Sen, A. (2005). Human rights and capabilities. *Journal of Human Development, 6*(2), 151–166.

Stigendal, M., & Novy, A. (2018). Founding transdisciplinary knowledge production in critical realism: Implications and benefits. *Journal of Critical Realism, 17*(3), 203–220. https://doi.org/10.1080/14767430.2018.1514561.

Streeck, W. (2019). Progressive regression. Metamorphoses of European Social Policy. *New Left Review, 118*(July/August), 117–139.

Uggerhøj, L. (2011). What is practice research in social work? – Definitions, barriers and possibilities. *Social Work & Society, 9*(1) Retrieved from: https://www.socwork.net/sws/article/view/6/22.

Wendt, W. R. (1981). Berufsakademie: Sozialarbeiter wie andere auch. Ein Plädoyer für Pluralität in der Ausbildung [Berufsakademie: Training social workers like elsewhere. A plea for plurality in training]. *Blätter der Wohlfahrtspflege, 128*(11), 268–271.

Ziegler, H. (2020). Social work and the challenge of evidence based practice. In F. Kessl, W. Lorenz, H.-U. Otto, & S. White (Eds.), *European social work – A compendium* (pp. 229–272). Opladen: Barbara Budrich.

Development of Social Work Practice and Education in Cyprus

Christos Panagiotopoulos and Agamemnonas Zachariades

1 Synopsis/Introduction

The evolution of social work education and the welfare system in Cyprus is inextricably linked to the country's recent turbulent history. Social work in the Republic of Cyprus, although shaped by the country's turbulent political past and present, is also influenced by Western theory as in many other countries on the Asian and African continents (Rankopo and Hwedie 2011; Yip 2007). In contrast with social welfare, which has a long history (since the late nineteenth century), social work education is still at an early stage of development in Cyprus – an unsurprising situation given that social work practice and education, in its early stages, is essentially a modernist Western invention that has a history of silencing marginal voices and importing, into diverse cultural contexts across the world, Western thinking, primarily from the UK and the US (Gray and Coates 2010). However, if social work of an indigenous nature is to be developed in Cyprus, and a more distinctive identity with regard to academic social work curricula is to be demonstrated, then Payne's (2001) views on social work knowledge need further exploration.

Therefore, in the following pages the reader will learn about the historical and scientific milestones that shaped and affected the development of social work practice and education and understand that social work education is still being questioned and trying to find its place among social sciences in tertiary education.

C. Panagiotopoulos (✉) · A. Zachariades
Department of Social Sciences, University of Nicosia, Nicosia, Cyprus
e-mail: Panagiotopoulos.c@unic.ac.cy; Zachariades.a@unic.ac.cy

© Springer Nature Switzerland AG 2021
M. Laging, N. Žganec (eds.), *Social Work Education in Europe*,
European Social Work Education and Practice,
https://doi.org/10.1007/978-3-030-69701-3_2

2   Process of Professional Social Work Development

2.1   Socioeconomic, Cultural and Political Context

2.1.1   Colonial Period: 1878–1950

In 1878, the British Empire declared and established a British protectorate over Cyprus by entering into negotiations with Turkey and concluded a treaty officially known as the Cyprus Convention (Neocleous 2014). The transition from Turkish to British rule could be characterised as sudden and abrupt without consideration for the Cypriot population (Neocleous 2014). The British primarily sought to declare freedom and justice since the focus of the ex-rulers in Cyprus was merely tax collection and investment avoidance in the development of the island (Neocleous 2014). That was illustrated by the lack of services, such as ports, roads, schools, water supply and other facilities, which could make everyday life easier (Triseliotis 1977). Even though the British administration had a vision of creating a prosperous future by imposing order on the indigenous chaos through formal rule (Neocleous 2014; Levine 2013; Hyam 2010) and the modernisation of the island, investments did not actually occur, at least to the extent that would begin to alleviate Cypriots' poor living standards (Neocleous 2014; Hook 2009). However, this vision constituted the first signs of social reforms aimed at policy formation for the construction of a social welfare model. During the Ottoman period, developments were limited and the Cypriot church was the main provider of some sort of informal social care assistance.

The British administration, therefore, introduced new 'welfare policies' by implementing the Infant's Estate Law of 1894, as well as criminal law, with the aim of strengthening family solidarity (Triseliotis 1977). In the years that followed additional legislation[1] was passed, such as the Children's Employment Law of 1928, the Mental Patients' Law of 1931 and the Juvenile Offenders' Law of 1935. The aim of these laws was respectively to protect female domestic servants from exploitation, provide mental health rehabilitation services and regulate the supervision of juvenile offenders (Neocleous 2014; Spaneas 2011). The end of World War II saw efforts to develop the first Health and Social Welfare Services. In particular, the Pan-Cyprian Federation of Labour set up an infant welfare centre and clinics in the main towns for the provision of free health and social care services (Neocleous 2014; Triseliotis 1977). A few years later, in the late 1940s, new developments in social welfare policy took place. In particular, several projects were undertaken to improve social conditions and promote social cohesion among the population. Systematic measures were specifically adopted to combat poverty, promote human rights and social justice and support community development (Panagiotopoulos et al. 2017; Spaneas 2011).

---

[1] The administration of Governor Ronald Storrs (1926–1932) implemented a number of important laws.

In connection with the field of social services, a more systematic effort can be identified in the 1950s with the introduction and establishment of the first Public Welfare Department in 1952 as part of a wider strategy that would offer psychosocial support services to various vulnerable groups, such as offenders, elderly people, families and children (Stampolis 1963; Social Welfare Services 2003; Panagiotopoulos et al. 2017; Spaneas 2011). The following year, 1953, a public assistance scheme was introduced to tackle the phenomenon of poverty (Stampolis 1963; Social Welfare Services 2003; Spaneas 2011). Subsequently, in 1954, the Children's Law Act was drafted which provided legal responsibility and executive power to the director of SWS to act as guardian in cases where vulnerable children needed immediate protection. Under the umbrella of the aforementioned legislation, the first children's homes, shelters, hostels and related institutions were built. The director of the public welfare department, through this legislation, concentrated executive power to decide on and place children in temporary foster care (Panagiotopoulos et al. 2017; Spaneas 2011; Neofytou 2011). Furthermore, in 1956, a public social officer was set up in an office established in London to act as a liaison between migrants and local social services (Neofytou 2011). All of the aforementioned initiatives of the period can be characterised as a replica of the British system, in which all services to individuals, families, groups and communities would be provided by only one organisation: the Public Welfare Department (Panagiotopoulos et al. 2017; Spaneas 2011).

The department's personnel at that time mostly consisted of teachers, policemen and administrative officers who acted informally as 'social workers' (Panagiotopoulos et al. 2017; Spaneas 2011). They were considered general practitioners capable of delivering a series of services to a wide range of vulnerable groups of people (Triseliotis 1977; Spaneas 2011). The selection process was based mostly on their ability to effectively utilise their soft and communication skills. However, the personnel's competence was questioned due to the increased workload in combination with the demand for effective case management and quality service. A number of gaps and omissions in the service delivery process were exposed. Therefore, it was acknowledged that the recruitment of a more qualified staff and the provision of specialised training were necessary. Thus, it was decided that social workers would be sent to Britain for a 2-year training course, either in social sciences or social administration (Panagiotopoulos et al. 2017; Spaneas 2011).

As Panagiotopoulos et al. (2017) pointed out, the provision of service delivery and social work was implemented without taking into consideration any of the country's specific indigenous needs. One could argue that the British administration was under the impression that social work is an international or universal profession. By extending this argument, other authors claimed that Western practices did not take into consideration the social and cultural environment. The established social work model was based on universal values, which excluded unique characteristics of the local context (Jönsson 2010; Triseliotis 1977; Panagiotopoulos et al. 2017; Spaneas 2011). At this point it is important to mention that the Western social work model is better characterised as an indigenous model of practice, rather than a universal one, which does not incorporate the wide range of worldviews and different discourses applicable to all regions (Spaneas 2011; Brydon 2011). Western social work education is mainly focused on the cultural aspects of individualistic communities, whereas in Southern communities, family and collective responsibility is valued more than individuality (Brydon 2011). As a result, the effectiveness of training abroad as well as the mechanisms of transferring the acquired knowledge into the local context could be debated (Jönsson 2010; Triseliotis 1977; Panagiotopoulos et al. 2017; Spaneas 2011).

Nevertheless, outreach welfare services were provided, where social workers undertook the responsibility of performing home visits to rural areas and villages so as to provide access to marginalised vulnerable people (Spaneas 2011; Triseliotis 1977). Moreover, in 1956 a number of voluntary organisations were established and the public welfare department was renamed to the Social Development Department in an attempt to promote and emphasise the need for better community planning (Stampolis 1963; Panagiotopoulos et al. 2017; Spaneas 2011).

However, all of the developmental effort and progress would be interrupted due to the inter-communal conflicts among Greek Cypriots (GCs) and Turkish Cypriots (TCs). When the inter-communal conflict reached its climax in 1958, the British administration of the island under the direction of British Prime Minister Harold MacMillan promoted the notion of segregating GCs and TCs. This attempt was called the MacMillan project for Cyprus. It is worth mentioning that this decision intensified the tensions and deepened the division between the two communities. Moreover, MacMillan's plans included, among other things, the separation of SWS. However, the project never materialised, so Greek and Turkish Cypriot social workers continued to work together under the same roof (Triseliotis 1977).

The late 1950s are characterised as a turbulent period for the island of Cyprus, marked as it was by the anticipated, human-caused ethnic violence among GCs and TCs and worsened after the island's independence in 1960. As Lange (2011: 382) highlighted, incompatible ideas of nation were at the heart of the conflict, with GCs desiring *enosis*,[2] with Greece, and the reactionary Turkish nationalism demanded the division of the island along ethnic lines. As Lange continues, the ethnic violence during that decade took the form of ethnic cleansing and Cyprus became a hyper-segregated island, with nearly all TCs living in one of 45 self-governed ethnic enclaves by 1964. Consequently, the inter-communal conflicts and hostile environment among the two communities overshadowed the efforts and any progress that took place in relation to the provision of SWS and social work.

The next section will attempt to elaborate on the most important developments that took place after the independence of Cyprus by presenting the crucial points that contributed to the formation of the social work profession and identity.

---

[2] Reunion in English.

2.1.2 Independence of Cyprus: 1960–1974

The first decade following independence in 1960 was quite unproductive since the Cypriot government was not committed to the development of a well-established social welfare state or to the introduction of a modern social policy. Furthermore, scepticism emerged around the welfare system as the newly appointed government lacked the experience to implement social welfare programmes (Panagiotopoulos et al. 2017; Spaneas 2011; Planning Bureau 1962; Triseliotis 1977).

The establishment of the Republic of Cyprus in 1960 nevertheless signified the development and drafting of international partnerships among SWS and international organisations with the aim of upgrading social policies, programmes and services for vulnerable groups such as the elderly, children and families, and people with disabilities (Social Welfare Services 2003; Panagiotopoulos et al. 2017; Spaneas 2011). Such partnerships included agreements with the United Nations (UNICEF, UNESCO), the European Council (later on), International Social Services and the World Health Organization (WHO) (Spaneas 2011; Social Welfare Services 2003). It is important at this point to mention that until 1963 both GC and TC social workers worked together despite a recommendation made by the Council of Ministers to separate the social service delivery process on an inter-communal basis (Panagiotopoulos et al. 2017; Spaneas 2011). Eventually, in 1963 Turkish Cypriot social workers withdrew at the peak of the inter-communal conflict and focused on certain areas by maintaining a separate welfare service (Panagiotopoulos et al. 2017; Spaneas 2011; Triseliotis 1977).

Three years later, in 1966, the Cypriot Association of Social Workers was established by the Greek Cypriot community. The primary aim of the association was to provide specialised systematic training to social workers, in collaboration with professionals from Greece and the UK (Neofytou 2011; Neocleous 2014). Subsequently, more social workers were recruited at the Ministries of Health and Justice (Neofytou 2011). In addition, in 1961, social workers who had graduated from Greece returned to Cyprus to be recruited into the SWS. In 1968, the Community Work and Youth Services programme was designed and implemented in order to improve the organisation of communities and voluntary organisations and, thus, to contribute to social development (Triseliotis 1977; Panagiotopoulos et al. 2017; Spaneas 2011). A few years later, in 1973, SWS supported the development of various community volunteer councils aiming to enhance social and community welfare (Neofytou 2011).

However, the devastating events of the military coup and the Turkish invasion in 1974 severely affected socioeconomic life in Cyprus and halted the progressive development of social prosperity. These events defined the history of the social work profession since there was a need for restructuring at a social policy and service delivery level in the face of a sudden increase in need for humanitarian assistance and high demand for social support.

2.1.3 Turkish Invasion and War Aftermath Period: 1974–1990

The war of 1974 constituted an enormous crisis associated with economic devasta-tion, which created severe social and demographic setbacks. The forced displace-ment of people and the severe destruction of the infrastructure caused significant changes in the structure of social welfare (Panagiotopoulos et al. 2017; Spaneas 2011; Neofytou 2011; Parlalis and Athanasiou 2015). Social work as a profession was affected by the political instability and the social crisis which violently dam-aged the island's socioeconomic conditions and welfare state. Social workers were neither trained nor equipped with the necessary knowledge and skills to face this humanitarian crisis and its adverse effects. Social work interventions in resolving crisis situations were deemed necessary. The priority of the state was shifted from social development to social restructuring. The primary purpose was the develop-ment of an organised social welfare contingency plan aiming to re-establish the various mechanisms of the SWS delivery process and secondly to alleviate the trauma of the forced displaced. Therefore, the extreme socioeconomic conditions influenced the evolution of the profession. The phenomenon of forced displacement created numerous social problems and increased dependence on the public social care system (Panagiotopoulos et al. 2017; Spaneas 2011). Therefore, SWS recruited additional personnel as social welfare officers from other non-related disciplines without proper professional qualifications. In that period, there was a lack of spe-cialised social work personnel to effectively address these new and very compli-cated social problems (Neofytou 2011). Consequently, this recruitment policy altered and distorted efforts to shape the social work identity and professional status.

The sudden increase of these new multifaceted psychosocial needs led to human-itarian community development programmes. The consequences of the invasion were reflected through the formation of a new vulnerable group, orphans, who demanded immediate attention. Accommodating and addressing the needs of these children constituted one of the major challenges for the SWS (Neofytou 2011). Therefore, the state assumed exclusive responsibility for providing SWS under a centralised system (Social Welfare Services 2008; Panagiotopoulos et al. 2017; Spaneas 2011). Social workers were dispersed to provide ad hoc psychosocial sup-port services within various 'refugee camps', in collaboration with other govern-mental departments (Panagiotopoulos et al. 2017; Spaneas 2011).

The formation of a centralised system defined the orientation and philosophy of the social welfare service delivery process. This restructuring is very well preserved to this day and has been the main target of criticism. For example, a number of authors characterised this philosophy as outdated and quite ineffective (Panagiotopoulos et al. 2017; Neocleous 2014; Parlalis and Athanasiou 2015; Spaneas 2011). One would have anticipated that the consequences of the Turkish invasion could have led to an upgrade and the evolution of the social welfare system and consequently of social work practice. Nevertheless, due to hasty planning, poor organisation and inadequate knowledge, the developments can be characterised as inefficient and limited. Hence, during this historic period the main focus of social work practice was to accommodate the refugees' needs and support their reintegration process in the southern part of Cyprus (Neocleous 2014; Ministry of Labour and Social Insurance 1980).

2.1.4 Towards Accession to the European Union: 1990–2004

During the 1980s and 1990s, Cyprus managed to bounce back and the economy flourished. Specifically, the World Bank characterised Cyprus as a high-income economy, and it was classified among the most advanced economies. Social prosperity was evident among the various social classes. This positive financial growth was reflected through the implementation of a newly introduced social welfare policy and the adoption of a flexible-distributive model in which the state generously offered social welfare benefits to the wider public (Panagiotopoulos et al. 2017; Spaneas 2011). In particular, the Law on State Aid and Services was amended in 1991 to ensure the provision of a wide range of allowances or benefits. For example, the state provided benefits in relation to maternity support, child support, single parent support, disability support, elderly support, student sponsorship, assistance for asylum seekers and people with international support schemes (Panagiotopoulos et al. 2017; Spaneas 2011). The criteria for providing those benefits were quite flexible, and sub-programmes were created to enhance the implementation of the various measures deriving from the new social policy. Accordingly, under the umbrella of this wider strategy, funds were allocated to NGOs for the development of community programmes and youth centres (Panagiotopoulos et al. 2017; Spaneas 2011). Moreover, SWS were restructured to adapt to new realities and the notion of the decentralisation of services was placed high on the agenda. However, a number of authors debated the extent to which the field of social work practice aligned with efforts to modernise and improve the service delivery process (Social Welfare Services 2003, 2004, 2007, 2008; Parlalis and Athanasiou 2015; Neocleous 2014; Panagiotopoulos et al. 2017; Spaneas 2011). Several obstacles and omissions were identified in the service provision process. For example, social workers faced a huge workload and management constraints, they were poorly equipped to deal with conflicts and set priorities, and they exhibited signs of burnout syndrome. As a result, service users were stressed and frustrated about the quality of the services provided. The service provision process and the behaviour of social welfare personnel were depicted in a negative light (Cyprus Commissioner of Administration 2007; Georgiou et al. 2006; Spaneas 2011). This negative image was, furthermore, promoted in the media (Cyprus News Agency 2011; Spaneas 2011).

A decade later, in 2000, social work academic qualifications were set and defined. Before that, a considerable majority of Cypriot social workers have been educated abroad, in particular in Greece, the UK and the US (Panagiotopoulos et al. 2017; Spaneas 2011). As Triseliotis (1977) points out, by 1974 only a third of social workers received higher education, those educational systems and models of practice facilitated their professional culture. In 2001 an attempt was made and the first native social work higher education programme became a reality. It was, however, mainly influenced by the Greek social work education model due to the friendly ties between the two countries.

The delay in introducing local social work academic educational programmes impeded the formation of a Cypriot social work professional identity. In that period, moreover, it is debatable whether any local think-tank institutions supported or explored the complex social conditions and cultural aspects of the island (Panagiotopoulos et al. 2017; Gray and Fook 2004).

After the accession of the Republic of Cyprus into the European Union in 2004, SWS as well as the social work profession made systematic efforts to harmonise its practices with EU standards in such aspects as decisions, directives and legislation.

Any progress made, nevertheless, would be affected severely in 2012, as the island would experience one of its worst financial crises. The gradual reduction in social welfare expenditures, the adoption of a more conservative residual welfare model and budget reductions in social care services had a significant impact on the profession of social work. The period was characterised by a sudden and unprecedented increase in the number of service users. SWS were not prepared to deal with this new phenomenon. The following section will attempt to determine the extent to which and how the financial crisis and economic recession affected the development of social work.

2.1.5   Economic Recession: 2013–2019

One of the most important focal points during the contemporary history of Cypriot social work was the financial crisis and economic recession which commenced in 2011 and resulted in rigorous austerity measures which severely affected the general public (Zenios 2013). However, the financial crisis reached its peak in 2013, when the banking sector was on the verge of collapse. As a result, the Republic of Cyprus once again went through one of its worst crises which was accompanied by severe socio-political and economic implications. To respond to this crisis, additional austerity measures were deemed necessary if the economy was to bounce back. Therefore, a series of memorandums and agreements were drafted and imposed by the International Monetary Fund (IMF) in the Republic of Cyprus. The most important measure was the haircut on bank deposits (Reuters 2013; IMF 2013a, b). These dramatic events were accompanied by a civil shock which caused social unrest and a number of social problems which posed some of the greatest challenges the social welfare system and the social work profession had ever faced (Balls 2013).

To be more specific, that period of time was characterised by a sudden increase in unemployment, a rapid increase in household debt, a sharp fall in monthly salaries, an abrupt decline in gross domestic product per capita, a higher dependence on public benefits and greater job insecurity (Parlalis and Athanasiou 2015; Naoumi et al. 2010). Moreover, due to the economic and financial adjustments made in the country, deriving from the agreements with the IMF, Cyprus experienced adverse changes in lifestyles and significant cutbacks in public funds, such as health, SWS and social protection. Nevertheless, the most important consequence of the crisis was the sharp increase in unemployment, the largest ever experienced in the country, which put people at risk of social exclusion (Parlalis and Athanasiou 2015).

The economic recession revealed the various gaps that existed in social welfare policy. Therefore, the state was called upon to tackle a double challenge: the financial crisis and the ability to provide services to groups of vulnerable people. According to Parlalis and Athanasiou (2015), the 2014 budget indicated a reduction of 13% for social benefits (€832,000) compared to the sum of €962,000 the previous year. This shift to a more conservative coverage model affected the delivery of social services in sectors such as SWS, local authorities, non-governmental organisations (NGOs), and voluntary organisations. In this context, social work had to evolve so as to respond to the newly emerging challenges.

Therefore, in an effort to upgrade the SWS provision, in 2014, the state decided to modify the public allowance scheme and introduce a guaranteed minimum income. The public allowance scheme was characterised as a time-consuming bureaucratic process in which frontline social workers had to neglect other traditional duties of social work such as counselling, case management and psychosocial support in order to satisfy the paperwork requirements of the scheme. This was considered the most important change and had a twofold meaning. On the one hand, the aim of the guaranteed minimum income (GMI) was to rationalise benefits provided to citizens and at the same time regulate public expenditure by limiting unnecessary spending. On the other hand, this new strategy aimed to change the work of social workers by having them assume more traditional social work roles and duties. Social workers are no longer in a position to directly decide whether someone will receive the GMI. Their role became more passive in terms of public benefits, since they only provided recommendations on an individual case basis to responsible authorities at the Ministry of Finance. In other words, it is understood that the role of social workers is largely 'advisory' rather than 'intrusive' (Parlalis and Athanasiou 2015; Panagiotopoulos et al. 2017; Spaneas 2011).

Furthermore, the economic recession severely affected the provision of the welfare state in which social work operates and exposed its major gaps and omissions. To provide a better understanding of this situation, the next section will attempt to define the Cypriot welfare model since it is inextricably linked to the development of social work in Cyprus.

2.2   Esping-Andersen's Concept of Welfare-Regime

In the case of Cyprus, there is substantial difficulty in precisely defining the welfare state in relation to Esping-Andersen's three welfare regime types. Throughout its history the Cypriot welfare state has undergone rapid reforms and structural reorganisation by strengthening its social policy so as to universalise the system as a whole (Shekeris 1998). Initially, due to the significant role of the family as an institution, the state was characterised as a conservative so-called corporatist one (Shekeris 1998). Conversely, a number of authors disputed this categorisation by including Cyprus as the fourth welfare regime in the Southern European Mediterranean (SE/M) (Gal 2010; Minas et al. 2013; Bettio and Plattenga 2004; Kääriäinen and Lehtonen 2006).

In particular, they argued that the description of the Cypriot welfare state could not rely on one pillar only. The SE/M's deeply embedded social features, such as the strong bond with religion, family and clientelism-particularism, are quite evident within the Cypriot welfare system (Minas et al. 2013). In addition, SE/M countries, like Cyprus, are criticised for their institutional favouritism and nepotism. In other words, the state is influenced by the governing party's values and policies, instead of making an effort to address purported gaps in the service delivery process (Minas et al. 2010). Omissions and discrepancies in relation to interagency collaboration, recruitment methods and case management can be identified within the Cypriot welfare system (Adascalitei 2012; Minas et al. 2013).

Moreover, the economic crisis in Cyprus diminished the welfare state by limiting budgets for social spending on health care and education, family and disability benefits, social security and fighting poverty (Minas et al. 2010; Babanasis 2012). Thus, the lack of social policy and SWS is replaced by primary social informal networks, such as intergenerational family and friendship ties (Minas et al. 2010; Babanasis 2012; Koutsampelas 2011; Iacovou and Skew 2010). However, these informal networks cannot provide long-term, steady, socioeconomic support and care to their dependent members. Therefore, such support is gradually transferred back to the public system, which sometimes is unable to attend to beneficiaries' specific, complex and demanding needs (Koukouli et al. 2008). As a result, one could argue that the nature of the welfare system has had consequences in many areas of social work, particularly in the governmental sector.

Consequently, increased social problems constitute an important challenge for social workers. Although social work plays a significant role in the resolution of social problems, increased bureaucratic control over practice and the gaps identified in the Cypriot welfare model prevent and limit scientific social work interventions. Social work personnel of the SWS can be characterised as a 'by-product' of the welfare regime, shaped more or less by the regime's main characteristics, which neglects the profession's scientific value and attributes (Bahle 2002; Munday and Ely 1996). In a nutshell, social work practice is inextricably linked to and affected by the social welfare model in which it operates. In Cyprus it is quite evident that the effects of bureaucratisation have distorted the development of the professional status of social work and at the same time restrained social workers' range of intervention. The next section will present some of the main social work areas as well as the duties and responsibilities of social workers.

3 Main Work Areas of Social Work in Cyprus

The validity and necessity of the social work profession in Cyprus has been heavily disputed and contested by society. Although historically there is some evidence of how social work has contributed to Cypriot society, its projected image, as Lymbery (2001) mentioned, is susceptible to public devaluation of the services it provides. Social work practice in Cyprus has been debated and subjected to public criticism. The profession's claims for professionalism are under threat (Lymbery 2001; Croisdale-Appleby 2014). Excessive bureaucratic procedures have reduced social workers' autonomy, making them state bureaucrats and restricting their traditional duties, roles and level of intervention. The poorly documented for professional autonomy and recognition and the negative depiction of the profession in the media have created a climate of uncertainty and eroded social work practice. This has had many consequences: a notable decline in employment satisfaction, a sharp rise in burnout and the fact that potential candidates of social work studies find the field unattractive (Lymbery 2014; McLean 1999).

SWS are the main provider of social care and the main employer of social workers at a pan-Cypriot level. In addition, SWS are provided at a pan-Cypriot level through the five major district offices and nine local offices in the respective cities. SWS offer a wide range of services, such as the coordination and provision of social services to the elderly and to people with disabilities, family counselling assistance, adoption, foster care and custody, protection of victims of sexual exploitation, protection of unaccompanied minors, and community projects such as state-funded schemes, and are responsible for compiling annual socioeconomic reports.

One of the most important recent developments is the introduction of a new funding policy system, the GMI, as described earlier. As a result of this policy, professionals from other disciplines have been employed to act as social workers (psychologists, sociologists, criminologists). This situation affects the quality of services since these professionals do not possess the skills and knowledge necessary to perform social work interventions, make referrals or undertake traditional social work roles such as advocate, mediator and facilitator. It has been asserted numerous times that the staff of SWS should include professionals from various disciplines. Nevertheless, the lack of professional boundaries, duties and responsibilities hinders the case management process, interagency collaboration and level of communication, thereby negatively affecting the social work development process (Ferguson and Woodward 2009). The organisational structure of SWS, therefore, diminished the roles of social workers by adopting a more bureaucratic posture and promoting theories of maintenance which do not seek to challenge the basic structure of society and apply innovative interventions (Lymbery 2001).

Furthermore, the increased level of bureaucratisation is evident within all aspects of social work practice in the Social Welfare Department. A broad literature review revealed that the domination of strict bureaucratic procedures over social work practice prevents social workers from upholding fundamental values such as viewing each case as unique or committing to social diversity so as to differentiate their approach and intervention methods (Howe 1992; Lymbery 2000, 2001; Wiliams 1996). For instance, the area of social work with families and children, which constitutes one of the main focuses of SWS in Cyprus, is dominated by a defensive need to follow rules by adopting a checklist mentality (Lymbery 2001). In addition, the daily practice of case management is guided by an administrative model, in which work becomes a routine task and most of the time does not respond to service users' particular needs (Lymbery 2001).

At the community level, social workers are employed in a number of programmes that have been subsidised and implemented by local communities and the SWS. Such programmes include multifunctional centres, which provide psychosocial services to vulnerable groups at a municipal level (i.e. the elderly, children, migrants and families). Such programmes allow more flexibility for social workers to take initiative and arrange a number of activities since they have the opportunity to design and implement social policy at a local level. The implementation of such policy is achieved through the provision of various social services with the aim of exploring and assessing the community's needs. An attempt was made to implement a programme under the principles of street social work. However, due to the poor design and implementation of the programme and due to the lack of training and inadequate results to justify its existence, the programme was discontinued. In terms of social work with people with disabilities and the elderly, service provision is implemented mostly by NGOs, which receive state funding (Parlalis and Athanasiou 2015). Social work intervention methods are family-orientated aiming to promote and encourage social inclusion through referrals, networking and interagency collaboration.

In the field of mental health, the number of social work practitioners and experts is quite limited. It is worth mentioning that mental health services are not available in primary care services but are provided via institutional and community settings. It can be argued that the absence of an advanced mental health system reduces opportunities for social work practitioners to get involved in the area (Panagiotopoulos et al. 2017). In addition, social workers, who serve as community liaison between the mental health system and general society and who could play a leading role in raising awareness either at the local (local authorities) or national (governmental policies) level, are absent from the community mental health network (Panagiotopoulos et al. 2017). In addition, social work practitioners are not adequately equipped to address the multifaceted needs of people with mental health disorders, nor are they actively involved in the decision-making process within this area of practice (Amitsis et al. 2009). Even though the effects of the financial crisis signalled the need for specialised clinical methods and targeted community action on the part of social workers, progress was quite limited at all levels (i.e. social policy, education, local prevention and interventions) (Asimopoulos and Teloni 2017). Various authors have observed that several socio-political factors may prevent the population from seeking any sort of psychological support services. Strong adherence to traditional social values and conservative cultural attitudes constitute some of these factors (Kokaliari et al. 2017; Madianos et al. 2012; Onoufriou 2009). To reinforce this argument even further, one major characteristic of the SE/M welfare model is a strong sense of connection with extended family, which acts as a psychosocial support mechanism. It can therefore be argued that the welfare model has restrained the development of such specialised social work methods and interventions.

An additional underdeveloped area is school social work. Only recently (2018) has this area been addressed by placing a number of social workers in various schools at a pan-Cypriot level, under the auspices of a co-funded project of the Ministry of Education. Social work interventions, therefore, are relatively new at a practical level. Social workers' duties include needs assessment, utilisation of diagnostic tools, formation of multidisciplinary teams, networking and referrals in order to prevent, identify and eliminate obstacles that interfere with children's education such as school violence and bullying. Furthermore, social workers in school settings act as a link between family and school.

One work area that has been quite developed is multicultural social work. Due to the increased numbers of migrants arriving in Cyprus, the state has used various funding opportunities from the Asylum, Migration and Integration Fund. Social workers were mostly employed within these programmes to offer psychosocial support services, such as assisting migrants in the social inclusion process.

4   Social Work Education in Cyprus: Is the Boom of Social Work Education Going to Last?

In contrast to social welfare, which has a long history (since the late nineteenth century), social work education remains at an early stage of development in Cyprus. More precisely, the first social work programme in tertiary education was established at the beginning of the twenty-first century. It is important to note that this programme was established by a private university,[3] and even today no public department has been established despite the obvious need for social work education at one of the three public universities.[4] Following that period and with no apparent reason, there seemed to be a boom in academic social work programmes. In fact, the launch of the first programme in 2001 was followed by two more social work programmes, all spearheaded by private initiatives. Despite that boom, still no robust social work education culture has been established. This may be due to the fact that social welfare has never been one of the priorities in the local political agenda. Therefore, the lack of social work programmes until the late twentieth century means that, in terms of social work, the current educational system represents a blend of various educational approaches and models from different educational systems (i.e. British, American) adjusted to the realities of the Cypriot context.

---

[3] Frederick University of Cyprus.
[4] University of Cyprus, Technological University of Cyprus, Open University of Cyprus.

Shardlow and Doel (2002) argue that social work resulted from the breakdown of traditional systems that supported and provided cohesion to social systems; these can include families, neighbourhoods and local communities. This took place irrespectively of differences in the socio-cultural context. The maturity of the social work education system in countries such as the US and the UK had an additional role to play in the transfer of knowledge to individual scholars with different cultural and educational backgrounds. Many academics and professionals in less developed or developing countries have been influenced by the US and UK models, and consequently these impacted upon their own countries and served as models of exemplary practices (Nimmagadda and Cowger 1999). This was also supported by the fact that most countries did not have a distinctive national or regional social work framework (Gray and Fook 2004). As a result, social work theories and models developed abroad were being embraced. While those influences were transformed into processes, they were adopted as a means of coping with the social consequences of accelerating economic change (Walton and Abo El Nasr 1988). This view has led Payne (2003) to argue that though there are different forms of social work, fundamentally they are all the same. However, Gray and Fook (2004) highlighted a number of authors (Hessle 2004) who have pointed to the need for 'liberating' social work from the dominance of Western philosophy. They suggested a number of possible approaches that allow and promote a flexible framework for universal social work (Gray 2005: 232). For those authors, a possible solution is to identify the elements of social work theories that transcend national boundaries. Other authors, in particular referring to less developed countries, take a more radical position (Fox 2010; Walton and Abo El Nasr 1988). They refer to the use of indigenisation in social work. They argue that societies need to define the terms of social problems, religion and social attitudes differently; in doing so there is a need for radical modifications of the ideas, values and methods of responding adequately to their needs and daily difficulties (Resnick 1995; Walton and Abo El Nasr 1988). The expressed dissatisfaction with the imported models is, at some point, transformed into actions towards the adjustment or modification of the incongruous components of the Western model to fit the country's socio-cultural environment and its cultural principles (Ferguson 2005; Walton and Abo El Nasr 1988).

Indigenisation is perceived as a process of developing necessary modifications to enable an imported model to be applied in a different cultural context (Yunong and Xiong 2008). In addition, it is utilised to reach an adaptive balance that fits the political and socioeconomic conditions and cultural aspects in the host country. Although there is no evidence for the need to enact new and genuine models by excluding any previous use of theory or experience from other countries, the perception is that internal (in the recipient country) theory is actually adopted (Panagiotopoulos et al. 2017).

Indigenisation does not contradict the internationalisation effort of social work (Gray and Coates 2010). The latter is understood to be an attempt to extend the sense that the principles of social work, wherever applied, are useful in addressing personal and communal challenges. For Gray and Coates (2010) the solution is to point to the need to promote and support the process of indigenisation along with that of internationalisation. They proceed to discuss the balance that needs to be struck between commitment to a culture and being open to incorporating external theory and practice which can be effective and culturally relevant.

4.1 Professional Practice in Cyprus and Social Work Education Since the 1950s

Theoretical frameworks (Midgley 1981; Yunong and Xiong 2008; Gray and Coates 2010) that developed the basis for indigenous social work underpin the situation of the Cypriot case as social work practice and education have never been questioned since their introduction in Cyprus. The political, economic and social conditions that affected the country heavily influenced the character of the social work profession. There was no attempt to evaluate the efficiency of practice for service users. In addition, the early life of social work education (since 2001) also had a major impact. It is therefore important to understand the link between professional practice and social work education, within the problems and challenges Cyprus is currently facing, so as to develop an indigenous character of social work education.

In an effort to address the observed gap in professional practice because of the lack of tertiary education on the island, social workers were trained abroad. The common approach was to send, on an annual basis, two employees to study in the United Kingdom in a 2-year course in social sciences or social administration (Clifford 1956). Upon their return they would also provide training to other employees in the services (Clifford 1956), acting as trainers. Their education included theories and practices tested and implemented in the UK, but with no reference to the local context. Needless to say that at that time Cyprus was under British hegemony and the socio-cultural context of the two countries was very different as Britain was a heavy industrial society, in contrast to Cypriot society, which was still an agricultural society heavily influenced by Eastern Mediterranean values and principles. Therefore and despite Cox et al. (1997), who claimed that 'the presence of multicultural, multi-ethnic and religious diverse population in many developing countries has also precipitated the indigenisation of the western social work model as well as the authentisation of native responses to the unique social problems of each country (p.2)', academic social work programmes implemented Western theories and practices with no adaptation to the country's needs, in light of the apparent belief that social work is an international or universal profession that transcends cultural differences.

Why did this occur? The unfiltered incorporation of academic knowledge into Cypriot reality had several causes. At the time of the establishment of the first programme there were no Cypriot academics in the field of social work (Panagiotopoulos et al. 2013). A situation very similar to that described by for Greece, where curricula were based on the norms, values and particular social and economic features of some Western Anglophone countries, the academic staff largely consisted of British and American academics, and textbooks were mere translations of American and British books (Ioakimidis 2012). With regard to social work education in Greece, the Royal Decree of 1963 represented the first attempt to standardise the operation of state social work schools, set the required qualifications for academics, establish a clear set of academic goals and curriculum, and establish a framework for student admissions and evaluations. In contrast with Greece, where social work education dates back to the 1950s, in Cyprus social work education begins, as stated earlier, in the early twenty-first century. Despite this initiative, the first steps in social work education were not as imagined. Academic programmes were populated by Greek academics who had retired from Greek social work programmes (TEIs)[5] in the 1980s and the 1990s.

The need for indigenisation (although at that time this theoretical approach did not exist) became apparent, as the suitability of foreign education and the appropriateness of mere transfer to the local context came under question. In addition, social work with vulnerable groups and community development projects was limited, partly because the importance of the family and strong collective (cooperative) bonds were being ignored. Despite the fact that the Cypriot, family-orientated context has traits similar to those of other southern European countries, i.e. Greece, Italy, Spain and Portugal, as defined by Flaquer (2000), the need to develop indigenous social work theories and practices shifted to social planning and advocacy. The question at that time and to this day might be how we can expect to observe and record important indigenous traits in the provision of local social work education at the tertiary level which could help in the building-up of knowledge derived from evidence-based practice and related to the local context. For example, social work programmes along with allied mental health professions continue to offer limited training in the understanding and treatment of NSSI. The lack of mental health social workers in particular prevents the development of such knowledge or the application of existing knowledge in a particular setting.

Despite the need for social work education, the absence of social work in tertiary education also led people who were interested in receiving social work education to travel abroad for social work studies. Thus, from the 1960s until even today, a great number of future social workers travelled to Greece, where the language and culture facilitated their studies. At this point, it is important to note that Greek social work programmes followed the North American curricula and experiences with regard to social work, as the majority of Greek social work scholars studied at North American universities (Kokkinaki 1986). Nevertheless, at the end of the twentieth century a milestone for current social work practice and education was reached in the form of the introduction of the first law recognising the profession (Registration Law for Social Workers 2000). For the first time, a law stated clearly that no one could pursue a social work job unless they held a degree in social work from a recognised tertiary education institution. This law was meant to be the dawn of social work

---

[5] The TEIs have a lower status and are considerably unprivileged compared to Greek universities resembling the divide between the ex-polytechnics (now referred to as new universities) and the older, more elite and established universities in the UK.

education, too. Under the same legislation, the Cyprus Registration Council for Professional Social Workers was also introduced.

4.2   A New Birth: The First Signs of Tertiary Education in Social Work

As stated earlier, prospective social workers had to travel abroad to receive training. However, in 2001 a private higher educational institution established a 4-year B.A. programme in social work in Cyprus. The curriculum was heavily influenced by the Greek educational system as no connection to the principles of local culture or practical paradigms were identified by members visiting from faculties elsewhere, especially compared with the heavy volume of teaching in other knowledge areas. Due to the absence of academic expertise and standing with regard to social work in Cyprus, the programme was run on an intensive model (i.e. blocks of teaching), but local social work experience continued to be largely ignored. However, these developmental limitations did not undermine the overall commitment to improvement in this new era of the social work profession in Cyprus. A boom in the number of social work students was noticed in 2005 when the first programme was officially accredited. It is important to note that no specific criteria were set at the time.

Following the birth of a 'new baby', private tertiary institutions established two new social work programmes. At the time all private universities considered social work a profitable academic sector. Thus, the second tertiary programme in social work was launched in September 2005 and the third in 2008. It was designed in line with doctrinal and operational educational standards. The main intention was to reflect a modern approach to social work – an applied social science with its own principles, values, theory and practice methodology. It took account of contemporary social risks and needs that question the adequacy of traditional policies and promote social policy and social protection, cultural diversity and the empowerment of individuals, families, groups, organisations and communities, while comparing local and international contexts. The programme focused on the combination of international theories and practices in relation to the local context.

Despite the time difference and the way they operated at their initial stages, the the aforementioned programmes gradually influenced the contemporary character of social work in Cyprus, cultivating within it a primary quality of indigenisation in a number of ways. This indigenous character was gradually developed as social work curricula incorporated recent evidence-based practice data derived from local research projects (Amitsis et al. 2009; Panagiotopoulos 2013; Ioannou et al. 2008; Panagiotopoulos and Nicolaidou 2007) and academic literature adapted to the local context. Additionally, social work practitioners were recruited to teach methods and supervise students during their practicum. Social work students attending these programmes have the opportunity to compare Cypriot and international contexts with regard to social work practice as they travel through Erasmus exchange programmes, participate in international projects and have the opportunity to present their research at conferences. It is believed that the development of local programmes and the involvement of a majority of non-Cypriot academics opened Cypriot social work students' minds and helped them understand what social work stands for.

Moreover, new knowledge in social work practice is being produced by scholars in Cyprus. This approach can be seen as one of the advantages of having local social work programmes recruiting academics based locally as they are able to link their academic future with the development of social work education and practice. Most of the research (Spaneas et al. 2012) conducted with regard to social work high-lights the lack of an indigenous character and the fact that social workers need to strengthen their position among other professionals in the health and welfare arena. In addition to research-generated findings, students achieve self-development through supervision sessions and, thus, started to explore matters related to preju-dice and other stereotypes. Additionally, graduate students as part of their disserta-tion projects started to research aspects related to social work practice.

This exchange of mutual learning helped both sides – academics and practitio-ners – to learn from each other. On the one hand, academics who had been trained and lived outside Cyprus became familiar with the local welfare regime (SE/M wel-fare regime), the challenges of social work practice and the culture of the country.

On the other hand, strong links among local academics and the Cyprus Association of Social Workers (CASW) were established in the early twenty-first century. This brought the academic community closer to practitioners. Exchange of experiences through training seminars and conferences and mutual collaboration in research and developmental project activities enhanced indigenisation (Panagiotopoulos et al. 2017). The lecturer-practitioner concept has been developed to combine professional activity in both the academic and practice components of the discipline by integrating theory, practice and the teaching of practice (Jarvis and Gibson 1997). In contrast to developments in the UK and the US, the local social work association does not have the power to assist, advise or even monitor social work programmes in terms of their aims, academic pathways, research output and contribution to local society. This lack of a regulatory body may create gaps in the provision of social work teaching programmes and clinical supervision to practitioners.

In recent years, the type of work described above has been mainly undertaken by evaluation committees of the Ministry of Education, which focus more on the tech-nicalities of programmes (numbers and quality of academic staff, research output and future vision) than on the indigenisation process itself. This fact and the lack of authority of the CASW largely confirm the view expressed by Payne (2001), who claims that 'in less regulated countries with regard to social work education, curri-cula are devised by particular educational institutions, and it is assumed that if their qualification is awarded the requirements for a professional social worker have been met'.

Although methods aimed at regulating and monitoring professional and educa-tional standards are widely implemented abroad, no one can argue that those types of procedures are not beneficial to this process. In particular, in a fast growing system, there is a need for a framework that will ensure the viability and quality of academic standards (Panagiotopoulos et al. 2017).

It is worth noting that at the time of the writing of this chapter, no social work programme existed yet at public universities, an absence that might be interpreted as unwillingness on the part of many governments to invest in social welfare and to equip social work practitioners with up-to-date knowledge derived from studying social work theories and having to experiment in practice. This lack of provision within public sector higher education has led to the development of social work education at private universities, and without the presence of a monitoring body similar to that found in the UK, US or even Greek system. Such a body needs to be established and should consist of both professionals and academics in order to enhance the indigenisation of social work teaching and ensure the quality of the education provided. It has been argued that the development of national standards applied and followed by all social work programmes would consolidate the professional reputation of social work and ensure the development of its distinctive character at both national and European levels (Panagiotopoulos et al. 2017).

Social work education in Cyprus has still not acquired its own defining features in terms of theory and practice, partly because it is still at an early stage of its development. Nevertheless, it has managed to produce enough academic output to provide a solid base for the continued development of Cypriot social work education and training. The gradual strengthening of the use of evidence-based practice (EBP), as presented earlier, in the day-to-day teaching of trainee social workers will ensure that psychosocial treatments and services with the most effective outcomes, as demonstrated by research and practice, will be part of the academic curriculum, and students will have the opportunity to engage with this process early in their professional life (Panagiotopoulos et al. 2017).

5 Critical Analysis of the Educational System: Will Social Work Practice and Education Find a Way to Co-exist?

Social work in its various forms has had a presence in Cyprus for almost 70 years. Its contribution to the growth of the welfare state and especially to community development within rural areas is undisputed. Unfortunately, the lack of formal social work education until the end of the twentieth century led to the overpopulation of social services by professionals who had neither appropriate training nor experience with the wide and complex range of social problems. It is an 'odd' situation that affects the profession and social work education to this day, because of the general perception that professionals in other fields can serve as social workers. Despite the gradual development of the profession through the years, social workers are still fighting to establish their professional identity among other psychosocial professionals (Panagiotopoulos et al. 2017).

Concrete examples of the foregoing statements can be found in the literature (Amitsis et al. 2009), which shows that other professionals, such as community nurses and occupational therapists working in mental health services, are doing what a social worker should do. Similar research findings (Spaneas et al. 2012) show the lack of clarity in the boundaries between social workers and other disciplines.

Askeland and Payne (2006) claim that social work education in Cyprus is founded on post-colonial ideology. Admittedly, social work education and practice were imported from and influenced by knowledge, ideas and practices derived from Western societies, particularly the British.

However, if an indigenous social work character is to be developed in Cyprus, and if a more distinctive identity with regard to social work curricula is to be demonstrated, then Payne's (2001) views on social work knowledge need further exploration. In particular, Askeland and Payne (2006) agree 'that either a practitioner or an academic may examine his or her own views in the light of a new understanding arising from a different culture or knowledge base. This may be valuable even if they interpret the new ideas through an overlay of their own culture, because some material is getting through to affect their existing thinking'.

Besides the importance of organisational politics within social services, social work in Cyprus faces many other challenges. Foremost among these is the viability of social work education in tertiary institutions; the current state of affairs is not auspicious. It is important to note that after 10 years of operation one programme has already been dropped due to decreased numbers of students. Especially during an era of economic and social downfall the assurance of the future of social work education is more imperative than ever. It is a rather paradoxical situation to have a discipline, such as social work, which fights oppression, for equal opportunities and a better world for vulnerable people while at the same time being offered by private universities, which focus more on their income than on whether or not a discipline will survive. Social work education is not as appealing as other related disciplines (i.e. psychology, nursing) in terms of future career prospects. As long as the government does not invest in social welfare, developing an indigenous character of social work as a component of social work education in the overall development of an indigenous social welfare character of a country poses an additional challenge.

Furthermore, contexts such as local authorities, street-based social workers, community mental health teams and schools are some of the areas where social work is still absent in Cyprus. Social work practice and, more importantly, education in Cyprus still has a long way to go in terms of developing its particular indigenous character and maintaining its existence. Nevertheless, indigenisation is a continuous process that needs to take into consideration theories, values and evidence-based practices in relation to the local context and how these three components can lead to local knowledge and innovative practices that have value and authenticity for local practitioners. Based on the preceding discussion and on what Ferguson (2005) claims in his proposal for a multidirectional model where all countries can be viewed as both donors and recipients of technology and ideas, it could be argued that Cyprus could build on that model and gradually strengthen its indigenous social work education and practice character in an era when it is needed more than ever.

References

Adascalitei, D. (2012). Welfare state development in central and eastern Europe: A state of the art literature review. *Studies of Transition Countries and Societies, 4*(2), 59.

Amitsis, G., Panayiotopoulos, C., & Stathakopoulou, E. (2009). *Evaluation of a vocational rehabilitation mental health unit.* Nicosia: Mental Health Services of the Republic of Cyprus.

Asimopoulos, C., & Teloni, D. (2017). Social work and the psychosocial effects of the economic crisis in Greece: Challenges for new radical directions in services, theory and values. *Comunitania-International Journal of Social Work and Social Sciences, 13*(1), 9–22.

Askeland, G., & Payne, M. (2006). Social work education's cultural hegemony. *International Social Work, 49*(6), 731–743.

Babanasis, S. (2012). *Από την Κρίση στη Βιώσιμη Ανάπτυξη* [From crisis to sustainable development]. Athens: Papazisis Publishers.

Bahle, T. (2002). The changing institutionalization of social services in England and Wales, France and Germany: Is the welfare state on the retreat? *Journal of European Social Policy, 13*(1), 5–20.

Balls, A. (2013). *PIMCO cyclical outlook for Europe: Rising political risk and ongoing economic weakness challenge a difficult journey to recovery.* UK: PIMCO.

Bettio, F., & Plattenga, J. (2004). Comparing care regimes in Europe. *Feminist Economics, 10*(1), 85–115.

Brydon, K. (2011). Offering social work education in an offshore context: A case study of an Australian programme delivered in Singapore. *International Social Work, 54*(5), 681–699.

Centre for Administrative Innovation in the Euro-Mediterranean Region. (2004). *Successes and future prospects for the Cyprus health policy.* Report, pp.15. http://www.innovations.harvard.edu/showdoc.html?id=9007. Accessed 22 June 2012.

Chou, Y.-C., Muhammad, M. H.-Y., Wang, F. T. Y., & Fu, L. (2006). Social work in Taiwan: A historical and critical review. *International Social Work, 49*(6), 767–778.

Clifford, W. (1956). *Cyprus annual report on social development for the year 1956.* Nicosia: Government Printing Office.

Cox, D., Pawar, M., & Picton, C. (1997). *Social development content in social work education.* Melbourne: RSDC, La Trobe University.

Croisdale-Appleby, D. (2014). *Re-visioning social work education: An independent review.* London: Department of Health.

Cyprus Annual Report. (1933). *Annual report of the government analyst for the year 1933.* Nicosia: Govt. Printing Office.

Cyprus Commissioner of Administration (Ombudsman). (2007). *Annual report 2007.* Nicosia: Antiracism and Discrimination Authority.

Cyprus News Agency. (2011). *Social worker was beaten by a service user.* http://www.sigmalive.com/news/local/386921. Accessed 15 May 2019.

Ferguson, K. M. (2005). Beyond indigenization and reconceptualization: Towards a global, multi-directional model of technology transfer. *International Social Work, 48*(5), 519–535.

Ferguson, I., & Woodward, R. (2009). *Radical social work in practice: Making a difference.* Bristol: Policy Press.

Flaquer, L. (2000). *Family policy and welfare state in southern Europe.* Barcelona: Institute of Political and Social Sciences, Autonomous University of Barcelona.

Fox, M. (2010). Post-colonialist practice: An Australian social worker in rural Zambia. *International Social Work, 53*(5), 720–731.

Gal, J. (2010). Is there an extended family of Mediterranean welfare states? *Journal of European Social Policy, 20*(4), 283–300.

Georgiou, D., Papadopoulou, A., & Polykarpou, D. (2006). *ENAR shadow report: Racism in Cyprus, European network against racism.* http://cms.horus.be/files/99935/MediaArchive/pdf/Cyprus_2006.pdf. Accessed 5 May 2019.

Gray, M. (2005). Dilemmas of international social work: Paradoxical processes in indigenisation, universalism and imperialism. *International Journal of Welfare, 14*, 231–238.

Gray, M., & Coates, J. (2010). 'Indigenization' and knowledge development: Extending the debate. *International Social Work, 53*(5), 613–627.

Gray, M., & Fook, J. (2004). Issues in defining "universal social work": Comparing social work in South Africa and Australia. *Social Work/Maatskaplike Werk, 38*(4), 363–376. https://www.researchgate.net/publication/238399599_The_quest_for_a_universal_social_work_Some_issues_and_implications. Accessed 13 May 2019.

Hessle, S. (2004). Editorial. *International Journal of Social Welfare, 13*, 277.

Hook, G. (2009). *Britons in Cyprus, 1878–1914*. Unpublished PhD thesis. Austin: University of Texas.

Howe, D. (1992). Child abuse and the bureaucratization of social work. *The Sociological Review, 40*(3), 491–508.

Hyam, R. (2010). *Understanding the British empire*. New York: Cambridge University Press.

Iacovou, M., & Skew, A. (2010). *Household structure in the EU*. Essex: Institute for Economic and Social Research, Essex University.

International Monetary Fund (IMF). (2013a). *IMF statement on Cyprus at the Eurogroup Meeting*. Press Release No. 13/80, March 16, 2013.

International Monetary Fund (IMF). (2013b). *IMF statement on Cyprus*. Press Release No. 13/91, March 24, 2013.

Ioakimidis, V. (2012). *Social work for social justice: Radical and critical theory – Practice – Examples*. Athens: Ion.

Ioannou, C., Shekeris, A., & Panayiotopoulos, C. (2008). Social policy in the shadow of the national question: The welfare system of Cyprus (in German). In K. Schubert, S. Hegelich, & U. Bazant (Eds.), *European welfare systems* (pp. 89–108). Wiesbaden: VS Verlag für Sozialwissenschaften.

Jarvis, P., & Gibson, S. (1997). *The teacher practitioner and mentor*. Cheltenham: Stanley Thornes.

Jönsson, H. J. (2010). Beyond empowerment: Changing local communities. *International Social Work, 53*(3), 393–406.

Kääriäinen, J., & Lehtonen, H. (2006). The variety of social capital in welfare state regimes – A comparative study of 21 countries. *European Societies, 8*(1), 27–57.

Kokaliari, E. D., Roy, A. W., Panagiotopoulos, C., & Al-Makhamreh, S. (2017). An exploratory comparative study of perspectives on non-suicidal self-injurious behaviors among social work students in the United States, Greece, Cyprus, and Jordan: Implications for social work practice and education. *International Social Work, 60*(4), 1015–1027.

Kokkinaki, S. K. (1986). Social work education in Greece. In H.-J. Brauns & D. Kramer (Eds.), *Social work education in Europe. A comprehensive description of social work education in 21 European countries* (pp. 249–278). Frankfurt: Eigenverlag des Deutschen Vereins für öffentliche und private Fürsorge.

Koukouli, S., Papadaki, E., & Philalithis, A. (2008). Factors affecting the development of social work and its professionalization process: The case of Greece. *International Journal of Social Welfare, 17*(3), 216–224.

Koutsampelas, C. (2011). Social transfers and income distribution in Cyprus. *Cyprus Economic Policy Review, 5*(2), 35–55.

Lange, M. (2011). Social welfare and ethnic warfare: Exploring the impact of education on ethnic violence. *Studies in Comparative International Development, 46*, 372–396.

Levine, P. (2013). *The British empire: Sunrise to sunset*. New York: Routledge.

Lymbery, M. (2000). The retreat from professionalism: From social worker to care manager. In N. Malin (Ed.), *Professionalism, boundaries and the workplace*. London: Routledge.

Lymbery, M. (2001). Social work at the crossroads. *British Journal of Social Work, 31*, 369–384.

Lymbery, M. (2014). Understanding personalisation: Implications for social work. *Journal of Social Work, 14*(3), 295–312.

Madianos, M., Economou, M., Peppou, L., Kallergis, G., Rogakou, E., & Alevizopoulos, G. (2012). Measuring public attitudes to severe mental illness in Greece: Development of a new scale. *The European Journal of Psychiatry, 26*(1), 55–67.

McLean, J. (1999). Satisfaction, stress and control over work. In S. Balloch, J. McLean, & M. Fisher (Eds.), *Social services: Working under pressure*. Bristol: The Policy Press.

Midgley, J. (1981). *Professional imperialism: Social work in the third world*. London: Heinemann Educational Books.

Minas, C., Jacobson, D., & Mavrikiou, P. (2010). *Household behaviour and home ownership: The case of Cyprus*. Paper presented at Eurasia Business and Economics Society annual conference, October, Athens.

Minas, C., Mavrikiou, P., & Jacobson, D. (2013). Homeownership, family and gift effect: The case of Cyprus. *Journal of Housing and the Built Environment, 28*(1), 1–15.

Ministry of Labour and Social Insurance. (1980). *National report for the year 1980*. Nicosia: Ministry of Labour and Social Insurance.

Munday, B., & Ely, P. (1996). *Social care in Europe*. London: Prentice Hall.

Naoumi, M., Papapetrou, G., Spyropoulou, N., Chryssakis, M., & Fronimou, E. (Eds.). (2010). *The social portrait of Greece*. Athens: Social Policy Institute, National Center of Social Research – EKKE.

Neocleous, G. (2014). *An account of the development of social insurance for Cyprus, 1878–2004; with particular reference to older people*. PhD thesis. York: University of York.

Neofytou, M. (2011). The development of social work in Cyprus. In T. Kallinikaki (Ed.), *Introduction to the theory and practice of social work*. Athens: Ellinika Grammata.

Nimmagadda, J., & Cowger, C. D. (1999). Cross-cultural practice: Social worker ingenuity in the indigenization of practice knowledge. *International Social Work, 42*(3), 261–276.

Onoufriou, A. (2009). 'Falling in love with someone from your own sex is like going against Cyprus itself' – Discourses towards heterosexual and female-to-female subjectivities at the University of Cyprus. *Journal of Gender Studies, 18*(1), 13.

Panagiotopoulos, C. (2011). Mandatory reporting in Cyprus: Barriers to its implementation and issues for future practice. *European Journal of Social Work, 14*(3), 379–402.

Panagiotopoulos, C., & Nicolaidou, M. (2007). At a crossroad of civilizations: Multicultural educational provision in Cyprus through the lens of a case study. *Journal of Intercultural Education, 18*(1), 65–79.

Panagiotopoulos, C., Pavlakis, A., & Apostolou, M. (2013). Family burden of schizophrenic patients and the welfare system; the case of Cyprus. *International Journal of Mental Health Systems, 7*(13), 1.

Panagiotopoulos, C., Spaneas, S., & Kerfoot, M. J. (2017). Social work education in Cyprus: Prospects and challenges in developing an indigenous character. *European Journal of Social Work, 20*(2), 277–287.

Parlalis, S. K., & Athanasiou, A. (2015). Social work during economic crisis. *Social Policy, 3*(Jan 2015), 73–92.

Payne, M. (2001). Knowledge bases and knowledge biases in social work. *Journal of Social Work, 1*(2), 133–146.

Payne, M. (2003). *Social work: Change and continuity*. Basingstoke: Palgrave.

Planning Bureau. (1962). *Five-year development plan 1962–1966*. Nicosia: Planning Bureau.

Rankopo, M. J., & Hwedie, K. O. (2011). Globalization and culturally relevant social work: African perspectives on indigenization. *International Social Work, 54*(1), 137–147.

Resnick, R. (1995). South America. In T. Watts, D. Elliott, & N. Mayadas (Eds.), *International handbook on social work education* (pp. 65–85). Westport: Greenwood Press.

Reuters. (2013). *Cyprus central bank announces 47.5 percent haircut on large Bank of Cyprus deposits*. Report. Accessed 23 Aug 2020.

Shardlow, S. M., & Doel, M. (2002). *Learning to practice social work. International approaches*. London: Jessica Kingsley Publishers.

Shekeris, A. (1998). The Cypriot welfare state: Contradictions and crisis. *The Cyprus Review, 10*(2), 112–134.

Social Welfare Services. (1998). *Annual report for 1998*. Nicosia: Ministry of Labour and Social Insurance.

Social Welfare Services. (2002). *Annual report for 2002*. Nicosia: Ministry of Labour and Social Insurance.

Social Welfare Services. (2003). *Annual report for 2003*. Nicosia: Ministry of Labour and Social Insurance.

Social Welfare Services. (2004). *Annual report for 2004*. Nicosia: Ministry of Labour and Social Insurance.

Social Welfare Services. (2007). *Annual report for 2007*. Nicosia: Ministry of Labour and Social Insurance.

Social Welfare Services. (2008). *Annual report for 2008*. Nicosia: Ministry of Labour and Social Insurance.

Spaneas, S. (2011). *Social work in Cyprus: The challenge of indigenization*. 9th Annual ESPAnet conference: Sustainability and transformation in European Social Policy. Valencia.

Spaneas, S., Cochliou, D., Themistocleous, S., & Vrasidas, C. (2012). *Evaluation of the Cypriot probation programme with an/or without the condition of community service*. Nicosia: Social Welfare Services.

Stampolis, A. (1963). *An analysis of the industrial relations system, the social legislation and welfare services of the island*. Nicosia: U.S. Educational Foundation in Cyprus and Ministry of Labour and Social Insurance.

The Registration Law for Social Workers. (2000). 173(I)/2000. Nicosia: Republic of Cyprus.

Triseliotis, J. (1977). *Social welfare in Cyprus*. London: ZENO, Booksellers and Publishers.

Walton, R. G., & Abo El Nasr, M. M. (1988). Indigenization and authentization in terms of social work in Egypt. *International Social Work, 31*, 135–144.

Williams, F. (1996). Postmodernism, feminism and difference. In N. Parton (Ed.), *Social theory, social change and social work*. London: Routledge.

Yip, K. S. (2007). Tensions and dilemmas of social work education in China. *International Social Work, 50*(1), 93–105.

Yunong, H., & Xiong, Z. (2008). A reflection on the indigenization discourse in social work. *International Social Work, 51*(5), 611–622.

Zenios, S. A. (2013). The Cyprus debt: Perfect crisis and a way forward. *Cyprus Economic Policy Review, 7*(1), 3–45.

Research-Based Social Work Profession in the Finnish Welfare State

Sanna Lähteinen and Aila-Leena Matthies

1 Introduction

This chapter examines the Finnish model of social work education from the perspective of European systems of higher education. The chapter is framed by the context of Finnish social work education and the development of the social democratic welfare state (Esping-Andersen 1990), including historical dynamics and current challenges. We also address the significance of the scientific discipline of social work and the strong research orientation in Finnish social work education.

In international comparison, Finnish social work education has been characterised as one that treats social work as an independent academic discipline studied at university (Shardlow et al. 2011), follows an integrated research model (Juliusdottir and Petterson 2003), and is developed in the framework of a national welfare state. Thus, social work as a scientific discipline includes all three levels of educational achievement: bachelor, master and doctoral levels. Only those who have studied social work for five years at university and completed both the bachelor's and master's degrees – a total of 300 European Credit Transfer System points (ECTS) points – can apply for a professional social worker's position in Finland (Lähteinen et al. 2017; Matthies 2011; Hackett et al. 2003; Shardlow et al. 2011; Urponen 2004). It is worth noting, however, that in Finland, formalised social worker education started at the School of Social Sciences in Tampere as late as 1942. Back then, the studies lasted two years and students completed a bachelor's degree in social work. This reflects the delayed development of the Finnish welfare state from the

S. Lähteinen (✉)
University of Lapland, Rovaniemi, Finland
e-mail: sanna.lahteinen@ulapland.fi

A.-L. Matthies
University of Jyväskylä, Kokkola, Finland
e-mail: aila-leena.matthies@chydenius.fi

© Springer Nature Switzerland AG 2021
M. Laging, N. Žganec (eds.), *Social Work Education in Europe*,
European Social Work Education and Practice,
https://doi.org/10.1007/978-3-030-69701-3_3

43

poorest Western European country of the 1930s into one of today's leading welfare states (The Guardian 2018; Matthies 2006).

Social workers occupy a core position in welfare state–based systems of social services, and they often work in a multi-professional setting that involves, for example, medical practitioners, psychologists, primary school teachers, practical nurses in early childhood education (day care) and experts in labour market services and rehabilitation. However, significant changes have occurred in social work because of ongoing comprehensive reforms in public social and health services aimed at the centralisation and integration of social and health services. Despite the high level of Finnish social worker education, many practitioners' positions in municipalities remain vacant. A high workload and bureaucratic-managerialist working environments strain practitioners, who claim that they cannot focus on systematic preventive work. This chapter will briefly discuss the opportunities and challenges of the situation.

The curriculum of Finnish social work education places a strong emphasis on research and a research-based understanding of social work. However, a broad multidisciplinary contextualization, particularly within social and behavioural sciences, typically frames study programmes. This chapter will discuss the meaning of the research-based orientation in social work as a profession and the concept of practice research. Finally, we will discuss the significance of active collaboration between the six university schools of social work in the Finnish National University Network for Social Work (Sosnet) that strongly affects disciplinary development, doctoral studies and the recently developed professional specialisation education programmes.

2   Development of Social Work Education

Although there are global standards and a rather broad global consensus on the purpose, content, values and implementation of the education and training of social work professionals, the regulation of the type and level of the degree is left to national authorities (Sewpaul and Jones 2005). Thus, a great deal of variety exists even within Europe (Matthies 2006, 2011). In international comparison, the master's-level qualification requirements of Finnish social workers are among the highest. However, in the Finnish context, this is not exceptional, since the master's degree sets a standard for most of the comparable welfare state–related professions, such as teachers in the comprehensive school system starting from primary school, speech therapists, special educators, psychologists, lawyers and managers of services. Thus, the Finnish welfare services and educational system have developed hand in hand, promoting the professionalisation and academisation of social, health and educational services, which are the most important employers of women in the country (Matthies 2006; Anttonen and Sipilä 1996).

The development of the Finnish welfare state and the formalised education of social workers started rather late, in the 1940s. However, Finland was included in the first record of international comparison of social work training produced in 1927 by Alice Salomon, German pioneer of social work education. According to the data collected by Salomon through her international contacts, a *spécialisation sociale* was established for young women at the Girls' High School in Helsinki, as well as a temporary course on social services by a Swedish-speaking women's association in Helsinki (Salomon 1927: 301). The first degree-oriented studies that can some-how be identified as systematic social work education started as early as 1928 at the Civic College – a public institution of higher education established in Helsinki in 1925. From the very beginning, social work education was thus provided at the university level as a one-year programme in child protection. From 1930 onwards, the Civic College was known as the School of Social Sciences. In 1966, the school was relocated and renamed to University of Tampere (Niemi 1997; Pohjola 1998, 2003; Kemppainen 2006).

The formalised education of social workers in Finland started in 1942 as a two-year bachelor-level degree programme offered by the School of Social Sciences. The programme was vocationally oriented and its main purpose was to provide municipalities with sufficient labour force. Therefore, the programme focused on juridical and administrative issues. Social workers were regarded as administrative officials and as servants to the welfare state and service system, an idea that was influenced by the German tradition of social policy (Niemi 1997; Pohjola 2003; Kemppainen 2006; Vuorikoski 1999; Matthies 1990). On the other hand, in the post-war period, Finnish social work education was also influenced by the US-based orientation toward social casework, especially in the healthcare sector. Along with many other European countries in the post-war period, Finland too was able to send young people to study social work in the US through a special fellowship. This took place especially in the 1950s and promoted a clinical and casework orientation in Europe (Satka 1994, 1995).

In 1975, the Finnish higher education system underwent comprehensive reform, which also elevated social work education to the master's degree level. This enabled social workers to receive a research-based education and to continue to a doctoral degree. However, the curriculum remained administrative and bureaucratic, with the main content focusing on the social welfare system that defined the tasks of social workers in society (Pohjola 2003; Kemppainen 2006). Thus, most of the teachers of the academic subject were still without special training in social work. At the begin-ning of the era of master's-degree-level education, social work was not yet an aca-demic discipline of its own, but instead social workers were educated through specific courses in a social policy master's programme. This solution is rather unique in international comparison, as many countries have incorporated social work education into the disciplines of, for instance, psychology, pedagogy or soci-ology (Matthies 1990; Pohjola 2003).

Slowly, from the 1970s onwards, social work started its process of academisa-tion. The first professor of 'social policy specialising in social welfare' was appointed at the University of Tampere in 1966, and later on, in 1970, the position was transformed to professor of 'social welfare. In the 1980s, social work education expanded to several other universities, so that in the early 1990s, altogether seven

Finnish universities offered master's-level degree programmes in social work (Matthies 1990; Pohjola 2003).

Social work became its own scientific discipline as late as 1994 (Urponen 2004), when a degree programme in social work with a major in social work was launched at three universities (the Universities of Kuopio, Lapland and Tampere). In 1999, the universities of Helsinki, Jyväskylä and Turku followed suit, and this transition was ratified in 1999 by a government decree stating that these six universities had an educational responsibility in social work. The decree also stipulated that the studies comprise basic, subject and advanced studies (approximately 100 credits) in the discipline of social work, including practice education and field placement (approximately 30 credits) and a master's thesis (Pohjola 1998; Kemppainen 2006; Karvinen-Niinikoski et al. 2007).

These main principles were ratified through the Government Decree on University Degrees 794/2004 in 2005 as part of an extensive reform of the Finnish higher education system carried out in compliance with the Bologna Process and the harmonisation of the European higher education system (Karvinen-Niinikoski et al. 2007). According to the decree, university studies are to comprise three cycles. Prior to this, university studies in social work consisted of a master's degree that was taken within 4–5 years and without having first obtained a bachelor's degree. Today, six Finnish universities award bachelor's, master's and doctoral degrees in social work.

It has been argued that the strong emphasis on social policy has prohibited social work education from developing its own characteristics (Matthies 1993; Pohjola 2003). On the other hand, the close connection to social policy supported the position of social work as an essential part of welfare services. This also meant that instead of social workers and social work academics, it was mainly state officials and social policy academics who defined the field and its education. Only after 1994 has social work education been able to develop its own theoretical, methodological and pedagogical solutions and to create a dialogue between education, research and social work practice (Urponen 2004).

Concomitantly with the Bologna harmonisation of the degree system, the status of a qualified social worker was regulated by the Act on Qualification Requirements for Social Welfare Professionals (272/2005). Gaining this status now required a master's degree with a major in social work which basically compelled students to have completed 300 ECTS of studies at the university. This qualification requirement was renewed in 2016 through the Act on Social Welfare Professionals (817/2015), with to the aim of improving the safety of service users and to protect their right to quality social welfare services. According to the new act, all professionals are entered in a central register of social welfare professionals maintained by the National Supervisory Authority for Welfare and Health (Valvira). Valvira has the right to withdraw one's right to practise the profession of social worker in certain cases, for example in cases of criminal offences or if a person is no longer capable of practising his or her profession due to the lack of professional skills (Pohjola 2019). Besides social workers, this act also concerns the registration of practical social service and elderly care professionals.

The Finnish system of tertiary education consists of two parallel sectors: universities and universities of applied sciences (or polytechnics). The tasks of these two sectors are to be clearly differentiated, and each has its own profile and strengths. University studies build on the connection between research and education, so the basic task of the two sectors is to conduct scientific research and use the best results in education. In general, polytechnics are multi-field, regional institutions of higher education whose activities focus on practical connections with the labour market and regional development.

What may cause confusion in international settings is that universities of applied sciences also offer education in social services, but the awarded degrees do not entitle students to the status of a qualified social worker. Instead, the degrees qualify them as social counsellors, who mainly work in the areas of service guidance, institutional social care, social pedagogy and early childhood education. In Finnish, social counsellors are referred to as *sosionomi*, and they are sometimes incorrectly assumed to have studied social work as well. However, the training of social counsellors is practice-oriented, not academic and research-based. Their tasks do not involve decision-making, and in most workplaces they are supervised by social workers. However, this task division is not very clear, and many social counsellors continue their studies at the university to become licensed social workers.

It can be argued that in Finland over the last two decades, the field of social welfare has developed a coherent system of education providing practical nurses, social counsellors and social workers with their own educational profiles and places in the world of employment (Pohjola 2019).

3   Postgraduate Opportunities in Social Work

Finnish higher education involves a system of postgraduate degrees that differs from that of other European countries. In Finland, social work graduates can continue their studies to a licentiate or a doctoral degree. The licentiate is an optional pre-doctoral postgraduate degree, after which one may continue to a doctoral degree. Although the licentiate is a Finnish specialty within the European degree system, it remained in the Decree on University Degrees even after the 2005 Bologna Process. In social work, the licentiate has become a postgraduate degree that qualifies a person for specialised tasks. It is an occupational postgraduate degree that emphasises the academic nature of the profession of social work. Its aim is to enable students to become highly competent within their specialised field. In addition to a licentiate thesis and supervised work practice within the chosen field, the degree entails the systematic deepening of a theoretical and practical understanding of one's specialised area. Research as well as specialised professional studies have thus been an important part of this degree (Vornanen et al. 2007). Social work is not, however, the only field that has offered specialised professional licentiate studies; psychology and logopaedics too have offered similar programmes (Government Decree on University Degrees 794/2004).

In the period 2000–2016, the six universities offering degree programmes in social work collaborated to organise professional licentiate degree programmes in five fields of social work (Hietamäki and Kantola 2010; Vornanen et al. 2007). In 2015, a new model of higher education replaced the programmes with specialisation education programmes. In Finland, universities offer these professional specialisation programmes to graduates who have already started working. The programmes aim to develop students' expertise and competence by providing education based on the research and focus areas of the universities. Only studies with requirements agreed upon in inter-university cooperation can be provided as professional specialisation programmes. Currently, the universities offer four professional specialisation programmes in social work: (1) welfare services, (2) empowering social work, (3) child, youth and family social work, and (4) structural social work. The scope of the studies is 30 credits, and the programme can be completed in 2.5 years while working full-time (Lähteinen and Tuohino 2016).

The six universities also have the right to award doctorates in social work (Karvinen-Niinikoski et al. 2007: 53). Prior to 1994, doctoral studies in social work were offered in the disciplinary frame of social policy and the number of students was low. Traditionally, in Finland, doctoral students study only part-time, which translates into long graduation times. Graduates also want to get work experience in social work before entering doctoral studies. A positive outcome of this tradition is that it may generate topics and ideas for research that might otherwise remain unthought-of by social work academics (Forsberg et al. 2019).

Overall, doctoral training in Finland has seen dramatic changes in recent decades. From the 1990s onwards, doctoral training has been systematically developed with the aim of rationalising it, strengthening its quality, shortening study times and lowering the average age of graduating PhD students. Meanwhile, emphasis has been placed on full-time study and practice that commit students to doctoral training. A significant contributor to the quantity and quality of doctoral training in social work was the establishment of national doctoral schools in 1995. These schools were financed and scientifically evaluated by the Academy of Finland. Thanks to financial resources and active national collaboration between universities, the number of graduating doctoral students increased rapidly. According to statistics collected from universities, a total of 180 people earned a doctoral degree in social work between 1994 and 2015. Of these, 55 graduated from the National Post-Graduate School for Social Work and Social Services coordinated by Sosnet. The doctoral education system has changed significantly since the graduate school reform in 2015, with universities now playing a greater role in the development of doctoral education. Despite this tendency, Sosnet has decided to continue collaboration in doctoral education. (Karvinen-Niinikoski et al. 2007: 53–57; Kananoja and Lähteinen 2017: 495–498; Forsberg et al. 2019).

Currently, students can apply to doctoral programmes after the completion of a relevant second-cycle degree (master's degree). PhD students are selected based on a written application and a research plan. The aim of doctoral education is to provide students with an in-depth knowledge of their field of research and capabilities to produce novel scientific knowledge independently. The focus is on independent research, which is chosen in most cases freely or according to the research field of the supervisor. The scope of the doctoral degree in the discipline of social work is 240 ECTS – that is, 60 ECTS more than in most European countries – wherein the scope of the PhD thesis is 180 ECTS. In principle, it takes approximately four years to complete the doctoral degree studying full-time, but in practice, it takes longer for most students to graduate. Doctoral studies can be completed full-time with a research grant or as a member of a research project. Some doctoral students study part-time while working or while teaching social work at a university. Universities have expressed their concern over the general cuts in research funding. The situation in social work research has been quite grim for a long time, and opportunities for securing research funding are scarce. The universities within Sosnet have collaborated actively to find a new financing instrument for social work research as a part of the national health, social services and regional government reform.

It can be argued that social work education has always faced new and emerging challenges, particularly in connection with the welfare state. The rapid development of the welfare state after World War II has played a dominant role in the development of social work education and professionalisation. The quality of Nordic welfare services is rooted in the high qualification and professional commitment of the predominantly female staff. In Finland, social work represents a core academic profession in social services comparable with the position of physicians in health services. There are also many other frontline professionals in public social, health and educational services who have a master's-level education, for example school teachers and psychologists.

4   The Current Educational Model in Finland

Thanks to government investment, the volume of social work degree students at all six universities promoting the discipline has grown rapidly in the last decade. This has been somewhat controversial, as there is pressure to reduce student admissions in social sciences. Currently, the annual admissions rate is around 350 new students, who earn the right to pursue both bachelor's and master's degrees majoring in social work.

Owing to the popularity of social work as a study option and the high number of applicants, students are selected through a demanding entrance examination process. However, this also in part ensures a low dropout rate and a motivated body of students. The majority of graduates are very satisfied with the contents and quality of their studies (Landgrén and Pesonen 2017: 35–36). Practically all the enrolled students obtain their degree –annually approximately 340 master's degree graduates are granted permission to apply for the right to serve as social workers.

Another special characteristic in Finnish social work education is that universities are autonomous institutions and thus have the freedom to decide on the content of the programmes they offer. Consequently, while general guidelines for the structure and contents of degrees are established by legislation, the authority to define the programme contents and target competencies of the degrees and individual courses remains with the faculties (Lähteinen et al. 2017: 4). This is to some extent inconsistent with the nature of social work education: each university should guarantee its graduates the same quality of education and level of expertise to practise as social workers. Collaboration within the National University Network for Social Work (Sosnet) is therefore essential because it enables active national steering and discussion regarding the structure and contents of social work degrees.

In Finland, a bachelor's degree comprises 180 and a subsequent master's degree 120 credit points (ECTS). To qualify as a social worker, one needs to earn a total of 200 ECTS points with social work as the major subject (Fig. 1). The study

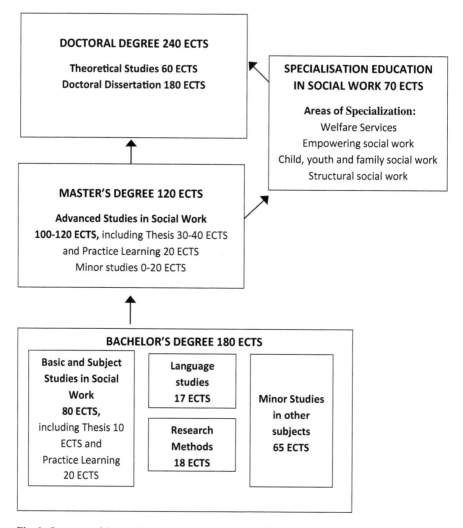

Fig. 1 Structure of degrees in social work education in Finland

programmes build on social work courses and broad multidisciplinary contextualization, particularly within social and behavioural sciences. In addition, there are courses on research methods, languages and other subjects. The degree programme as a whole has been designed to provide students with sound skills and a broad scientific base of education. Subjects that are offered as a minor play a key role because they allow students to complete their studies in the major and to pursue themes reflecting their individual interests and the direction they may take in their future work. The minor studies included in the bachelor's degree are usually chosen by the student in one or two different disciplines (Lähteinen et al. 2017; Lähteinen and Tuohino 2013).

Social work education builds on university studies in the social sciences. In addition to providing students with professional-practical expertise and the status of a qualified social worker, it develops one's academic capabilities and research skills, thereby giving a firm footing in the social sciences. Central to the curriculum is an understanding of society as a whole, combined with scientific, theoretical and critical thinking (Pohjola 2003). Hence, it has been argued that the Finnish system of social work education represents an integrated research model (Juliusdottir and Petterson 2003), where research is integrated into the education programmes. In many ways, social work education looks to the standards of other university programmes, using them as an important indicator of quality.

The Finnish scholar Synnöve Karvinen-Niinikoski (2005) has argued that since the 1980s, the concepts of research-oriented social work and practitioners as researchers have been central to the Finnish debate on social work education. In addition, various concepts of research-based social work have been used recently (Pohjola et al. 2012; Hämäläinen 2014). As social workers practice the only social welfare profession requiring a university-level education, the discipline has a crucial responsibility as regards the creation of research-based knowledge in social welfare and the systematic development of the field (Lähteinen et al. 2017). According to Finnish policy, qualified social workers are to have a master's degree. This idea stems, on the one hand, from the old professional tradition that academic professions are based on a master's degree and, on the other hand, from the vision of social work as a profession that requires research-based knowledge-production and reflective practice- and context-oriented expertise (Karvinen-Niinikoski 2005). Finnish social work education follows this reasoning, although there is a constant struggle for a balance between academic expertise and research skills (Kemppainen 2006).

The curriculum of social work places strong emphasis on research, a research-based understanding of social work, and three practice placements during the programme. Practice education and field placement are a statutory requirement (Government Decree 794/2004, section 15) in social work education, and therefore both bachelor and master programmes contain courses to be completed in workplace contexts. According to an agreement among universities in Sosnet, altogether a minimum of 30 ECTS points' worth of courses involve direct practice learning and field placements. Additionally, during the first year, students perform introductory practice learning (5–10 ECTS) in the field without their own hands-on work input. Thus, the ratio of direct field practice is approximately 30–40 ECTS points out of a total of 300 ECTS points for the qualification of social worker. In Finland, the concept of practice education includes theoretical studies and seminars at the university as well as field placements in social work practice (Karvinen-Niinikoski et al. 2007; Lähteinen et al. 2017). Therefore, practice and academic learning are not actually strictly separated, since the academic parts of studies, especially research for the bachelor's and master's theses, often include direct involvement in practice as practice-research. On the other hand, learning during field placements involves integrating the idea of research-based practice (Julkunen and Uggerhoej 2016).

Students' field placement is thoroughly informed and guided by research, which means that it is an integral part of theoretical and scientific teaching. It follows that professional practices, theoretical knowledge, a research-oriented approach to one's work and knowledge production all combine to form a competency in social work that evolves in keeping with the principle of cumulative and trialogical learning throughout the student's education. Through practice education, students acquire data for research and find topics to explore in their bachelor's and master's theses. Overall, cooperative relationships between universities and professionals in the field are well established, as they have been developed systematically over the decades. Efforts are also made to integrate service users as experts by experience into education and research (Lähteinen et al. 2017; Tuohino et al. 2012; Karvinen-Niinikoski et al. 2007: 36).

The curriculum is designed to prepare graduates for the following tasks:

– analysing and understanding clients' different life situations,
– meeting clients and defending their social rights,
– raising social awareness,
– influencing political decision-making,
– writing reports and other documents,
– planning and leading projects,
– cooperating across multiple professions,
– Judicial reasoning of the field and
– applying legislation (Sosnet 2003).

In the framework of Sosnet, social work schools have jointly nominated the main goals and areas of competency to be achieved in social work programmes. The impetus for this project was to reflect upon the state of social work education at Finnish universities today and to consider how social work education should be developed to provide the expertise needed to meet the pressures brought on by future changes in society (Lähteinen et al. 2017: 4).

Figure 2 shows the knowledge of and skills in social work to be gained through the completion of bachelor- and master-level social work education. This is described through a number of areas of expertise that social workers need to employ in their work. In addition, social workers usually need expertise in their specialised areas of social work depending on the type of tasks they perform and on the organisation in which they work (Lähteinen et al. 2017: 12).

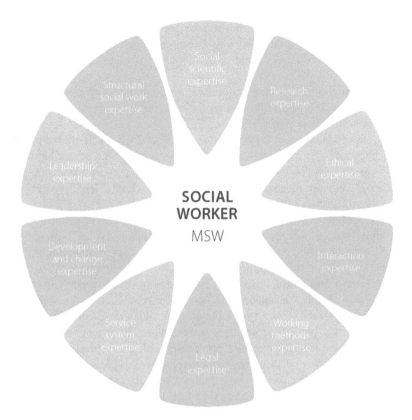

Fig. 2 Areas of expertise to be gained through social work education (reprinted with permission from Lähteinen et al. 2017: 13)

Completion of the bachelor's and master's degree programmes in the discipline of social work provides the student with the following expertise:

- **Social scientific expertise** is the core of the knowledge and skills created by social work education. This relates to the rational view of the individual as part of society and its communities, institutions and systems. The tasks of a social worker require analysing and understanding how the phenomena addressed by social work are situated in relationships between the individual and society.
- **Research expertise** is crucial in equipping graduates with the skills needed to analyse and produce research knowledge on social service users, social work practices, the system of services, the impact of the work and the phenomena that social work addresses.
- **Ethical expertise** is a crucial aspect of social work. It requires professional confidence as well as an understanding and consideration of the sensitive, personal and human qualities of the encountered phenomena. An ethically competent person is also capable of professional discretion in demanding client situations.

- **Interaction expertise** is required because the phenomena addressed in social work involve human relationships and communities. Social workers need this skill to encounter difference and difficult situations in an ethically sustainable and problem-solving manner.
- **Working methods expertise** requires a solid command of relevant working methods, especially the skills needed for assessment, evaluation, psychosocial support and social advocacy.
- **Legal expertise** is one of the cornerstones of social work and needed to further and safeguard basic and human rights. Social workers should be familiar with the legal environment of their work and their role as persons exercising public authority. They are responsible for ensuring their clients' legal protection and assessing the impact of their legal decisions on the clients.
- **Service system expertise** requires a sound understanding of clients' different life situations, the phenomena that social work addresses and how these are linked with the service system. Social workers play a key part in developing the service system to meet the future needs of service users and society.
- **Development and change expertise** is based on a social worker's expertise in dealing with change – a capability building on an analytical and research-based understanding of the service system, legislation and complex life situations. The social worker's profession requires a readiness to develop innovative and forward-looking working methods, procedures and service processes and to network with partners to develop new approaches.
- **Leadership expertise** means that social workers are capable of managing and directing service processes based on their education. Social workers are required to have a good command of the processes and content areas pertaining to management, finances and administration.
- **Structural social work expertise** requires the ability to identify the processes and problematic situations and misconduct in society that lead to exclusion and deprivation. This work calls for skills in producing knowledge of these problems and proposing solutions to them. It also requires an understanding of the ways in which the political system functions. Structural social work often involves social advocacy, as social workers must have the skills necessary to contribute to social development and to engage in public debates.

    (Lähteinen et al. 2017: 14–16.)

5 Finnish Social Workers in the Labour Market

The labour market situation of Finnish social workers is exceptionally good in the European context. In fact, there is a need for qualified professionals, and graduates can choose their place of employment after completing their studies. Notwithstanding some regional fluctuation, social workers are actively recruited in both metropolitan and rural areas. The social welfare sector also offers social workers diverse opportunities for employment in professions other than that of a social worker. They can work as experts on social issues, for example in research and development, administration, education, quality management, social impact assessment and supervision. (Lähteinen et al. 2017: 12). Hence, graduates may find employment in a wide range of state, municipal, third-sector and private organisations and workplaces.

Most Finnish social work students start to work in a position related to their field of interest already during their studies, which helps them find a job right after graduation. In 2015 and 2016, 65% of the graduates had a social work position prior to graduation. Of those who worked during their studies, 85% found a job within one month and 93% within three months of graduation. The corresponding percentages are lower for those who did not work during their university studies, but still nearly half of them were employed within a month and 66% within three months after completing a master's degree in social work. Approximately 90% of the graduates worked under the title of social worker (Landgrén and Pesonen 2017: 12, 19).

According to recent studies, the majority (94%) of Finnish social workers are employed by social welfare services in municipalities, which legally oversee financing and provision of most social, health and educational services for citizens (Landgrén and Pesonen 2017; Vuorijärvi et al. 2019). Private commercial businesses and third-sector organisations have a complementary role in providing social services – a situation that the ongoing reform of social and health services is not likely to change. There are approximately 4700 permanent positions for social workers in municipalities, of which over 80% are occupied by qualified and licensed social workers. The positions temporarily without a licensed social worker are occupied mainly by master's-level social work students (Vuorijärvi et al. 2019).

Until the late 1990s, social services and social work were organised by municipalities for local residents without differentiating between target groups or the nature of their social problems. Consequently, social workers had a comprehensive, community-oriented understanding of issues. On the other hand, extensive competence was also required of social workers in organising services. In the last two decades, most municipalities have reorganised their social welfare services according to the lifecycle model (based on age group) and centralised them. This enables them to specialise their services based on the life phases of target groups: families with children, adults and the elderly. However, this approach may also prevent municipalities from addressing their local communities in a comprehensive manner.

Following this specialisation of services according to the lifecycle model, more than a third (35%) of social workers are in child welfare and family services (Vuorijärvi et al. 2019). These services include child protection, casework and support measures in open (preventive) care, residential care, foster care, family work and legal family services (Pösö et al. 2018; Juhasz and Skivenes 2017). In this operating environment, a multi-professional and cross-sectoral approach is needed to address family health care, early childhood education, schools, psychological services, and child and youth psychiatry.

The second largest sector after child welfare services is social work with adults, which employs 13% of all social workers (Vuorijärvi et al. 2019). This work in fact covers all types of social work that do not address child welfare, families or the elderly. It consists of counselling and diverse measures to promote social inclusion and participation among people between working age and 64 years of age. Most of this work is still focused on poverty, income, and housing, but it also includes the broad spectrum of tasks pertaining to labour market inclusion, training and rehabilitation prevention and treatment of substance abuse, and mental health care.

Social work with immigrants is mainly organised as part of the work with adults. The work with refugees and recognized asylum seekers started systematically 30 years ago. In towns, integrations services organize the social work with forced migrants (Turtiainen 2012). Regarding work with forced migrants, social work very concretely faces the double role of acting as an agent of state policy while being one of the weightiest advocates of rights for forced migrants.

The third largest employer of social workers is health care (11% of social workers) and the fourth largest is work among people with disabilities (5% of social workers) (Vuorijärvi et al. 2019). Other areas include, for example, gerontological social work, emergency social services and administrative social work. School social work is also an important field, but in most municipalities, it is nowadays organised as part of educational services. The availability of school welfare services, including social work, is a statutory requirement at all levels of education, and they are mainly organised as community-based, multi-professional teams consisting of a school social worker, a school nurse, a psychologist and special education teachers (Puronen 2019).

Finally, it is worth noting that especially social work graduates with an interest in research and development can employ themselves in a variety of projects funded by the state, the European Union or various foundations. Finland's 11 regional Centres of Excellence on Social Welfare play an important role as agencies developing social services and connecting research, education and the practice of social work. Practice research in social work may represent an inspiring field to continue one's education into professional specialisation and doctoral studies.

Recent years have seen intensive and critical discussions on social workers' well-being at work and working conditions, especially in child welfare services. The nature of the work is considered one of the core reasons why there is a lack of workforce despite the fact that the number of qualified and registered social workers is sufficient. In analogy to the British so-called Baby P case, Finland has its own cases where children have died as a result of tragic incidents while being service-users in child welfare services. These cases have led to a widespread public discussion on the operating conditions within child welfare services and especially on social workers' excessive workload and high turnover. To tackle these problems, a national reform was recently launched in child welfare services with early support and prevention at its core and with the aim of minimising the growing need for child welfare services. The key part of the reform has been to prioritise and strengthen the basic services that address public health, social affairs and education and to coordinate them into a family centre model enabling early prevention and more systematic and multi-professional group work. An investigative report also proposed that the number of clients per social worker be restricted to 25 (Lahtinen et al. 2017; Kananoja and Ruuskanen 2018; Kananoja and Ruuskanen 2019).

In addition to the discussion on child welfare services, there has been public discussion on what constitutes a sufficient number of available social workers and the high turnover of workers. Around 50 social worker positions in metropolitan regions of Finland and 220 in the entire country are currently vacant (duunitori.fi). Through newspapers and social media, Finnish social workers have started to express their concern over the heavy workload, illegal and unethical practices, misconduct and other problems they encounter in daily work (Tiitinen and Lähteinen 2014). Municipalities currently face challenges in preventing employees from leaving and in recruiting new ones. On the other hand, the public discussion on the shortage of social workers is somewhat controversial, since there are approximately 7000 licensed social workers in Finland and slightly less than 5000 positions for them to fill (Pohjola 2019; Vuorijärvi et al. 2019).

According to a recent study on newly graduated social workers, 91% regarded their work as interesting and 93% as responsible and independent. As many as 88% considered their duties varied and challenging. On the other hand, 68% felt that their workload was too heavy, and 52% reported that their work was mentally draining. Because of the heavy workload and low salary, social workers have started to consider changing their workplace within social services or seeking employment in some other field (Landgrén and Pesonen 2017: 28–32). The results of this survey are in line with previous studies on social workers' work-related well-being (Mänttäri-van der Kuip 2015) and on the factors affecting employees' decisions on whether to continue in child welfare services or leave the field (Matela 2011).

6 Current Challenges of Social Work Education in the Transforming Finnish Welfare State

We have highlighted the ambitious Finnish goal of educating social workers who are able to base their work on research. The question arises, however, whether a research orientation is in fact applicable, needed and wanted in the practice of social work. As a result of the ongoing reform aimed at the integration of social and health services, voices within the government and social work administration are getting louder, demanding that interventions in social services be based on research evidence similar to that established in health services. According to advocates of this line of thought, the impact of the interventions should be known in advance, as has been the case in health services. It is very challenging to point out in this context that owing to a lack of research funding and a late entrance into academia, social work and social services have never had an equal chance to develop a body of research knowledge that would allow us to examine the Finnish social services in a comprehensive manner. Therefore, scholars and professionals are now making political efforts to significantly increase government funding for social work research. Furthermore, research-based knowledge is understood very differently in social sciences than in medical science. Instead of listing standardised and evidence-based interventions, social work refers to the best available knowledge that includes the voices of service users, the silent knowledge of practitioners, and scientific knowledge – and constant critical reflection thereof. Reflective practice and thinking are regarded as the most important scientific tools for social workers because each case faced in practice is complex and unique (Wilson 2013; Blom and Morén 2010). Optimistically, future social work education will be even more connected to practice research, as it would provide new knowledge of specific social work issues and develop academic skills in critical reflection (Gredig and Sommerfeld 2008).

As Tuomo Kokkonen and Kati Turtiainen (2018: 177) stated, the neoliberal transformations of the Finnish welfare state are giving rise to an increasing number of tasks in social work that contradict the humanistic and emancipatory nature of social work itself. When reflecting critically on the current education of social workers in Finland in terms of the changes and challenges of the welfare state, two types of shortcomings become apparent. On the one hand, many types of new social problems and challenges cannot be addressed with the competencies provided by current training. On the other hand, social worker education should provide students with the needed courage and skills to defend the rights of service users more effectively, to work in a more client- and community-oriented manner in a bureaucratic setting and to adopt a more preventive work approach at the levels of policy making, public debate and civic engagement (Kairala et al. 2012; Tapola-Haapala 2014). These shortcomings call forth the idea of structural and preventive social work (Närhi and Matthies 2016). We discuss this dilemma through the cases of child welfare and combating poverty.

6.1 Moving Towards Preventive Child Welfare Instead of Corrective Child Protection Involving Constant Crisis Intervention

The economic crisis of the 1990s brought about serious cuts to a significant number of preventive services for children and families. Simultaneously, the services became more difficult to reach and their quality decreased. This has been the case in practical family work and household support, municipal youth work, school social work, school health care and day care. Although the economic situation in Finland has improved remarkably, preventive welfare services never returned to what they were before the crisis. On the contrary, the new managerialist style of governing and organising services has reduced professional autonomy and split the tasks of child welfare and family work into separate, standardised service chains. The policy has greatly affected Finnish families, increased workloads and raised costs, especially in substitute care. People say that instead of doing preventive work, child welfare is nowadays only able to react to crises (Lith 2018). Since 2016, a broad national multi-professional and multi-disciplinary programme has focused on ways to provide more preventive and child-oriented services for children and families.

6.2 Financial Social Work as a Means to Prevent Social Inequality

One of the most significant reforms of social work practice was introduced in 2017, when the distribution of needs-tested social assistance as the basic form of income security was transferred from municipalities to the Social Insurance Institution of Finland (Kela) that provides the service mostly online. Kela is also in charge of most of the other forms of income security, including pensions, unemployment benefits, home child care allowance, student financial aid and health insurance–related benefits. It was expected that the transfer of income security from the municipalities to Kela would simplify the system, reduce bureaucracy, remove the stigma of being a recipient of social benefits and normalise the system of basic social assistance that is yet to be used to a full extent. In addition, social workers had expected to finally be able to focus on 'real social work' with people in need, instead of verifying their right to financial assistance, which had resulted in major workloads and dominated discussions with service users. However, they discovered that the complex issues of poverty and marginalisation could not be addressed using a nationwide, standardised online service system of financial assistance. Therefore, the option remains for clients to apply for temporary and complementary assistance from municipal social services. This has highlighted the need for specific financial social work (Wolfsohn and Michaeli 2014) that helps to lift people out of poverty and improve the financial situation of individuals and households (Viitasalo 2018). Emphasis should also be placed on the structural root causes of inequality and poverty in society (Krumer-Nevo et al. 2009).

Manifesting current developments in the Finnish welfare state, the examples of child welfare and financial social work demonstrate the importance of reconciling the need for more focused, well-scheduled and individual work practices with community and policy interventions. Furthermore, it is also of great significance to address this issue in social work education.

References

Anttonen, A., & Sipilä, J. (1996). European social care services. Is it possible to identify models? *Journal of European Social Policy, 6*(2), 87–100.

Blom, B., & Morén, S. (2010). Explaining social work practice – The CAIMeR theory. *Journal of Social Work, 10*(1), 98–119. https://doi.org/10.1177/1468017309350661.

Esping-Andersen, G. (1990). *The three worlds of welfare capitalism*. Princeton: Princeton University Press.

Forsberg, H., Kuronen, M., & Ritala-Koskinen, A. (2019). The academic identity and boundaries of the discipline of social work: Reflections of social work professors on the recruitment and research of doctoral students in Finland. *British Journal of Social Work, 49*(6), 1509–1525. https://doi.org/10.1093/bjsw/bcz069.

Gredig, D., & Sommerfeld, P. (2008). New proposals for generating and exploiting solution-oriented knowledge. *Research on Social Work Practice, 18*(4), 292–300. https://doi.org/10.1177/1049731507302265.

Hackett, S., Kuronen, M., Matthies, A.-L., & Kresal, B. (2003). The motivation, professional development and identity of social work students in four European countries. *European Journal of Social Work, 6*(2), 163–178. https://doi.org/10.1080/1369145032000144421.

Hämäläinen, J. (2014). Tiedontuotanto sosiaalityön rakenteellisena kysymyksenä [Knowledge production as an issue of structural social work]. In A. Pohjola, M. Laitinen, & M. Seppänen (Eds.), *Rakenteellinen sosiaalityö. Sosiaalityön tutkimuksen vuosikirja 2014* [Structural social work. Yearbook of social work research] (pp. 64–86). Kuopio: UNIpress.

Hietamäki, J., & Kantola, H. (2010). Sosiaalityön ammatillisen lisensiaatinkoulutuksen arviointitutkimus [Evaluation research of the professional licentiate degree in social work]. *Sosiaalityön julkaisusarja no. 7.* Jyväskylä: University of Jyväskylä.

Juhasz, I., & Skivenes, M. (2017). The Population's confidence in the child protection system – A survey study of England, Finland, Norway and the United States (California). *Social Policy & Administration, 51*(7), 1330–1347. https://doi.org/10.1111/spol.12226.

Juliusdottir, S., & Petterson, J. (2003). Common social work education standards in the Nordic countries – Opening an issue. *Social Work and Society, 1*(1), 1–16.

Julkunen, I., & Uggerhoej, L. (2016). Negotiating practice research. *Journal of Teaching in Social Work, 36*(1), 6–10. https://doi.org/10.1080/08841233.2016.1119625.

Kairala, M., Lähteinen, S., & Tiitinen, L. (2012). Rakenteellisen sosiaalityön osaaminen sosiaalityön opetuksen käytäntöyhteydessä [Structural social work competence in practice education]. In N. Tuohino, A. Pohjola, & M. Suonio (Eds.), Sosiaalityön käytännönopetus liikkeessä [Changing Practice Education], *SOSNET julkaisuja 5* (pp. 36–55). Rovaniemi: Valtakunnallinen sosiaalityön yliopistoverkosto Sosnet.

Kananoja, A., & Lähteinen, S. (2017). Tutkiminen ja kehittäminen sosiaalialalla [Research and development in social work]. In A. Kananoja, M. Lähteinen, & P. Marjamäki (Eds.), *Sosiaalityön käsikirja* [Social Work Handbook] (pp. 487–501). Helsinki: Tietosanoma.

Kananoja, A., & Ruuskanen, K. (2018). Selvityshenkilön ehdotus lastensuojelun laatua parantavaksi tiekartaksi. Väliraportti [The Rapporteur's proposal for the roadmap for improving the quality of child welfare. Intermediate report]. *Sosiaali- ja terveysministeriön raportteja ja muistiota 31/2018.* Helsinki: Sosiaali- ja terveysministeriö.

Kananoja, A., & Ruuskanen, K. (2019). Selvityshenkilön ehdotukset lastensuojelun toimintaedellytysten ja laadun parantamiseksi. Loppuraportti [Investigator's suggestions for improving the quality and operating conditions of child welfare]. *Sosiaali- ja terveysministeriön raportteja ja muistiota 2019:4.* Helsinki: Sosiaali- ja terveysministeriö.

Karvinen-Niinikoski, S. (2005). Research orientation and expertise in social work – Challenges for social work education. *European Journal of Social Work, 8*(3), 259–271. https://doi.org/10.1080/13691450500210756.

Karvinen-Niinikoski, S., Hoikkala, S., & Salonen, J. (2007). *Tutkintorakenneuudistus sosiaalityön koulutuksessa. Sosiaalityön valtakunnallinen hanke 2003–2006* [The Bologna process in social work education. The national project 2003–2006]. Rovaniemi: SOSNET Julkaisuja 1. & University of Lapland.

Kemppainen, T. (2006). Sosiaalityöntekijät 2015. In M. Vuorensyrjä, M. Borgman, M. Mäntysaari, T. Kemppainen, A. Pohjola (2015), *Sosiaalialan osaajat 2015. Sosiaalialan osaamis-, työvoima- ja koulutustarpeiden ennakointihanke (SOTENNA): loppuraportti* [Social welfare professionals in 2015: Foresight study on the expertise, labour force and educational needs of social welfare professionals] (pp. 230–284). Jyväskylä: Sosiaalityön julkaisusarja 4. University of Jyväskylä.

Kokkonen, T., & Turtiainen, K. (2018). Social work education in Finland. In M. Kamali & J. H. Jönsson (Eds.), *Neoliberalism, Nordic welfare states and social work. Current and future challenges* (pp. 171–181). London: Routledge.

Krumer-Nevo, M., Monnickendam, M., & Weiss-Gal, I. (2009). Poverty-aware social work practice: A conceptual framework for social work education. *Journal of Social Work Education, 45*(2), 225–243.

Lähteinen, S., & Tuohino, N. (2013). Kahden sosiaalialan korkeakoulututkinnon suorittaneiden käsitykset alan korkeakoulutusten tuottamasta osaamisesta [Conceptions of higher education and expertise in the social services and social work education]. *Janus, 21*(1), 41–58.

Lähteinen, S., & Tuohino, N. (2016). Sosiaalityön erikoisosaamista vahvistamassa – erikoissosiaalityöntekijän koulutus vastaamassa toimintaympäristön muutoksiin [Strengthening the special expertise in social work – Specialisation education in social work responding to the changes in the environment]. *Janus, 24*(2), 185–193.

Lahtinen, P., Männistö, L., & Raivio, M. (2017). *Kohti suomalaista systeemistä lastensuojelun toimintamallia. Keskeisiä periaatteita ja reunaehtoja [Towards a Finnish systemic child protection operating model. Key principles and boundary conditions].* Työpaperi 7/2017. Terveyden ja hyvinvoinnin laitos: Helsinki.

Lähteinen, S., Raitakari, S., Hänninen, K., Kaittila, A., Kekoni, T., Krok, S., & Skaffari, P. (2017). Social work education in Finland: Courses for competency. In *SOSNET julkaisuja 8.* Rovaniemi: Valtakunnallinen sosiaalityön yliopistoverkos Sosnet & University of Lapland.

Landgrén, S., & Pesonen, T. (2017). *Vastavalmistuneiden urapolut 2017. Vuosina 2015–2016 valmistuneiden Talentian jäsenten sijoittuminen työelämään* [Career paths of the newly graduated in 2017. The career paths and access to working life of the newly graduated members of Talentia trade union in years 2015–2016]. Helsinki: Talentia. https://www.talentia.fi/wp-content/uploads/2017/11/vastavalmistuneiden_urapolut_2017.pdf. Accessed 1 June 2019.

Lith, P. (2018). *Lastensuojelun painopiste on kriiseissä, ei niiden ehkäisemisessä [The emphasis of child protection on crises, instead of their prevention].* Asiantuntija-artikkelit ja ajankohtaisblogit: Helsinki. https://tilastokeskus.fi/tietotrendit/artikkelit/2018/lastensuojelun-painopiste-on-kriiseissa-ei-niiden-ehkaisemisessa-1/. Accessed 1 June 2019.

Mänttäri-van der Kuip, M. (2015) Work-related Well-Being among Finnish Frontline Social Workers in an Age of Austerity. *Jyväskylä Studies in Education, Psychology and Social Research, 524.* Jyväskylä: University of Jyväskylä.

Matela, K. (2011). Viihtyvät ja vaihtuvat. Lastensuojelun sosiaalityöntekijöiden työssä pysymiseen ja työstä lähtemiseen vaikuttavat tekijät [Those who thrive and those who leave. Factors affecting the child protection social workers' intention to leave or stay in work]. Pohjois-Suomen sosiaalialan osaamiskeskuksen julkaisusarja 33. Oulu: Pohjois-Suomen sosiaalialan osaamiskeskus.

Matthies, A. -L. (1990). Arjen ja tieteen välissä. Sosiaalityön akatemisoitumisen tarkastelua. Suomalainen sosiaalityö [Between everyday life and science. Adressing the academisation of social work]. *Sosiaalipolitiikka, 1990*(2), 25–39. Helsinki: Sosiaalipoliittisen yhdistyksen vuosikirja. Sosiaalipoliittinen yhdistys.

Matthies, A.-L. (2006). Wohlfahrtsstaatliche Aspekte des finnischen Bildungssystems in vergleichender Sicht [Welfare state related aspects in the Finnish educational system in a comparative perspective]. In A.-L. Matthies & E. Skiera (Eds.), *Das Bildungswesen in Finnland* (pp. 33–43). Bad Heilbrun: Klinkhardt.

Matthies, A.-L. (2011). Social service professions. Towards cross-European standardisation of qualifications. *Social Work & Society, 9*(1), 89–107.

Närhi, K., & Matthies, A.-L. (2016). The ecosocial approach in social work as a framework for structural social work. *International Social Work, 61*(4), 490–502. https://doi.org/10.1177/0020872816644663.

Niemi, V. (1997). Miten sosiaalityöntekijöiden koulutus Suomessa alkoi [How did social worker's education begin?]. In "Valitse sosiaalihuolto elämäntehtäväksesi" Sosiaalihuoltajakoulutus 1942–1995 [Choose social welfare as your life's calling. Social work education in years 1942–1995]. *Tampereen yliopiston sosiaalipolitiikan laitoksen julkaisu C-sarja, no 9. Sosiaalihuoltajat ry 9*, 5–28. Helsinki.

Pohjola, A. (1998). *Sosiaalityön yliopistollisen koulutuksen kehittäminen*. *Koulutus- ja tiedepolitiikan osaston julkaisuja 52/1998* [Developing social work university education]. Helsinki: Opetusministeriö.

Pohjola, A. (2003). Sosiaalityön koulutuksen tila ja paikka [The stage and place of social work education]. In: M. Laitinen, & A. Pohjola (Eds.), *Sosiaalisen vaihtuvat vastuut* [The shifting social responsibilities] (pp. 145–165). Jyväskylä: PS-kustannus.

Pohjola, A. (2019). *Sosiaalihuollon ammattihenkilölain (817/2015) muutostarpeita koskeva selvitys*. *Selvityshenkilöraportti* [Investigation on needs for reform in the Act on Social Welfare Professionals (817/2015)]. Investigator's report 2019:16. Helsinki: Sosiaali- ja terveysministeriö.

Pohjola, A., Kemppainen, T., & Väyrynen, S. (2012). Vaikuttavuus on monta [Many ways to understanding impact]. In A. Pohjola, T. Kemppainen, & S. Väyrynen (Eds.), *Sosiaalityön vaikuttavuus* [Impact in Social Work] (pp. 347–352). Rovaniemi: Lapland University Press.

Pösö, T., Pekkarinen, E., Helavirta, S., & Laakso, R. (2018). 'Voluntary' and 'involuntary' child welfare: Challenging the distinction. *Journal of Social Work, 18*(3), 253–272. https://doi.org/10.1177/1468017316653269.

Puronen, H. (2019). What School Social Work is like in Finland. Electronic Newsletter April 2019. International Network for School Social Work. http://internationalnetwork-schoolsocialwork.htmlplanet.com. Accessed 1 June 2019.

Salomon, A. (1927). *Die Ausbildung zum Sozialen Beruf* [Education of social professions]. Berlin: Carl Heymanns Verlag.

Satka, M. (1994). Sosiaalinen työ peräänkatsojamiehestä hoivayrittäjäksi [Development of social work from looking after to care entrepreneur]. In J. Jaakkola, P. Pulma, M. Satka, & K. Urponen (Eds.), *Armeliaisuus, yhteisöapu, sosiaaliturva. Suomalaisen sosiaaliturvan historia* [Charity, community support and social security. The history of Finnish social security]. Helsinki: Sosiaaliturvan Keskusliitto.

Satka, M. (1995). *Making social citizenship. Conceptual practice from the Finnish poor law to the professional social work*. Diss. Jyväskylä: University of Jyväskylä.

Sewpaul, V., & Jones, D. (2005). Global standards for the education and training of the social work profession. *International Journal of Social Welfare, 14*, 218–230. https://doi.org/10.1111/j.1468-2397.2005.00362.x.

Shardlow, S., Scholar, H., Munzo, L., & McLaughlin, H. (2011). The nature of employer's involvement in social work education: An international exploration. *International Social Work, 55*(2), 205–224. https://doi.org/10.1177/0020872811418993.

Sosnet. (2003). *Academic social work education in Finland*. Description of social work education in Finland prepared by the Finnish National University Network for Social Work (Sosnet). https://www.sosnet.fi/In-English/Undergraduate-Studies/Social-work-education-in-Finland.

Tapola-Haapala, M. (2014). Social work education and political action. In T. Harrikari, P.-L. Rauhala, & E. Virokannas (Eds.), *Social chance and social work* (pp. 68–85). Farnham: Ashgate.

The Guardian. (2018). *Safe, happy and free: Does Finland have all the answers?*. https://www.theguardian.com/world/2018/feb/12/safe-happy-and-free-does-finland-have-all-the-answers. Accessed 1 June 2019.

Tiitinen, L., & Lähteinen, S. (2014). Julkisen viestinnän keinoilla toteutetun rakenteellisen sosiaalityön tavoitteet [The aims of media advocacy in structural social work]. In A. Pohjola, M., Laitinen, & M. Seppänen (Eds.), *Rakenteellinen sosiaalityö. Sosiaalityön tutkimuksen seura* [Structural social work. Year book of social work research] (pp. 191–212). Helsinki: UNIpress.

Tuohino, N., Pohjola, A., & Suonio, M. (2012). *Sosiaalityön käytännönopetus liikkeessä* [Changing practice education in social work]. In *SOSNET julkaisuja 5*. Rovaniemi: Valtakunnallinen sosiaalityön yliopistoverkosto Sosnet.

Turtiainen, K. (2012). Possibilities of trust and recognition between refugees and authorities: resettlement as a part of durable solutions of forced migration. Diss., Jyväskylä studies in education, psychology and social research 451. Jyväskylä: University of Jyväskylä. Retrieved from: http://urn.fi/URN:ISBN:978-951-39-4912-9. Accessed 7 Sept 2020.

Urponen, K. (2004). Finland. In A. Campanini & E. Frost (Eds.), *European social work. commonalities and differences* (pp. 71–77). Carotti: Roma.

Viitasalo, K. (2018). *Äitien pyrkimykset ja toimintamahdollisuuksien valikko. Käsitteellinen tutkimus äitien taloudellisista toimintamahdollisuuksista* [Aspirations and Capability. Set of Mothers A Conceptual Study on Mothers' Financial Capabilities]. Diss., Jyväskylä Studies in Education, Psychology and Social Research 606. Jyväskylä: University of Jyväskylä. Retrieved from: http://urn.fi/URN:ISBN:978-951-39-7340-7. Accessed 7 Sept 2020.

Vornanen, R., Törrönen, M., Lähteinen, S., & Pohjola, A. (2007). Professional postgraduate studies in social work: The Finnish example and European challenges. In E. Frost, M. J. Freitas, & A. Campanini (Eds.), *Social work education in Europe* (pp. 117–131). Roma: Carocci editore.

Vuorijärvi, P., Raappana, M., Kinnunen, P., & Kostamo-Pääkkö, K. (2019). *Sosiaalihuollon ammattihenkilöstö- ja tehtävärakenneselvitys 2018. Sosiaali- ja terveysministeriö* [Investigation of social welfare professionals and their division of labour]. Unpublished report.

Vuorikoski, M. (1999). Sosiaalityön professionaalistuminen ja koulutus [Professionalisation and education of social work]. *Acta Universitatis Tamperensis, 687*.

Wilson, G. (2013). Evidencing Reflective Practice in Social Work Education: Theoretical Uncertainties and Practical Challenges. *British Journal of Social Work, 43*, 154–172. https://doi.org/10.1093/bjsw/bcr170.

Wolfsohn, R., & Michaeli, D. (2014). Financial social work. In *Encyclopedia of social work*. https://doi.org/10.1093/acrefore/9780199975839.013.923.

Legislation

Act on Social Welfare Professionals (817/2015)
Act on Qualification Requirements for Social Welfare Professionals (272/2005)
Government Decree on University Decrees and Specialisation Education 794/2004

Social Work Education and Training in France: A Long History of Being Energised by an Academic Discipline and International Social Work

Robert Bergougnan and Florence Fondeville

1 High Level of Social Protection

Over the years, France has established one of the most developed social protection, social action and social assistance systems in the world. As a product of this history, French social work (SW), like a vine, has its roots in the deep strata constituted by the long movement of French political, economic, geographical and technical development, by which the forms of aid, reception and support for the most vulnerable have been structured. The current quantity of systems, services and forms of solidarity actions that result from this is as much a strength – diversity – as a weakness – compartmentalisation. The technological and eco-social transformations under way, which are giving rise to new social needs and aspirations associated with national and international observations of the United Nations (UN) and Council of Europe (CoE), highlight the shortcomings and risks of the French system. This system focuses on curative approaches and provides the "means to survive but without the prospect of going out and being autonomous through work" (Buzyn 2018, Minister of Solidarity and Health in the government of Prime Minister Edouard Philippe). The aim is to renew French SW, its methods and tools through a strategy to prevent and fight against poverty.

France, as a member of the Council of Europe, ratified the European Social Charter in 1973 and the Revised European Social Charter in 1999 as a whole. By this act, the French states undertake to respect European standards in terms of protection and social action. Thus, evaluations are carried out to support the practical and positive effects of these commitments. These assessments regularly highlight the shortcomings or difficulties of each state in relation to these standards. France has seen progress in the field of child care (prohibition of work for children under

R. Bergougnan · F. Fondeville (✉)
ERASME, Toulouse, France
e-mail: rbergougnan@erasme.fr; ffondeville@erasme.fr

© Springer Nature Switzerland AG 2021
M. Laging, N. Žganec (eds.), *Social Work Education in Europe*,
European Social Work Education and Practice,
https://doi.org/10.1007/978-3-030-69701-3_4

65

15 years of age), the health of foreigners (state medical assistance), and housing (definition of decent housing and implementation of the eviction prevention system), but also defaults with regard to the European Social Charter.

The National Association of Social Service Assistants (ANAS 2015) pointed out situations that were the subject of a reminder from the European Committee of Social Rights for non-compliance with the recommendations of the charter, for example, "The minimum amounts of invalidity and reversal pensions are clearly insufficient", "young people under 25 years of age are not entitled to sufficient social assistance", "the granting of the minimum integration income to non-Community foreigners holding a temporary residence permit is subservient to the completion of a five-year period of residence on French territory" and finally, "it is not established that the right of appeal in matters of social assistance is effective" (ANAS 2012).

This book is being published in a political period (influx of migrants, Brexit, European elections in May 2019 against the backdrop of populism and a crisis within the Council of Europe) which aims to give momentum to the European dimension of social work (SW) training and which seems to be marked by a historical constant: the perennially repeated promise to eradicate poverty, discrimination and inequality at a time when the gap between the rich and the poor keeps widening incessantly. In this context, movements such as "the yellow vests" and numerous analyses are emerging in France that also highlight the precariousness of social workers, their exhaustion and suffering.

Therefore, the question arises: how can French SW education and training provide answers to these challenges and contradictions and how to go about it?

The modern structuring of social action in the form of SW began in France in the nineteenth century within the dynamics of the industrial revolution, as in other countries (UK, Belgium, Germany, USA). Overall, during a period of population displacement from rural agricultural areas to industrial cities, the aim was to address the following issues:

– the massive precariousness of the population which was the workforce for the emerging industry, the proletariat;
– the breaking of traditional collective solidarity ties affecting the proletariat, who mostly came from the agricultural world and emigrated to industrial cities (Pascal 2014).

Systemic changes in technology and the economy generate tensions and violent conflicts among social classes that require profound political transformations. In France, the stabilisation of the republican state was necessary a century after the French revolution.

"In this 19th century, it is a question of finding solutions to solve what is defined as 'the social question'. The solutions differ, but the target stays the same: the proletariat, which, deprived of the protection that property constitutes for the bourgeoisie, is left to various hazards such as unemployment, illness, old age, not to mention that wages are insufficient to ensure the minimum subsistence that are food and housing" (Pascal 2014).

Donzelot (1984) and Castel (2009) also showed how this transformation into the social state, also called the welfare state, was structured and how it led to the emergence of SW in France.

The French social state model has been described as a "conservative-corporatist" welfare state or "insurance model" in the classification of Esping-Andersen (1990), along with those of Germany, Austria and Italy. It is characterised by the historical effects of the central role of the state, strong left-wing political mobilisations, corporatism or Church influence. It differs from two other types. The "liberal" welfare state, or "residual model" in the United States, Canada and Australia, in which assistance is based on the central consideration of an individual's resources with little or no transfers such as social insurance. The Affordable Care Act, more generally referred to and known as Obamacare, which came into effect on October 1, 2013, completed this. Finally, the "social democratic" welfare state or the "universal model" established in the Scandinavian countries is based on principles of universalism and *demarchandisation* in order to enable individuals, within certain legal frameworks, to partially free themselves from the constraints of labour market values for their survival and so be able to receive sufficient replacement resources through a generalised social security system.

Thus, in the French social protection model, the state is considered a legitimate provider of well-being. The resulting statism is reflected in a Bismarckian-type social protection system: an insurance system backed by paid employment which aims to partially maintain the income of working people when circumstances (accident, illness, old age, unemployment) exclude them from the labour market. The state thus maintains the specific characteristics of socio-professional categories, which gives it its corporatist character and redistributive limits (maintenance of acquired interests and specific statutes). Canvassing is limited to the impossibility of working. In this context, redistribution is in fact not very effective, and social stratification is only slightly modified: the preservation of socio-professional structures and acquired advantages limits the redistribution and equalisation of situations.

But subsequent developments in social protection systems have led to a hybridisation between the corporatist principle of affiliation through work and that of affiliation through citizenship. Today, European systems, while still subject to dissimilar political inspirations, have moved closer together in terms of how they operate. Differences in principle are now more important between branches (e.g. sickness, pensions, disability, unemployment, minimum income) than between different countries' models. Benefits that depend on the income of insured persons (pensions, unemployment) are quite naturally financed by contributions, which is in line with the contributory nature of the corresponding schemes. On the other hand, schemes that provide benefits unrelated to insured persons' incomes (e.g. health care, disability) are logically increasingly financed by taxes. This development has been particularly characteristic of France since the mid-1980s. As a result, the differences between the Bismarckian, Scandinavian and Beveridgean systems are fading in favour of a certain homogenisation of the principles that guide the development of social protection (Cornilleau 2019).

Thus, we must consider that the French system, like some other European systems, is moving towards a hibridisation between an insurance system and a tax system. One example of this movement is the creation of the *Revenu minimum d'insertion* (RMI) (minimum insertion income) in 1988.

2   Two Historical Social Professions and a Functionalist Logic

The first and main group of social workers are women, and its activities were first visible at the end of the nineteenth century, when the first "social house" was created in 1896. They were middle-class women who demonstrated a strong commitment both to asserting their autonomy and to their convictions concerning social welfare (Ruggero 2016).

In 1905, France imposed a separation of church and state, which came to dominate social action, mainly oriented towards family policy. This followed closely on the heels of the 1901 law establishing freedom of association, which had an important influence on the structuring of civil society initiatives in the field of social and medico-social action.

The first School of Practical Social Work was created in 1913, followed by the School of Training for Factory Superintendents in 1917. Together they launched a movement that would continue throughout the twentieth century. The social workers these professionals worked with factory workers and within families to ensure a good education, hygiene and health monitoring and home management by mothers and wives. The diploma of social worker was created in 1932: the *diplôme d'etat d'assistant de service social* (DEASS).

> After World War I, the acceleration of the development of schools of social services (between 1924 and 1937, the number of schools increased from five to eleven), and the methodical organisation of their teaching on a model that tends to become similar (lessons, conferences, internships), give concrete expression to the construction of a common identity for social workers. Training will be the vehicle for transmitting shared references and values to future professionals. These are of four types: moral values that refer to the vocation, selflessness, loyalty, altruism, empathy that the social worker must show in his activity; the social worker's attitude towards the people whose situation he aims to improve and the institutions he works with. Social training protects professional secrecy and ethics in social action; reference to academic and professional knowledge; schools of social work provide their students with theoretical, methodological and practical scientific knowledge; the practice of work-study alternation, an essential reference in any social training, with practical application of the knowledge taught (Delaunay 2007).

During World War II, under the so-called Vichy regime which cooperated with the German occupying force, family-oriented policies were developed and the field of ill-adapted childhood emerged and developed under the particular impetus of child psychiatrists. After the war, in 1945, France introduced the *sécurité sociale* and structured child protection through ordinances passed in 1945 (Chauvière 1980).

The Vichy regime was very quickly confronted with a rise in both juvenile delinquency (which tripled between 1939 and 1942) and in numbers of children in danger (the number of vagrants and children at moral risk would reach 600,000 by the end of the war). Prisons were full and, in any case, in the hands of the occupying power. The Ministry of National Education, which to that point had dominated child welfare, was discredited in the eyes of the regime, which accused school teachers of being responsible for the lack of patriotism and, therefore, for defeat.

The Ministry of Health took the initiative in placing so-called ill-adapted children under the tutelage of medical doctors, and in particular psychiatrists, rather than into the care of specific SW organisations. In this context the principle of observation and sorting became generalised with respect to responding to an astonishing project whereby a distinction was made between "constitutional perverts", i.e., children incapable of rehabilitation, and other perverts who could be rehabilitated.

Two professions then emerged in the service of this identification activity: psychologists and educators, placed under the authority of a psychiatric doctor in charge of synthesing the data thus collected.

Based on the ideal of recovery to create a new person, boy scouts and pathfinders provide the first leaders. Their values at the time were in line with the regime: a call to a sense of honour, a permanent example of a leader, a patriotic spirit. He introduced emotional attachment and life in small groups, including minors, and influenced the standard profile of an educator (leadership, virility, self-control, morality, personal commitment). The 1942 law on delinquent children largely inspired the law of 2 February 1945, which organised the juvenile criminal justice.

Institutions for children and adolescents labeled as being ill-adapted developed with the profession of specialised educator who, in contrast to social assistants, saw significant male involvement. Coming from scouting, the army and youth movements, these new professionals recruited from many social strata were involved in the daily lives of these children and adolescents. A large institutional reception system had developed, "educators, a status that precedes the profession", wrote Bourquin (1998).

Thus, the first educators in the ill-adapted childhood sector and the first schools to train them appeared in 1942–1943, and the first diploma of Specialised Educator was introduced in 1969, *diplôme d'etat d'educateur spécialisé* (DEES).

Beyond these original professions, new professional qualifications developed very quickly according to a logic partitioned between specific actions and stratified between differents levels of qualifications. The implementation of the RMI in 1988, and the insertion services extended this. During the 1980s, these developments lead to the emergence of the notion of social intervention, which, while providing a convenient language tool, makes it possible to broadly embrace a set of professional groups, or professional identities, without having to consider the practical and corporatist issues that affect them. In doing so, this two-dimensional theoretical and organisational dynamics led to circumscribing and limiting SW in a specific area of institutions and an instrumental and executive position.

In this context, it appeared that all actors fully adhered to this designation, so SW research did not really address the question of the limits that this caused for a true update of SW. Therefore, two approaches are principally highlighted in terms of the socio-political and cultural determinants of domination and social capital, in reference to Pierre Bourdieu, or on the side of the clinical practice of professionals through approaches focused on the analysis of the activity and suffering of SW from the perspective of the sociology of the actor and social psychology. As for the rest, it is the socio-historical analysis of public policies that mobilises researchers. French SW research has remained impervious to the theories and research of international SW published in English. For example, in France nobody knows who Walter Lorenz is.

This can be interpreted either as a result of the lack of institutionalisation of SW research or as the main cause of its difficulty in establishing itself in the academic landscape. In doing so "the social intervention approach" fuel a permanent backdrop of jamming.

Today, research is developing on the SW professionalisation process under the influence of international collaborations with French speaking countries (Association Internationale pour la Formation, la Recherche et l'Interventions Sociale, AIFRIS), with Belgium, Switzerland, Canada-Québec, African countries and ERASMUS programmes.

3   Main Work Area and Institutional Framework of Social Work

The French political system and its administrative framework are structured at four levels: state-national level, regional level, departmental level and city-municipal level.

Social assistance and social action in France account for 10% of social protection expenditures and 3.2% of gross domestic product. These are mainly managed by departments. At the end of 2016, the departments provided 4.1 million social assistance benefits, for a net annual expenditure of 37 billion euros, an amount that increased by 2% in one year and 13% in five years (Fig. 1).

- **State competences – national level**

   Social assistance:
   Legal assistance, minimum income assistance, adult allowance and guaranteed resources for disabled workers. Support for institutions and services for disabled workers and centres of housing and social reintegration (CHRS) for homeless people.

   Social and medico-social institutions and services:
   Schéma national d'organisation sociale et médico-sociale, participation in the departmental social and medico-social organisation framework, authorisation and price setting of some social and medico-social establishments; price

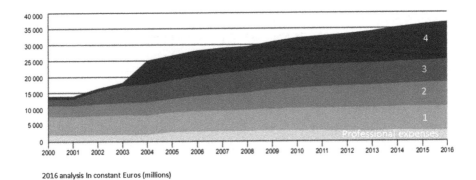

2016 analysis in constant Euros (millions)

Fig. 1 Evolution of net social assistance expenditure of departments in France, 2000–2016 (DREES 2018)

setting of the "care" portion, control and supervision of establishments and services.

Social action:

Emergency accommodation and social emergency measures, management of warning and emergency plans for the benefit of elderly or disabled persons in cases of exceptional risk.

- **Regional council competences**

Regional councils are in charge of the organisation and finances of schools for social workers and nurses and of programmes for the professional integration of young people. It has no power over SW.

- **Departmental council competences**

At the territoriral level, in departmental councils, the so-called *chef de file* of social action is in charge of the social and medico-social (SMS) action policy. It organises the development and implementation of departmental schemes of SMS organisations and the coordination of actions carried out in these areas within its territory. It authorises the creation or transformation of SMS establishments that provide services. It also sets prices for services provided. Its actions concern:

1. **child protection**: child and family welfare and unaccompanied migrant minors,
2. **disability compensation benefit**, with the departmental house of disabilities and allocations,
3. **assistance to the elderly,** with social assistance for residential care and the personalised independence allowance for the elderly at home (APA),
4. **Active Solidarity Income** (RSA, for the French *Revenue de solidarité active*).

At the end of 2016, departmental services included 65,000 professionals, distributed as follows:

– 34,700 administrative and technical staff in the social and medico-social field; they accounted for 44% of all staff in this field, excluding family assistants;

– 29,400 staff members, or 38% of the total number, accounted for social and educational staff, the second largest category; so-called **socio-educational counsellors and assistants,** whether Social Service Assistants (ASS), Specialised Educators (ES) or Family Social Economy Counsellors (CESF), made up 96% of these employees.

- **City competences**

- The Communal Council in Social Action is a local institution for social action and as such implements a series of general prevention and social development actions in the municipality in which it is based while collaborating with public and private institutions at other levels. To this end, it develops activities and missions (within the legal and optional framework) aimed at assisting and supporting the populations concerned, such as the disabled, families with difficulties or the elderly, by administering useful services such as *crèches*, day-care centres or retirement homes.
- **Associative action**

Social activities are not directly organised by public institutions; a number of them are coordinated by associations and foundations. They work with public institutions.

They represent

– 35,120 private institutes for social and medico-social activities
– 1,124,130 salaried workers including social workers and support workers
– 24.4 billion euros in total salary.

There are no accurate statistics on the number of social workers in this field because, but the UNIFAF organisation estimated that social workers accounted for around 30% of salaries (UNIFAF 2017).

4 History and Context of Social Work and Social Intervention Training

As we saw previously, SW training in France was established in 1938, when the DEASS was created along with studies of "visiting" nurses. The first ES schools appeared in 1942 and DEES was institutionalised in 1967.

These schools have remained independent of universities to this day. In 1986, regional institutes of social work were created in many French regions, but this process did not spread to all regions, which weakened the position of the schools and, more importantly, hindered the development of research in SW.

The implementation of the two basic SW training courses was followed by the creation of 11 additional diplomas covering six fields (Tables 1 and 2). These 13 diplomas range from level 1 to level 7 of the European Qualifications Framework (EQF).

Table 1 Level 6 EQF bachelor's in SW - 180 ECTS points

Diploma	Curricula
State Diploma for technical Educators Diplôme d'État d'éducateur technique spécialisé (DEETS) SW with disabled workers in adapted companies	3 years 1200 school hours + 15-month internship
State Diploma for Educators for Early Childhood Diplôme d'État d'éducateur de jeunes enfants (DEEJE)	3 years 1500 school hours + 15-month internship
State Diploma for Specialised Educators Diplôme d'État d'éducateur spécialisé (DEES)	3 years 1450 school hours + 15-month internship
State Diploma for Family Social Economy Counsellors Diplôme d'État de conseiller en économie sociale familiale (DECESF)	3 years 540 school hours + 560 internship hours
State Diploma for Social Service Assistants Diplôme d'État d'assistant de service social (DEASS)	3 years 1740 school hours + 12-month internship
Certificate of suitability for management and leadership positions social intervention unit Certificat d'aptitude aux fonctions d'encadrement et de responsabled'unité d'intervention sociale (CAFERUIS)	400 school hours + 420 internship hours
State diploma for family mediation Diplôme d'état de médiateur familial (DEMF)	490 school hours + 105 internship hours

Table 2 Level 7 EQF

Diplomas	Length of training
State Diploma in Social Engineering Diplôme d'État d'ingénierie sociale (DEIS) social work research curricula	700 school hours + 175 internship hours
Certificate of Suitability for the Position of Headmaster or Social Intervention Service Certificat d'aptitude aux fonctions de directeur d'établissementou de service d'intervention sociale (CAFDES)	700 school hours + 510 internship hours

4.1   Levels 3 and 4 EQF

In the field of social care, four diplomas are granted at SW schools: a state diploma for family assistants (DEAF), a state diploma for educational and social support (DEAES), a state diploma for technicians of social and family intervention (DETISF), *Moniteur Educateur* – daily-life educators in specialised homes (DEME).

In 2009, the *Union nationale des acteurs de formation et de recherche en intervention sociale* (UNAFORIS 2018), the French association of schools of SW, was created as a unique national network of schools of SW and social intervention. It was formed in order to reinforce the particular features of these SW schools and their recognition as higher education and research institutions. It was also intended to recognise degrees in SW. This level licence (level 6 of the EQF) was established in 2018. Today UNAFORIS represents all SW schools and care worker training institutions and aims to promote links between evolving skill needs and training responses and to support cooperation and mutualisation between training organisations.

The professionalisation of the field is the result of various developments in SW and marks not only a lack of dichotomy between SW and social intervention but also a strong fragmentation between diplomas, schools and professions. Indeed, the French system features is a strong link between diplomas and jobs. Thus, the notion of social intervention, which covers a broader field in the area of social action, has blurred the boundaries of SW.

However, on 1 July 2016, France's government created a High Social Work Council – *Haut conseil du travail social* (HCTS), an advisory body close to the Ministry of Social Affairs. Within the HCTS, under the impetus of UNAFORIS, the government decided to take into consideration the international definition of social work adopted by the International Federation of Social Work (IFSW) and the International Association of Schools of Social Work (IASSW) General Assembly on 10 July 2014 in Melbourne, Australia. Indeed, France has chosen to include in the Code of Social Action and Families, which is the legal framework for SW, not a translation but a transposition of the international definition of SW. Thus, the first sentence, "Social work is a professional practice and a discipline" (international definition of SW IFSW and IASSW), was modified to avoid or simply dismiss the question of the scientificity of SW. While some commentary explains the elements of this choice, it provides no clarification on institutional guidelines that would make it possible to specify the framework and timetable for this structuring.

Caught between the notion of social intervention and the management of services, French SW thus remains within a very operational and instrumental framework, which characterises the difficulties of French schools in participating in and contributing to exchanges, the international production of knowledge and the evolution of practices.

However, SW has a presence in higher education, at the undergraduate and post-graduate levels, from the bachelor's (*licence* in France) to master's degree. There is no PhD-level education in a specific SW discipline.

5 Developments in Social Work Training at the Higher Level

The French SW study system is based on two dimensions that complement each other: school-based training and on-the-job training (internships). The duration varies according to each diploma, but practice placement always constitutes a significant part of the programme.

Various training reforms in France (2007, 2011 and 2018) have led training centres to redesign their programmes in line with changes in practices and organisations following a repositioning of diplomas at the European level, which allows for mobility and the acquisition of 180 to 240 European Credit Transfer and Accumulation System (ECTS) points.

It was at the end of the 2011 reform that SW training was introduced at the European level with a modular division allowing the acquisition of 180 ECTS points and therefore a positioning at the bachelor level (*licence* degree in France). The notion of a personal career path is reinforced with the possibility of building bridges between European diplomas or in any case obtaining European credits. Students can obtain these ECTS points at European schools in conjunction with their training (ERASMUS mobility).

We will set out three structural elements of these training reforms, as follows.

The establishment of professional references of skills, activities and training and certification systems – from 2007 –structured diplomas since all training is organised on the basis of skill areas. This represented "a fundamental change in the culture of social work professionals" (Jaeger 2009). And, although the arrival of standards may have been considered too technical by social workers (Jaeger 2006), it is now accepted and allows modularisation, opening one of the paths of access to European mobility and a more individualised educational career pathway.

The individualisation of training paths is now a central element of training courses, raising the need for organisations to think about the content and structure of training in a way that is linked to students' paths and no longer through a uniform model of a global training programme for validation. Student must be able to enhance – or even certify – previously acquired skills and develop new ones through gateway systems.

A new approach to alternation training has arisen that represents the last key element of reform, which seems central because it contributes to the transformation of the professionalisation process. Internship sites have become a qualifying space: the internship field must now be in a contractual relationship with the school of SW. Work-linked training is based on a tutoring system and the fields must make internship proposals based on the areas of expertise in which they can train students. These elements give a new position to the professional field in a reverse approach, based on the lessons learned during training. The locations of internships have always played an essential role in the training of social workers, but the latest reforms structure and reinforce the modalities and spaces of articulation between theoretical and practical acquisitions.

Today, following the 2014 *Etats généraux du travail social* (General States of SW) and the 2015 inter-ministerial action plan for SW and social development, a new reform places social workers at level 6 of EQF and promotes the transition of SW schools from SW training institutions to higher education institutions.

This reform repositioned the place of research in training and paved the way to new skills for these social workers.

5.1 Links Between Social Work Research and Training: Objects and Status of Knowledge

The historical anchoring of SW in work-linked training (as we have seen, the internship is an integral part of the training of canonical SW professions) and the transition of some of the training courses to higher education raise the question of the place of knowledge and its construction in training and its links with research and the field. The transition from the training of social workers to level 2 raises questions about the internship as the principal means for professionalising workers and the place of scientific knowledge in the training of social workers. There is a real challenge here today in linking the different types of knowledge in the professionalisation processes.

5.2 Concerning the Alternation Process and the Place of Professional or Practical Knowledge

A recent note from UNAFORIS (2016) presents various possible ways of professionalising these different skills. Professionalisation methods, based on integrative work experience as "a professionalisation process centred on the person in training who will carry out apprenticeships, build [students'] project from reflective work on their experience and the transformation of these experiences into knowledge" (Cornier 2012).

These modalities should make it possible to overcome a double challenge:

– Moving from "training" to "education" in the sense that the structuring of skills is no longer conceived of exclusively in the field but in other areas of experience;
– Constituting spaces of reflexivity that are linked with social, organisational and practical evolutions and allow a hybridisation of knowledge that constitutes new professional identities.

5.3 The Place of SW Research and the Relation with the University – the Place of Scientific Knowledge

As we have seen, French SW in its historicity remains stuck between social intervention and service management in a very operational framework, and the scientificity of SW remains a complex issue. The transition from SW training institutions to the higher education level therefore directly affects these imperatives and spurs ongoing debate.

Thus, research has difficulty positioning itself in the social field and defining its disciplinary field(s), its objectives and its referent knowledge. A 2011 consensus conference raised several salient points of debate that, in our opinion, illustrate well the challenges and current structure of SW research (Jaeger 2013a, b): "How to define the relationships between knowledge and professional activities? Is there any professional knowledge? Can we talk about one or more social work sciences? What are the links between research and the aims of social and medico-social action? What are the complementarities between professional and social science knowledge for social work? What is the place of interdisciplinarity in social work research?"

In these elements of debate, SW research in France today must clarify its positions on different models:

- Research by social workers or research by scientists from different disciplines who "observe and translate" SW: this has given rise to the debate on research IN – INSIDE OF or ON SW. Let us explain what we mean. Here, IN refers to the construction of a discipline in SW, and INSIDE OF refers to the researcher's position. Researchers are social workers and conduct research in their practice. In this case they use Action research methods. ON also refers to the position of researchers and the objectives of their research; researchers are external scientists and treat SW as an object.
- Collaborative action research as a feature of SW research or empirical research. These research methodologies legitimately refer to the researcher's place according to her discipline and purpose.
- Finally, in recent years, the place of the relevant people as service users, in particular their experiential knowledge in research on SW, has also emerged.

These different models of research are being invested differently by the actors of SW research and are giving rise to different collectives or research groups that promote and defend each issue. This is indicative of polymorphic and non-convergent research and complicates the structuring of the field and its relation to SW education and training.

Finally, it is important to add that these elements of debate obviously intersect with the institutional and legislative dynamics that are also trying to structure the field: the creation of a chair of SW at the *Conservatoire national des arts et métiers* (CNAM) in 2000 in the field of sociology; the creation of UNAFORIS in 2009, which aimed to strengthen the particular features of SW schools and their recognition in higher education and research institutions; the 2002 law on the participation of service users, which promoted quality and qualification; the establishment of the Platform for Research in Social Action Training (PREFAS) in 2007, which aimed to pool, initiate and promote SW research and the establishment of scientific interest groups (SIG) in 2017. Four SIG were involved when UNAFORIS organised a special event to valorise the research activities of French SW schools in December 2018.

Today, the accreditation of training institutions as institutions of higher education and the transition to the bachelor's degree for higher education courses accelerate the necessary positioning of schools of SW on SW research. France hosted an international conference on SW education of the European Association of Schools of Social Work (EASSW) in Paris in June 2017.

6 Current Social and Societal Trends Are Subject to Uncertainty and Instability

What is the expected role of social work in addressing these trends and developments?

The plan and strategy to reduce poverty, in particular, which was launched in 2018, strengthened various areas of social workers' activity and skills, some of which were already highlighted in the 2015 inter-ministerial action plan for SW and social development – collective SW and social development, the participation of the people concerned, SW and territory, digital and SW and moving towards it. Thus, the notion of social intervention is removed to give way to that of SW (National Strategy for the Prevention of Poverty Reduction).

This strategy identifies several areas of transformation and progress to develop, which are reflected in the following five commitments:

- Commitment No. 1: Equal opportunities from the very first steps to break the cycle of poverty.
- Commitment No. 2: Guaranteeing the fundamental rights of children on a daily basis.
- Commitment No. 3: Guaranteeing a training path for all young people.
- Commitment No. 4: Establishing more accessible and equitable social rights activity incentives.
- Commitment No. 5: Investing in universal job search assistance.

These commitments are broken down into 21 specific measures and 15 national thematic groups present in each region. All these themes integrate the challenges of training social workers, and one group reframes these questions of SW education and training.

In the strategy, the training of social workers is considered in two dimensions: initial training and lifelong learning, while six specific new patterns of social intervention appear to be enhanced:

1. Social development, collective intervention
2. Participation of individuals concerned
3. Digital society
4. Moving towards "*Aller-vers*"
5. SW and territories
6. Socio-professional integration in an inclusive dynamic

6.1 Social Development, Collective Intervention

Capabilities and skills to:

(a) **Conduct a social development project:** Social development is a process of mobilising individuals, groups and territories, mobilising the capacities of inhabitants to act to create a collective and enable citizens to participate in democratic life and social action to be more preventive, participatory and inclusive.

(b) **Conduct a collective intervention project:** The development of "collective actions" leads professionals to follow certain rules: collective information, animation and SW with user groups, networking organised around projects. In addition, these activities, which are focused on the needs of users to create and promote the conditions, allow them to be fully involved in the transformation of their situation.

Contextual Elements Resulting from community SW in reference to the work of Saul Alinsky and Paulo Freire, collective SW has developed in France since the events of May 1968. The social intervention of collective interests is defined as "considering the living conditions of a population in a given territory, which aims to take into account collective interests, understood as factors likely to facilitate the social communication of various groups and, by so doing, to help control daily life, in its various dimensions" (Nouveau dictionnaire critique d'action sociale 2008, translated by the authors).

Collective SW has a particular interest in questioning the collective dynamics of a given territory and aims to develop the relationship between a defined population and its local and institutional environment. This concept is therefore strongly linked to local social development, "which is a method of approaching and understanding local problems in a comprehensive way that can be applied both to sectoral social policies (housing, employment, culture) and to priority groups (young, inactive, elderly, early childhood)" (Godet 2008).

As we can see, these elements of the SW approach are not new and are now being used as part of the renovation of SW. The logics of systems presented earlier reposition social workers in coordination logics which, in fact, requires repositioning people as actors but also placing them at the heart of territories constituted by a multiplicity of actors and institutions in an empowerment strategy. These notions are based on new political aims, in particular the creation and promotion of conditions that allow accompanied persons to be fully involved in their lives and situations, with all the ambiguities that this can lead to (liberal logic).

In our opinion, these aims can also develop citizenship: since this approach is repositioned as one of the essential methods for developing the power to act by the people concerned, it puts the group back at the heart of SW as a vehicle for socialisation and development. We are part of an "ethics of care": we are not a single individual without others; "ethics of care" refers to the notion of interdependence and social links where the territory becomes a vector for mobilising the capacities of its inhabitants to create collectives and participate in democratic life as defined by Carol Gilligan. Initiatives for inclusive territories are emerging, often on the initiative of associations strongly linked to the groups of people concerned. These emerging collectives become levers for social action. This is one of the most relevant and crucial dimensions in SW today because these collectives emerge and structure themselves around the issues they face, and it is also a political issue.

6.2 Participation of Individuals Concerned

Capabilities and skills to energise the co-construction of personal paths. Application of the principle of citizen participation, which considers all stakeholders in decision-making processes at the same level.

Participation should be promoted in three aspects:

- Co-construction with the person of their project and life course, as part of individual or collective support;
- Participation in the governance of national and local, consultative or decision-making bodies, in the social and medico-social field;
- Co-training of social workers (with reference to the POWER-Us model).

Contextual Elements This question is not a recent one in practical guidelines. Already in 1982, Nicole Questiaux, Minister of National Solidarity, addressed it extensively in a circular written for social workers. In recent years, the issue has continued to grow: on the one hand, through the various political orientations mentioned earlier, but on the other hand, through the structuring of groups of supported people. The growth of these groups makes it possible to make their voices heard and facilitates their participation in various institutional (social life councils) and political (HCTS) bodies. We will also mention the National Council of Accompanied Persons (CRPA), the *Association départementale des personnes accueillies à la protection de l'enfance* (ADEPAPE) (representative of former child protection) or Aide à Toute Détresse Quart-Monde (ATD Fourth World) (international non-governmental movement which aims to influence political decisions in consultation with people affected by precariousness and poverty).

The participation and proposals of the groups of people concerned in political logic lead to collaborative work on different levels:

1. In the implementation of new social intervention measures. This is the case of experimentation with course referents that will be set up where CRPA has a presence. This is also the case with the "one home first" system, which experiments with peer support in support systems for people suffering from psychological disorders and living in precarious situations. These mechanisms are now in place.
2. In training orientation since modalities for the participation of individuals concerned in training programmes have been defined – in particular by UNAFORIS – Guide 2018 – and in the Inter-Ministerial Action Plan for Social Work and Social Development 2015. The ERASME school in Toulouse is part of the Power-Us project.
3. In the participation of individuals concerned in political bodies since the persons concerned now have a presence in inter-ministerial bodies (groups of the High Council for Social Work 2017).

6.3 Digital Society

Capabilities and skills to:

(a) **Integrate a digital culture.** The use of social networks is transforming communication patterns and social connections. Digital technology can generate social innovation and enable positive changes in professional practices.

(b) **Identify the uses of digital technology and its effects on citizenship.** The dematerialisation of many public services and the computerisation of data have an impact on access to the rights of accompanied persons and raise questions about the confidentiality of personal data.

(c) **Act as a digital assistant.** Digital technology can further exclude the most vulnerable who do not have access to computer equipment or the skills to use it.

Contextual Elements The rapid evolution of digital tools is also disrupting the practices of social workers. Being themselves subject to professional changes caused by the development of digital tools and the industrial revolution they bring about, they raise new ethical and professional challenges. From the point of view of the people concerned, the stakes are also high, questions of access and cost, equipment and understanding arise and cast doubt on the republican principle of equality. The dematerialisation of many public services and the computerisation of data have a strong impact on people's rights.

As the Council of Europe emphasised in 2016, there is a social and societal challenge that goes beyond SW, and the concept of digital citizenship is at the heart of an intergovernmental project entitled Digital Citizenship Education (Council of Europe n.d.). This project aims to contribute to "redefining the role of education in enabling all children to acquire the skills they need as digital citizens to participate actively and responsibly in a democratic society, whether offline or online".

Since September 2017, the HCTS has been proposing to reflect on ways to support changes in practices in order to (enrich and) conceive of digital technology as a vector of the power to act, of allowing people to exercise their rights as part of a shared vigilance and analysis – respecting the legal framework, ethical and deontological references, and values to be shared.

6.4 Moving towards "Aller-vers"

This concept includes capabilities and skills to:

(a) **Evolve practices and organisations to better meet needs.** The aim is to address the problem of the "non-use" of social rights by developing a proactive culture of SW and spaces that are closer to the population.

(b) **"Moving towards" people with unmet support needs**, sometimes isolated, in withdrawal or struggling to make a request, to identify their rights or to present themselves at the right counter. This approach is a response to the increasing complexity of administrative procedures and the complexity of precarious situations experienced by people living in poverty.

Contextual Elements The profound transformations of our society, the rise of precariousness and the isolation of different groups linked to the increasing complexity of solidarity systems have generated new forms of isolation: poverty, unemployment and increased homelessness, for example.

Although "moving towards" is already a skill of social workers, the aforementioned forms of isolation and the diversification of the groups concerned require new modalities of intervention, in particular allowing for the exercise of rights. Often associated with marauding or specialised education in an open environment, *moving towards* is nowadays at the heart of different and new organization or new social services and therefore aimed at a wider audience. Thus, Marie Paule Cols, Vice-President of HCTS, reminded us on World Social Work Day in 2019 that we are in the process of "putting a certain number of values and fundamentals back into the profession, while society around us is changing" (Cols, 2019, translated by authors).

Thus, moving towards, as a constitutive mission of SW, can be characterised as a proactive approach to reaching out to people who do not necessarily make requests. It requires action according to the basic principles of intervention but also combining theoretical and methodological approaches to the development of the power to act and the logic of territories.

6.5   Social Work and Territories

This includes the capabilities and skills to:

(a) **Adapt and strengthen SW in social housing neighbourhoods or in situations of urban relocation.** Difficulties that are more significant here than in other territories and can be quantified (higher unemployment rate, more frequent school drop-out rates and, overall, less favourable poverty indicators). Without falling into clichés, social workers may be confronted with more significant difficulties in these territories with specific social and cultural codes (e.g. greater gap between generations, risks of more radicalisation, violence).

(b) **Adapt and strengthen SW in remote rural areas.** Social workers working in isolated rural areas must deal with the need to provide care for groups of people who are more often confronted with problems of mobility and difficulties in accessing certain public services, which are less present in rural areas, and the phenomenon of impoverishment that is less visible because of the isolation of the people concerned.

Contextual Elements Working on the territorial dimension now seems essential in view of the particularities and significant differences between certain territories: rural areas, working-class districts or urban areas.

For example, some neighbourhoods are ghettoised, isolated and the result of a continuous deterioration towards which policies have been less supportive and for which funding is lacking. Rural areas are also becoming isolated territories with increasing impoverishment, difficulties in access to employment and public services, and high levels of isolation. This raises the issue of access to digital technology.

Social intervention must respond to these new territorial logics by combining various methodologies and theoretical fields of collective work, local social development and empowerment development.

6.6 Socio-professional Integration in an Inclusive Dynamic

This concept includes the capabilities and skills to:

(a) **Act efficiently and consistently to promote employment.** SW have to strengthen their role and place, as actors in ensuring access to work and the collective utility of the most vulnerable people, in an inclusive dynamic.
(b) **Place the User at heart of the system:**

- take the whole situation into consideration,
- support individual and collective pathways to promote social/vocational integration or mobility of public applicants in the fields of employment, access to the law, health, housing, citizenship or vocational training.

Contextual Elements Under the impetus of public policies and in a constraining economic context, structures in the fields of health and social services are now in an era of decompartmentalisation and transversality. The logics seen earlier – territorial logics, development of partnerships, networking – are all indicators of these changes and a new organisation of institutions that disarticulate institutional logics.

The various testimonies of the people concerned contribute to this redefinition by pointing to institutional logics of organisational silos and denouncing compartmentalised and stacked care.

Professional practices are now guided by the most personalised considerations possible with regard to the persons concerned and by two major principles: **inclusion and continuity of support** – at different scales: territorial, between different sectors or within the same institution. Thus, coordination missions are developing strongly. This is the case, for example, in the establishment of career path referents in 2019; unlike with case managers, the career path referent is intended to "offer reinforced support to people in great social difficulty and aims to do so by improving cooperation between professionals in charge of monitoring the same person, by actively involving the latter in decision-making. The challenge is to ensure the continuity of the accompanied person's journey, by eliminating the direct or peripheral obstacles they encounter, and by proposing coherent actions corresponding to their needs". (Ministère des Solidarités et de la Santé 2019, translated by the authors)

These **changes in professional paradigms** entail the need to clarify the coordination roles and missions of social workers at levels 6 and 7 (EQF) and to consolidate or develop skills currently taught in training centres (e.g. multidisciplinary and interdisciplinary teamwork, partnerships, communication, professional writing).

All these orientations indicate a desire to profoundly transform SW approaches. This in itself is a good approach because French SW has indeed remained in a state of withdrawal into itself and is strongly marked by instrumental policies and institutional logics, corporatism and claim dynamics rather than by social empowerment and social development. This is probably very strongly influenced by an industrial model and a centralised state.

Today, the movement being created, in the context of a significant transformation of the role of the state under the presidency of Mr Macron, is opening up opportunities for SW to occupy a new place in social development. However, there is a real risk of devaluation of the role of SW. Indeed, the promotion of other approaches, such as commercial privatisation of social action in the forms of social and charity business through the implementation of social impact contracts in the name of efficiency goals, plays a role in this.

7 Challenges and Perspectives: Moving Closer to International Standards and Developing Collaborations and Research

We have seen that SW in France has a long history. Over the years, it has developed a knowledge base and a strong professional ethic. The values that inspire professionals in the field are legitimate and consistent with major international institutions such as the UN, UNESCO and the Council of Europe to which France is committed. We talked about the wealth of this knowledges and also pointed out its weaknesses. It is too segmented, too immersed in social intervention and too isolated from international relations and research. In recent years, France has become aware of these difficulties and has embarked on a process of transformation.

As we saw, France has classified SW degrees based on 180 ECTs (bachelor level). Training programmes include two areas of skills common to all SW curricula which complement the more traditional skills centred on being attentive to each individual's situation. They replace them in more general and collective contexts of social development.

These areas are as follows:

Professional SW communication.

> Develop, manage and transmit information.
> Establish a professional relationship.

Involvement in dynamic partnerships and inter-institutional collaborations.

> Develop actions in partnerships and networking.
> Ensure a mediation function.
> Register in teamwork.

Mobility is sought on local and international scales.
The practice of alternating between school and work is reinforced.

These transformations require the establishment of educational approaches that allow:

- The capacity to link conceptual theoretical approaches and field investigations. The inductive approach needs to be prioritised and complemented by a deductive approach.
- The reflexive analysis of work by group situations.
- Cooperation between schools and social services upon agreement.
- The encounter of different practices by local and international mobilities.

Faced with complex social phenomena and policies that seek short-term effectiveness, French SW is fragile, because it is exposed to economics and political evolutions. Thus, it must find and impose the modalities to ensure its reinforcement. A number of paths remain to be explored:

Strengthen the Role and Place of SW and SW Education
- Quickly give a clear and specific position to SW within social intervention and create a common code of ethics for a large and unified professional community.
- Reinforce the status of higher education institutions of SW schools in each regional territory with official research activities and teacher-researchers as universities of SW.
- Recognise a qualification system as a whole: bachelor's degree – master's degree – PhD in SW.

Strengthen Innovation and SW Research
- Recognise and structure a specific field of research in SW.
- Support incubators of collective projects involving professionals, stakeholders, students and teacher-researchers.
- Create a PhD in SW.

Open French SW to the Dynamics of International SW and Its Objectives
- Develop practices for the translation of foreign language theories and material on SW.
- Integrate international social work learning into curricula.
- Integrate the question of eco-social transition, climate change, migration, crises.
- Strengthen mobility and international cooperation between schools.

In France, as in other countries, the activities of SW are often subjected to the pressure of economic and social problems. Thus, the activity of SW needs to be renewed constantly. This is also determined by political choices, particulary in times of populist political movements. The autonomy of SW is more or less real depending on the context and the period. This is an important reason to work and cooperate on an international definition of SW and standards for SW education, research and comparative methods of education and training. The time has now returned for French SW to move from the Gallic village of Asterix into the global village (Rollet 2016).

References

ANAS. Association Nationale des Assistants de Service Social [ANAS. National Association of Social Service Assistants], 2015. https://www.anas.fr/

ANAS. (2012). Congress of the International Federation of Social Work *"Strengthening the voice of social work and giving it new direction"*.. Available at: https://www.anas.fr/Intervention-de-l-ANAS-au-Congres-de-l-International-Federation-of-Social-Workers-IFSW-a-Stockolm_a841.html. Accessed 26 Aug 2020.

Bilan associatif de l'emploi sanitaire et social [Association review of health and social employment]. 2018. Available via: https://recherches-solidarites.org/wp-content/uploads/2018/09/Bilan-2018-de-l-emploi-associatif-sanitaire-et-social.pdf. Accessed 26 Aug 2020.

Bourquin, J. (1998). *La Revue d'histoire de l'enfance "irrégulière"* [The Children's History Review "irregular"]. Available via: La protection de l'enfance: regards https://journals.openedition.org/rhei/12. Accessed 26 Aug 2020.

Buzyn, A. (2018). *Stratégie nationale de prévention et de lutte contre la pauvreté « Investir dans les solidarités pour l'émancipation de tous »* [National stratégie to prevent and fight against powerty "To invest in the solidarities for emancipation of all]. Available at: https://solidarites-sante.gouv.fr/actualites/presse/dossiers-de-presse/article/strategie-nationale-de-prevention-et-de-lutte-contre-la-pauvrete. Accessed 26 Aug 2020

Castel, R. (2009). *La montée des incertitudes. Travail, Protection, Statuts de l'individu* [The rise of uncertainties. Work, Protection, Status of the individual]. Paris: Editions du Seuil, Coll. La couleur des idées.

Chauvière, M. (1980). *Enfance inadaptée: l'héritage de Vichy* [Unsuitable childhood: the legacy of Vichy]. Paris: Les Éditions ouvrières.

Cols, MP (2019). *World social work day 2019 Paris - Aller Vers ou Revenir aux fondamentaux. 19 Mars 2019* Available at: https://www.lemediasocial-emploi.fr/article/journee-mondiale-du-travail-social-aller-vers-ou-revenir-aux-fondamentaux-2019-03-20-07-00. Accessed 26 Aug 2020.

Conférence européenne EASSW-UNAFORIS. *Les formations en travail social en Europe: faire bouger les lignes pour un avenir durable* [EASSW-UNAFORIS European Conference. Social work training in Europe: moving the lines for a sustainable future], June 2017. Available via: https://evenements.unaforis.eu/. Accessed 26 Aug 2020.

Cornier, C. (2012). L'alternance intégrative, une notion fondamentale dans le processus de professionnalisation des travailleurs sociaux [Integrative alternation study/practices, a fundamental notion in the process of professionalization of social workers]. In G. d'Allondans (Ed.), *Sites qualifiants. Etablissements de formation en travail social. Une nouvelle dynamique de l'alternance*. Paris: Editions Taraedre.

Cornilleau, G. (2019). *L'état Providence: Quelles interrogations?* [The welfare state: What questions?]. Available via: https://www.vie-publique.fr/parole-dexpert/269721-etat-providence-quelles-interrogations. Accessed 26 Aug 2020.

Council of Europe. (n.d.). Digital Citizenship education. Available at: https://www.coe.int/en/web/digital-citizenship-education/home. Accessed 26 Aug 2020.

Définition du travail social. Rapport adopté par la commission permanente du 23 février 2017 du HCTS [ANAS. National Association of Social Service Assistants, 2015 . Definition of social work. Report adopted by the HCTS Standing Committee of 23 February 2017], Paris. Available via: https://solidarites-sante.gouv.fr/IMG/pdf/definition_du_travail_social-2.pdf. Accessed 26 Aug 2020.

Definition of International social work approved by the IASSW General Assembly and IFSW General meeting in July 2014 Melbourne.Available via: https://www.iassw-aiets.org/global-definition-of-social-work-review-of-the-global-definition/. Accessed 26 Aug 2020.

Delaunay, B. (2007). La formation initiale en service social, une instance de professionnalisation [Initial training in social service, a professionalisation body]. *Vie Sociale, 4*, 59–78.

Etats Généraux du Travail Social [States General of Social Work] (2015). https://solidarites-sante.gouv.fr/affaires-sociales/travail-social/archives/article/rapports-des-egts Accessed 26 Aug 2020.

Donzelot, J. (1984). *L'invention du Social. Essai sur le déclin des passions politiques* [The invention of the Social. Essay on the decline of political passions]. Paris: Editions Fayard.

DREES. (2018). L'aide et l'action sociales en France. Vue d'ensemble Fiches thématiques Annexes. Ministère des Solidarités et de la Santé. https://drees.solidarites-sante.gouv.fr/IMG/pdf/ve-8.pdf

Esping-Andersen, G. (1990). *The three worlds of welfare capitalism.* Princeton University Press.

European qualifications framework. Available at: https://ec.europa.eu/info/education/skills-and-qualifications_en. Accessed 26 Aug 2020.

Fiches métiers du travail social [French Social work job technical sheets]. 2014. https://solidarites-sante.gouv.fr/metiers-et-concours/les-metiers-du-travail-social/. Accessed 26 Aug 2020.

Godet, J. M. (2008). Préambule. Quelle formation pour le développement social local? [Preamble. What training for local social development?] In J. M. Gourvil, & M. Kaiser (Eds.), *Se former au développement local.* Paris: Dunod.

Haut Conseil du Travail Social [High Council for Social Work]. (2016). Available via: https://solidarites-sante.gouv.fr/ministere/acteurs/instances-rattachees/haut-conseil-du-travail-social-hcts/presentation-du-hcts/. Accessed 26 Aug 2020.

Jaeger, M. (2013a). A propos de la formation des travailleurs sociaux: une histoire à redécouvrir [On the training of social workers: A story to be rediscovered]. *Vie sociale, 4*, 191–215.

Jaeger, M. (2013b). Conférence de consensus. La recherche en / dans / sur le travail social. L'avis du Jury, 22 juin 2013 [Consensus conference. Research in / in / on social work. The opinion of the Jury]. *VST, 120*, 82–89.

Jaeger, M. (2006). Les référentiels pour la formation des travailleurs sociaux: une affaire d'import-export [Standards for the training of social workers: An import-export affair]. *Vie sociale, 2*(2), 57–65.

Jaeger, M. (2009). La formation des travailleurs sociaux: nouvelles configurations, nouveaux questionnements [The training of social workers: New configurations, new questions]. *Caisse Nationale d'Allocations Familiales, 2*(152), 74–81.

La Participation des Personnes Ressources Concernées aux Formations à l'Intervention Sociale. Guide UNAFORIS [Participation of Relevant Resource Persons in Social Intervention.

La Participation des Personnes Accompagnées aux instances de gouvernance et à la formation des travailleurs sociaux. Synthèse du groupe de travail adopté par le HCTS en séance plénière le 7 juillet 2017 [Participation of Supported Persons in governance bodies and in the training of social workers. Summary of the working group adopted by the HCTS in plenary session on July 7], Paris. Available via: https://solidarites-sante.gouv.fr/ministere/acteurs/instances-rattachees/haut-conseil-du-travail-social-hcts/rapports-et-publications-du-hcts/rapports/article/participation-des-personnes-accompagnees-aux-instances-de-gouvernance-et-a-la. Accessed 26 Aug 2020.

La professionnalisation dans les formations en travail social. Des modalités diverses. Note du groupe de travail Professionnalisation de l'UNAFORIS [Professionalisation in social work training. Various modalities. Note from the UNAFORIS Professionalisation working group], November 2017, Paris. Available via: https://www.unaforis.eu/sites/default/files/public/fichiers/telechargements/unaforis_professionnalisation_221116.pdf. Accessed 26 Aug 2020.

Le, S. (2018). L'arroseur arrosé – Quand le travail souffre de précarité [The watered sprinkler – When work suffers from precariousness]. In *4(64)*.

Ministère des Solidarités et de la Santé. (2019). *Guide d'appui à la démarche du référent de parcours, ANDASS et DGCS* [Guide to support the pathway referent approach, ANDASS and DGCS]. Paris. Available at: https://solidarites-sante.gouv.fr/ministere/documentation-et-publications-officielles/guides/article/guide-d-appui-a-la-mise-en-oeuvre-de-la-demarche-du-referent-de-parcours. Accessed 26 Aug 2020.

Nouveau dictionnaire critique d'action sociale. (2008). Paris: Bayard.

Pascal, H. (2014). *Histoire du travail social en France. De la fin du 19ème siècle à nos jours* [History of social work in France. From the late 19th century to today]. Paris: Presses de l'EHEPS.

Plan d'action interministériel en faveur du travail social et du développement social [Interministerial action plan for social work and social development], 2015, Paris. https://solidarites-sante.gouv.fr/affaires-sociales/travail-social/article/plan-d-action-interministeriel-en-faveur-du-travail-social-et-du-developpement. Accessed 26 Aug 2020.

PREFAS Midi Pyrénées: Actes de séminaire du PREFAS, Professionnalisation des travailleurs sociaux [PREFAS seminar proceedings, Professionalisation of social workers], 2017, Toulouse. Available via: http://www.prefas-mp.fr/sites/prefas-mp.fr/files/actes_semininaire_du_2_decembre_2017_-_professionnalisation_des_travailleurs_sociaux.pdf. Accessed 26 Aug 2020.

Pourquoi et comment les travailleurs sociaux se saisissent des outils numériques. Rapport du Haut Conseil en Travail Social [Why and how social workers are embracing digital tools. Report of the High Council for Social Work]. 2019, Paris. Available via: https://solidaritessante.gouv.fr/IMG/pdf/pourquoi_et_comment_les_travailleurs_sociaux_se_saisissent_des_outils_numeriques.pdf. Accessed 26 Aug 2020.

PowerUs. Available via: https://powerus.eu/

Ruggero, I. (2016). Des « héritières » dans la formation d'assistante de service social? Aspiration au travail social et reclassement ["Heiresses" in the training of social service assistant? Aspiration to social work and reclassification]. *Revue Française de Pédagogie, 2*(195), 37–50.

Rollet, C. (2016). *Du village Gaulois au village global. Points de repères pour le travail social* [From the Gallic village to the global village. Benchmarks for social work]. Paris: L'harmattan.

Stratégie Nationale de Prévention de Lutte contre la Pauvreté. Investir dans les solidarités pour l'émancipation de tous [National Strategy for the Prevention of Poverty Reduction. Investing in soilidarities for the emancipation of all], 2018, Paris. https://solidarites-sante.gouv.fr/affaires-sociales/lutte-contre-l-exclusion/lutte-pauvrete-gouv-fr/. Accessed 26 Aug 2020.

UNAFORIS. (2018). *La PARTICIPATION des personnes ressources concernées aux formations à l'intervention sociale*. Paris: https://www.unaforis.eu/sites/default/files/public/fichiers/telechargements/2018_09_unaforis_guide_participation_version_papier_vdef.pdf. Accessed 26 Aug 2020.

UNIFAF. (2017). Enquête-Emploi. Diversité des emplois et leurs caractéristiques. https://enquete-emploi.unifaf.fr/resultats/diversite-des-emplois-et-leurs-caracteristiques

Social Work and Social Work Education in Germany: Development and Challenges in a Scientific and Practice-Based Profession and Its Education

Marion Laging, Peter Schäfer, and Miriam Lorenz

1 Introduction

This chapter examines the extent to which social work education in Germany is able to reflect on and respond to the current challenges facing social work today.

Research has shown that we are witnessing a rapid societal and political transformation with widening social and economic disparities. This may affect social work as an academic discipline and profession as well as the living conditions of the people who are the recipients of care provided by social workers. Against this background, we have conducted a comprehensive analysis that focuses on historical and current social and socio-political transformations and their effects on social work as well as its educational structures. Specific emphasis is placed on the results and the potential of the process of academisation and the level of internationalisation that social work education has achieved over the last years.

This chapter consists of four sections.

First, before the presentation of the current situation, we describe and analyse significant steps of the historical process of professional social work development in Germany. This part includes a review of the particular socioeconomic, political and cultural context in which social work arose and is currently embedded.

The original version of this chapter was revised: Incorrect URL was placed for the reference Schäfer and Bartosch (2016) in the reference section which has been corrected now. The correction to this chapter is available at https://doi.org/10.1007/978-3-030-69701-3_12

M. Laging (✉) · M. Lorenz
Hochschule Esslingen, University of Applied Sciences Esslingen, Esslingen, Germany
e-mail: marion.laging@hs-esslingen.de; miriam.lorenz@hs-esslingen.de

P. Schäfer
Hochschule Niederrhein, University of Applied Sciences, Mönchengladbach, Germany
e-mail: peter.schaefer@hs-niederrhein.de

© Springer Nature Switzerland AG 2021, corrected publication 2021   89
M. Laging, N. Žganec (eds.), *Social Work Education in Europe*,
European Social Work Education and Practice,
https://doi.org/10.1007/978-3-030-69701-3_5

Second, a description of the main work areas and methodology of social work in Germany follows. We will point out what kinds of professional orientation (e.g. case management, advocacy, community work) are discernible and what kind of work areas and professional activities have recently become more or less relevant.

Third, the current model of social work education in Germany is described in detail. We provide clear insight into the classic and main developments of social work education, particularly the main contents and characteristics and the level of academisation social work education has achieved.

Finally, against this background, we analyse whether there are discrepancies between what educational institutions both aim for and achieve and what the practice field demands. To what extent has the academisation of social work supported practitioners in this regard? What roles do or could European and global perspectives play in this process?

2 History, Framing and Structures of Social Work in Germany

The history of social work in Germany started with the establishment of civic society at the beginning of the nineteenth century. For large sections of the population industrialisation brought with it a degree of poverty and misery which could no longer be seen as naturally occurring phenomena (Hammerschmidt et al. 2017: 9).

Poverty and misery were not new phenomena, but at this time they became framed by capitalism. People were seen as subjects to the market and were expected to survive and procreate within the mediums of exchange governed by market mechanisms. However, this happened in the absence of any safety nets that might otherwise have been provided by pre-industrial society – safety nets such as those provided by familial relationships, guilds, churches, or the like. Put another way, especially in terms of the labour market, there was no guarantee that people would be able to sell their labour; and if they could sell their labour, there was no guarantee that they would get what they needed for a decent life. The huge number of problems, risks and uncertainties about such situations created a breeding ground for what became known as the *Soziale Frage* (social issue) (Hammerschmidt et al. 2017: 17f).

The theories that tried to explain the conditions and causes were diverse and contradictory. However, the debates surrounding social issues brought the questions of poverty out of the individual moral realm and into the world of social theories (Wendt 2017a: 112ff).

But neither the aristocracy nor the urban middle classes were able to significantly improve the living conditions of the working poor, nor were they able to cope effectively with the steadily worsening socioeconomic tensions that consequently arose. This became obvious during the famine revolts and during the Silesian Weavers' Uprising of 1844. Furthermore, the conflicts between the aristocracy and the aspiring middle classes became more and more severe and culminated in the March Revolution of 1848 (ibid.).

Against this background, social-reform politics for the *Unterbürgerlichen* (sub-bourgeois) seemed to be necessary for the urban middle classes in order to stop the destructive power of unbridled economic liberalism. Furthermore, the organised labour movement emerged and the bourgeoisie found itself caught between two fronts: on the one hand, the labour movement, and on the other hand, the aristocracy. The middle classes found themselves politically impotent at state level, but nevertheless powerful and active on the municipal level due to local self-governance. This allowed them to fashion the idea of creating a better society (Hammerschmidt et al. 2017: 21).

The municipalities were in charge of caring for the poor, and they developed a multiplicity of caring approaches. However, step by step, the Elberfeld System for the relief of the poor, whose main principles are still partially valid today, became the dominant model. Volunteers – but only men – would look after a maximum of four poor men and their families in a given district. During regular visits the needs of the family were assessed systematically. Additionally, an evaluation was made as to whether other claims existed. On that basis it was decided whether and to what extent benefits would be granted. A controlling, educating and disciplinary intention can easily be identified: for example, whoever refused to work was reported to the police (Hammerschmidt et al. 2017: 22f; Wendt 2017a: 301f; Hering and Münchmeier 2014: 33ff).

The administration of relief for the poor was supplemented by the engagement of the educated middle classes, who were organised in associations, as well as by the social charitable engagement of confessional groups. At that time, this kind of engagement was called *Privatwohltätigkeit* (private charity); in 1920 it was renamed to *Freie Wohlfahrtspflege* (non-statutory welfare), the current overarching term for social associations in the private sector in Germany (Hammerschmidt et al. 2017:24).

Philanthropic motives were important within these associations, but they also aimed to impose the norms and values of the middle classes upon the working classes, not least via social control. The current discipline of social pedagogy has its roots in the work of these associations. The aim of social pedagogy was to foster integration through education. The danger of "mob rule" could be averted and inculcation in the values of liberal democracy achieved. These activities can be viewed as a means for enforcing the "cultural hegemony" of the middle classes, which has also been characterised as colonialism or secular missionary work (Hering and Münchmeier 2014: 36f).

But all these developments and achievements were insufficient in terms of pacifying the working poor. The labour movement became organised into multiple associations and parties, which strove for a new fundamental societal change. Therefore, Otto von Bismarck, Chancellor of the German Empire, developed a twin-track strategy that included both massive intimidation of the working classes and the erection and establishment of a social security system at the same time. In 1878, anti-socialist laws were passed. They aimed to cripple the labour movement through various means. The new social security system included insurance for health care, accidents and pensions. One crucial characteristic of this system was the legal right to demand support in case of unemployment or incapacity, so this system should not have had discriminative and humiliating effects. But insurance-based support was often not sufficient to meet the needs of those affected, and the pre-existing forms of help within the municipalities remained important (Wendt 2017a: 382fff; Hammerschmidt et al. 2017: 64f).

Therefore, the social sector which exists today has been influenced and shaped by the structures and systems which were conceived during the early years of the German Empire (1871–1918). Specifically, a dual structure emerged that contains both insurance against the basic risks of life and at the same time social work and social pedagogy in the form of counselling, support and education, for example (Wendt 2017a: 382fff).

These were mainly organised in associations of the urban middle classes, and over the following years these associations developed a rich plurality of different approaches and perspectives. At that time, socio-critical movements also arose, such as the women's and youth movements, that also influenced society until World War I.

The initially free and unbounded engagement led first to a confusing jumble of activities and measures. For a more desirable rational and effective/systematic design of offering help and education, umbrella organisations were increasingly founded at the municipal and national levels. These umbrella organisations aimed at organising effective information exchange and collaboration, as well as engaging in strong and close collaborations with the public sector. Furthermore, as these associations became more and more funded by the public sector, civil society engagement was increasingly incorporated into the state. On the other hand, the associations were able to influence politics through their umbrella organisations (Hammerschmidt et al. 2017: 49ff).

In 1894, the *Bund Deutscher Frauenvereine* (Federation of German Women's Associations) was founded as an umbrella organisation of 65 associations; in 1912, 2200 associations were members. These associations focused on fields of education and social affairs (education, parenting, social issues). Alice Salomon, a pioneer within the women's movement, started by developing lecture events, followed by a 1-year course; then in 1908 she founded the first formal educational institution for social work, the *soziale Frauenschule* (the Social School for Women), which turned out to be a milestone in the history of the profession of social work in Germany (Wendt 2017a: 440ff).

In 1917, Alice Salomon also initiated the Conference of German Women's Social Schools in which representatives of the ministry participated, in addition to the schools of social work. While the conference developed guidelines for the main features of social work education, the state started to regulate the education of social work in 1918 (Wendt 2017b: 86ff).

The range of social help increased sharply during World War I. The Federation of German Women's Associations aimed to receive acknowledgement and to achieve rights by taking over duties during the war. The vast majority of the professionals in the social field did not oppose the war, and the youth movement shared the general enthusiasm in 1914 when patriotism and militaristic tendencies were growing stronger (Wendt 2017b: 152ff).

In those days, social help started to become differentiated into three large sectors, which remain relevant today: (1) *Kinder- und Jugendfürsorge* (services for children, young people and families), (2) *Sozialhilfe* (social assistance), and (3) *Gesundheitshilfe* (health care), as will be described in more detail.

After World War I, under the Weimar Republic, the most important legal foundation and organisations for social work were established.

Although financial restrictions riddled the social sector, politics at that time aimed to take over responsibilities and to anchor social rights and duties in the constitution. An increase occurred in voluntary and public welfare, and there emerged an interwoven structure of private and public welfare work, which exists to this day. The voluntary welfare organisations, as umbrella associations, represented a plurality of approaches, initiatives and interests groups in the field of social help, which were as follows: (1) *Innere Mission* (now *Diakonisches Werk*: Diaconal Charity of the German Evangelical Church), (2) *Deutscher Paritätischer Wohlfahrtsverband* (now *Paritätischer Wohlfahrtsverband*: German Parity Welfare Organisation), (3) *Arbeiterwohlfahrt* (Workers' Welfare Association), (4) Caritas, (5) *Deutsches Rotes Kreuz* (German Red Cross), and (6) *Zentralwohlfahrtsstelle der deutschen Juden* (German Central Jewish Welfare Office) (Hering and Münchmeier 2014:128).

These six organisations were coordinated in a further, still existing umbrella association, the *Deutsche Liga der freien Wohlfahrtspflege* (German Federation of Voluntary Welfare Organisations).

At the same time, social work became a state-recognised qualification (Hammerschmidt et al. 2017: 59–79).

In 1933, the National Socialists came to power under Adolf Hitler, marking the end of the Weimar Republic.

In the name of eugenics and race hygiene, "valuable" humans were separated from the "inferior". Disabled, mentally ill, homosexual and "antisocial" people were segregated and finally eliminated. Social legislation measures generally remained in force, but in those days, social politics and social work focused on *Volkspflege*, which meant that only the "Aryan master race" – as a race, not as individuals – should be fostered and should benefit from social politics and means (Hammerschmidt et al. 2017: 80f; Wendt 2017b: 174).

Gesundheitsämter (public health departments at the municipal level) played a crucial role in putting this ideology into practice. Step by step, social politics became eradication politics. By 1945, 400,000 people had undergone forced sterilisation and over 210,000 of the handicapped and mentally ill had been murdered in Germany and Austria alone (Hammerschmidt et al. 2017: 85f).

Social workers were part of this cruel process – as long as they themselves were not discarded for political reasons or because of their Jewish ancestry. Leading figures, such as Alice Salomon for example, had to flee. However, the vast majority of social workers continued to work within the system of social help, as described earlier, but under the rule of the Nazi ideology at that time (Hammerschmidt et al. 2017: 80f; Wendt 2017b: 175f).

After World War II and all its devastation, the conviction gained recognition that democracy included social responsibility of the state. The western part of Germany (BRD) developed a system that tried to combine capitalism with social equity and which since that time has been referred to as a social market economy. The constitution declared the republic to be a social state, governed by the rule of law as a social, constitutional state (Wendt 2017b: 199ff).

The type of welfare in western Germany that had emerged by that time has been characterised by Esping-Andersen as a conservative welfare regime. The other two types are called social-democratic and liberal regimes (Wendt 2017b: 209; Esping-Andersen 1990: 25ff).

Welfare regimes refer to all the norms, rules and laws that determine social policy in a state. Each welfare regime is characterised by its relationship between state, market and civic society (NGOs and family) in terms of being responsible for social security, social equity and providing social help (ibid.).

One of the main features of the conservative welfare regime is statutory social security which is linked to gainful work. The principle of equivalence is central: the more one has paid, the more one is going to get paid. Therefore, the conservative welfare regime is to a large extent characterised by monetary transfer. Furthermore, the associations of churches and of civic society are included in the care system and play an important role. Hence, this kind of welfare regime is also called a corporatist welfare regime (Wendt 2017b: 210).

The relationship between the public sector and the voluntary sector (at that time mainly associations of churches and civic society) became organised by the principle of subsidiarity, reaffirmed by a Constitutional Court decision in 1967. The principle of subsidiarity gives a subordinate position to public bodies, to the effect that public bodies should only be active in providing social help in cases where private bodies are not able or willing to do so. Nevertheless, public bodies are obliged to fund private initiatives and social services (Aner and Hammerschmidt 2018: 145). The so-called principle of subsidiarity was anchored in the two precursors of today's Child and Youth Welfare Act (SGB VIII) and the Social Welfare Act (SGB XII). According to this principle, which was shaped by Catholic social teaching, public institutions should refrain from establishing their own social facilities and services if charitable facilities could be used. At the same time, the public sector was obliged to reimburse the assigned institutions for the cost price. This principle has strengthened the voluntary welfare sector in Germany but has also been criticised: The primacy of the voluntary sector leads to an inclusion of the voluntary sector in statutory regulations, and the voluntary sector is in danger of losing its independence and autonomy (Wendt 2017b: 209).

Against this background, the voluntary welfare sector is the major employer of social work in Germany: In 2016 there were 1,912,665 employees active in 118,623 facilities and services (BAGFW 2018: 6).

Following the introduction of re-education programmes by the American military authorities, with which the Americans and the British wanted to "democratise" the Germans, social work had (again) found its way to western Germany. Social workers who had emigrated in the Nazi era now returned to contribute to the reintroduction of social work. There was an opportunity to study American methods of casework, group work and community work. In Germany, these practices were – just like democracy – willingly accepted without immediately taking root.

Less based on those methods than on an American understanding, "social worker" soon began to be used as a job title. The social educational intention remained (as a pedagogical reference). In 1950, the National Association of Social Work, *Deutscher Verband der Sozialarbeiterinnen* (German Association of Social Workers) was re-founded out of the former *Verband der deutschen Sozialbeamtinnen* (Association of German Social Civil Servants) – initially without allowing men to become members (Wendt 2017b: 203).

The federal German policy initially focused on material transfers. The German *Wirtschaftswunder* ("economic miracle") allowed a comparatively generous, i.e. primarily quantitative, expansion of social protection with regard to the standard risk, with continued sick pay, child benefit regulations (family benefits compensation) and changes in statutory health insurance (Wendt 2017b: 205f).

The 1970s brought a multi-faceted scene of political initiatives and self-help groups, which significantly influenced social work. The peace movement, gay and lesbian movements and various self-help groups in the cultural and health sectors also performed practical activities with a social work character, such as women's shelters and drug facilities (Hammerschmidt et al. 2017: 114). Reform schools were gradually closed and alternative forms of housing developed (Hammerschmidt et al. 2017: 107f). A strong self-help movement unfolded in the field of mental health problems, HIV and AIDS; the disability movement questioned the traditional paternalistic system of services for disabled people (Hammerschmidt et al. 2017: 117; Wendt 2017b: 274–280).

In the 1980s, social work lost its reputation because it (1) was perceived critically by the self-help movement as a professional coloniser, (2) had to deal with charges of its own ineffectiveness and (3) became subject to questioning of its methodological and professional autonomy. After the widespread, much criticised failure of social work in the 1970s, where it pursued an approach of societal change by class struggle and community work and identified new target groups of social work, many social workers now sought the "path inwards". A psychotherapeutic approach, also called "psycho-boom", with a variety of different forms of therapy and schools, provided a wealth of therapeutic techniques whilst criticising and devaluing the classic methods of social work (see Sec. 3.5, "Methods of Social Work"). While the professionals were aiming for therapeutic competence, the contracting authority, under the influence of neoliberal economic theory, urged for more efficiency in the services. It encouraged organisations providing social work to follow the management practices of commercial enterprises. In the last decade of the twentieth century, managerial thinking and action entered into the organisation and procedures of human services (Wendt 2017b: 301–337).

At the end of the twentieth century, the diversity of social professions continued to increase, and common understanding within the field of social work declined. It became even more difficult for professional social workers to locate themselves in the range of employees with different types of education and identities (Wendt 2017b: 332ff).

In addition, the increasingly differentiated practice of social work (see Part 3, "Fields of Social Work in Germany") meant that many employees in special services no longer identified as social workers. They regarded themselves as debt counsellors, professional guardians, mediators, addiction consultants and so forth, or as supervisors, leaving the domain of social work completely (Wendt 2017b: 334). Accordingly, social work was held together only as an ensemble of social activities with specific social tasks. Furthermore, there was a lack of a common horizon or direction, and in particular, a link between "direct" social work and the level of programmes, initiatives and political representation (Wendt 2017b: 336).

Against this backdrop, a heated debate about social work science was sparked in the 1990s. In 1989, the German Association of Social Work (now DGSA) was founded. In addition to the professional associations Deutscher Berufsverband der Sozialarbeiterinnen (DBS) and Berufsverband der Sozialpädagogen/Sozialarbeiter und Heilpädagogen (BSH) at that time, and independently of them, the theory of the profession as well as the whole scope of social work was to be reflected and represented in a specialised political field (Wendt 2017b: 333).

The representatives of academic social pedagogy denied, however, that this was needed and in turn raised the claim that their humanistic approach to social pedagogy also provided the theory and science for social work. This specifically German (and exclusively German-speaking) discourse was factually unsubstantiated but should have rather been considered as a result of the academic localisation of social pedagogy. Nonetheless, there was a good deal of seriousness in the German academic terrain in distributing and defending their academic property (Wendt 2017b: 333f). The controversy gradually faded around the year 2000, when all groups agreed on the generic term *Soziale Arbeit* (social work) (for both *Sozialarbeit* (social work) and *Sozialpädagogik* (social pedagogy)).

It was urgent to clarify (1) the perspective of social work research, which had become more important in the quest for effectiveness and efficiency; (2) the relationship of occupational social work to civic engagement; (3) the intersection of social work sciences with health sciences and care, which in turn reached the level of science; (4) the ethical and economic dimensions of social work and (5) how the science of social work was to be linked to social informatics due to its increasing involvement in data processing, information networking and virtual communication (Wendt 2017b: 334).

These discourses took place in the context of the increasing appearance of neoliberal policies, which again challenged the self-identity of social work (see Part 5, "Current Developments and Challenges for Social Work Education").

3   Fields of Social Work in Germany

In Germany, various approaches have been taken systematically to present the fields of social work in Germany. The most common ones are from Aner and Hammerschmidt (2018), Thole (2012) and Otto et al. (2018); in addition to these researchers, others systematise the working areas of social work. The following part, Part 3, which gives an overview of the fields of social work in Germany, is based on the system proposed by Aner and Hammerschmidt (2018), which is oriented towards historical development and divides social work into four major sectors:

1. General and economic assistance
2. Children's services
3. Health-related assistance
4. Further differentiated fields of work.

3.1   General and Economic Assistance

General and economic assistance is part of the municipal services of general interest, which are provided as cash benefits, benefits in kind, or services. They include very different kinds of support and benefits that have arisen from the welfare of the poor.

General and economic assistance includes both non-specific support (often in the form of counselling and care) as well as highly specialised services for specific problem areas or groups of people. Poverty is the central dimension of assistance. Since 1961, the government has granted the legal right to access welfare benefits. In addition, it was determined that benefits were based on the principle of human dignity, which includes the sociocultural minimum subsistence level in setting the basis for calculating benefits. However, social assistance has not proved effective in combating poverty, as the gap between social assistance and average income is too large.

For people in specific social situations, the following social assistance is provided (Aner and Hammerschmidt 2018: 14f):

(a) Inpatient facilities such as shelters, supportive housing, e.g. for vulnerable adults, and aftercare facilities.
(b) Day care facilities, e.g. day care centres for specific groups (e.g. migrants), employment and qualification facilities and special schools.
(c) Consultation services and community-based services such as counselling for specific groups (e.g. those with hazardous substance use), legal advice centres and outpatient supportive housing.

It is true that the development of general and economic assistance is closely linked to the process of so-called normalisation of welfare and of the welfare state support system. However, they followed the development of poverty in the Federal Republic more than other fields did at the same time.

Although Germany is one of the richest countries in Europe and in the world, according to the Federal Statistical Office, 15.3 million people in Germany were affected by poverty and social exclusion in 2018, which corresponds to 18.7% of the population (Statistisches Bundesamt 2019). Some social groups were particularly affected by poverty: those living alone, 32.9%; single parents, 32.5%; those with low levels of education, 30.9%; and the unemployed, 70.5% (Aner and Hammerschmidt 2018: 17f).

Today, it needs to be taken into account that the boundaries between these groups and the rest of society and, thus, between those claiming benefits and those not claiming them have become increasingly fluid because population groups formerly considered secure are now exposed to an increasing risk of poverty.

3.2 Children's Services

Children's services are the largest field of work for social workers and social pedagogues in the Federal Republic. About one third of social workers and social pedagogues are employed in institutions for children's services. Children's services are regulated by law nationwide.

In 1990, a paradigm shift in children's services was initiated, and the hitherto strong control and intervention orientation of the previous Child and Youth Services Act was transformed into a modern benefits law, which provides support and assistance to children, adolescents and their parents.

It is noteworthy that the legal basis for welfare assistance also stipulates that it is the task of children's services to prevent and reduce disadvantages and to contribute to positive living conditions for young people (Aner and Hammerschmid 2018: 30f).

Basically, the law (SGB VIII) distinguishes between "services" and "other tasks". The service provision takes place predominantly and in accordance with the principle of subsidiarity, not by the municipality as a public institution itself, but by independent agencies. The other tasks are carried out by the municipalities themselves, because these are so-called sovereign tasks that cannot be delegated to independent agencies. For example, only a public institution may, under certain conditions, intervene in basic rights, such as parental rights within the framework of the public guardianship (*staatliches Wächteramt*). Only qualified, state-approved social workers are entitled to perform these tasks.

Assistance ranges from family support to removal of a child to a place of safety.

Children's services are an area of tension, influenced by various conflicts of objectives. A fundamental conflict of objectives exists through the obligation, on the one hand, to promote the general welfare of children, adolescents and their families and, on the other hand, to provide individual assistance and carry out protective measures (due to concerns about a child's welfare).

Another conflict of objectives arises from the financial situation of the municipalities. Economically and financially weak municipalities tend to focus on particularly urgent children's services or on those associated with directly enforceable legal rights which are necessary for the protection of a child's well-being. As a consequence, the social infrastructure cannot be further developed, which again can lead to professional problems within children's services. This can be seen in communities, for example, where the services of existing youth centres have been reduced, although professionally extended services or even an additional youth centre is required. While there were still 33,300 employees in children's services in 1998, this number was reduced to just over 17,500 at the beginning of 2015 (Aner and Hammerschmidt 2018: 36ff).

3.3   Health-Related Assistance

Health-related assistance takes place both inside and outside the healthcare system. Social workers are partly involved in treatment processes directly (as clinical social workers). However, they mainly take over tasks of health promotion, education and counselling in the public health service or within independent agencies (Aner and Hammerschmidt 2018: 52f).

Social work's understanding of health is based on a holistic and life course approach in which health is seen as an event of one's own lifestyle or a healthy environment that is adapted to the needs of the disabled.

Traditional areas of health-related social work are hospital social work and social work in public health services, and in particular, work with mentally ill or addicted people and with children, young people and families (health promotion).

Recently developed areas are specialised advice centres (on the subjects of drugs, AIDS, pregnancy/abortion), work with self-help groups, workplace health promotion, health promotion in old age and (municipal) planning and networking of health-related assistance.

The organisational assignment of these newly created areas varies within municipalities. Services such as AIDS prevention, addiction prevention and counselling, and legally required "pregnancy conflict counselling" preceding abortions are mainly offered by voluntary welfare organisations (Aner and Hammerschmidt 2018: 54f).

Social work in the healthcare sector takes place, for instance, in hospitals, mental health clinics and nursing homes. In health-related areas of social work it is performed, for example, as part of services for disabled people, as drug and addiction help (outpatient, inpatient, semi-stationary, outreach) and in hospice care. Social work in non-health-related areas of social work can take place in pre-schools, community or neighbourhood work and adult education centres (Aner and Hammerschmidt 2018: 56).

3.4   Other Differentiated Fields of Work (Older People's Services, Disabled People's Services, Family Support)

This subchapter outlines the three fields of social work, which were initially part of the general social assistance, but after World War II gradually evolved into specific fields of work: older people's services, disabled people's services and family support.

3.4.1 Older People's Services

The practice of social care for the elderly in municipalities is inconsistent across the different federal states and municipalities. This is not only a consequence of weak legal requirements, but also of different financial resources of the municipalities. In most cities and towns, the proportion of older people in the total population has been increasing for some time and will continue to do so for the foreseeable future. Although this requires appropriate planning of the infrastructure, it is not a problem in itself. But at the same time there is increasing old age poverty. The poverty rate for those aged 65 and over was 15.9% in 2014, and a total of 7.6% of the elderly were socially deprived in at least three out of nine areas of life (Aner and Hammerschmidt 2018: 67f).

3.4.2 Disabled People's Services

Disabled people's services is a generic term for state-guaranteed social services for people whose needs for special support are the result of a disability. Its goal is to avoid or compensate for disability-related disadvantages so as to enable self-determination and participation.

This field of work is wide-ranging, because it covers not only very different needs but also the entire lifespan. The following section outlines four areas of the field in which social work professionals work together with other professionals.

The area of early childhood education aims to minimise the consequences of disability (Aner and Hammerschmidt 2018: 72). Another major field is the support of disabled people in vocational training and employment, with their education taking place in a so-called dual system where their special conditions are taken into account. Supportive housing, another field of support for disabled people, has recently experienced a shift away from total institutions providing all services to the provision of outpatient care only. Further fields of work include outpatient assistance, services and counselling centres initiated by self-help and disability movements (Aner and Hammerschmidt 2018:74).

3.4.3 Family Support

Services for the promotion of family education in particular are types of family advice which address the needs and interests as well as experiences of families in various life situations and educational settings. They further enable the family to cooperate with educational institutions and empower them for forms of self-help and neighbourhood assistance and help young people to prepare for marriage, partnership and living together with children.

3.5   Methods of Social Work

Social work in Germany is characterised by a great variety of methods. However, the three classic methods of casework, social group work and community work are still fundamental. They have been supplemented and modified by a variety of other methodological approaches since the 1980s, but they remain classic methodological components of education and practice in social work.

Casework, the oldest method of social work, was already implemented and supplemented by Alice Salomon in Germany. Nowadays it is used in many different fields of social work to address various issues (Belardi 2017: 72–74). It is best known in fields related to family support, especially in social pedagogical family support (Belardi 2017: 75–76).

A special form of casework for case management in Germany was developed by Wolf Rainer Wendt, whereby the social worker primarily acts as a service coordinator and broker (Belardi 2017: 75).

Social group work has its roots in the youth movement in Germany at the beginning of the twentieth century (Müller 2017: 79). After World War II, in the democratic reorientation, it was considered an effective method in social work to impart democratic values and humanistic ideas to the new generation (Müller 2017: 80).

This method of social work is represented particularly in youth work, generating new social skills and initiating processes of learning and instruction among peers, in contrast to *Individualpädagogik* (individual pedagogy) (Müller 2017: 86).

Community work in particular has been experiencing a boom in Germany since the 1960s as an "approach to improving living conditions in deprived neighbourhoods" (Hinte 2017: 88, author's translation). It was seen as a kind of "resistance from below" (ibid.) and a "form of social commitment" (ibid.). Economic and social conditions were to be changed through community work with a focus on the most affected and disadvantaged people (ibid: 89). In the practice of social work, though, community work-oriented approaches have played a rather subordinate role. However, many of the principles of community work have been retained in today's specialised concepts of *Stadtteilorientierung* ("neighbourhood work") and *Sozialraumorientierung* ("person-in-environment approach") (Hinte 2017: 95f).

Based on the three classical methods, a variety of other methods have been developed and taught, such as methodical approaches in children's services planning, quality management, public relations, evaluation and experiential education (cf. Kreft and Müller 2017: 99–173; Puhl 2017: 157–160; Michl 2017: 126–129).

The general discourse on methodology in social work revolves around two core arguments: on the one hand, a strong focus on methods implies technocratisation, standardisation and a lack of focus on the individual case; on the other hand, one hopes to establish strong professionalisation, profiling and recognition by a clearly identified, elaborate range of methods which are exclusive to social work (Kreft and Müller 2017: 12–26).

4 Social Work Education in Germany

Developments in social work education are closely interwoven with the development of the profession, as the earlier historical review clearly showed. Furthermore, social work education in Germany is an important part of the whole profession with all its current problems and challenges.

The social work academisation process, which started in the 1970s, is important for the present understanding of the structures and conditions of social work education. As universities of applied sciences became established, they started to offer social work programmes. Today, they are almost universally called universities of applied sciences (UAS). Here, initially the programmes of social work and social pedagogy were located in accordance with their historical development (see earlier discussion). Within the next 30 years, these programmes merged into social work degree programmes almost everywhere. However, within the field of social sciences, there continue to be many different subjects and degree programmes related to social work. That is why statistics incorporating current data on students studying social work are hard to find. A special feature in Germany is the educational science degree programme with a focus on social pedagogy, which can be studied at universities. Occasionally, social work at universities can also be studied without a disciplinary connection to educational sciences.

In the summer semester of 2019, there were 132,362 students studying social sciences in Germany (including social work, social pedagogy, social sciences and sociology, but excluding educational science) (Statistisches Bundesamt 2020: 22); of these students, 94,801 were women (Statistisches Bundesamt 2020: 24), which shows that in Germany it is still a female-dominated profession.

It should also be noted that social work in Germany is studied largely at UAS, which are organised by the state, the church, and increasingly also through private sponsorship. For years, the number of students has been rising steadily. With the Bologna reform of 1999, the UAS were also enabled to develop and offer master's programmes, and the degree programmes of the UAS and universities were equalized in terms of their academic degrees. By now, almost all UAS offer master's programmes in social work. Because the universities' right to award doctorates has only been granted to universities of applied sciences for a limited number of cases, the associated generation of junior researchers in the discipline of social work is still primarily to be found at universities. Consequently, universities still have a high level of influence on the development of social work. In addition, doctoral degrees are predominantly located in the so-called reference disciplines, such as educational science, sociology, psychology, law or political science, not in social work. Since the UAS have been given the right to award PhDs independently, their influence on the profession may gradually change.

Another crucial and efficacious factor in the difference between the two types of higher education institutions is the difference in structural standards regarding the teaching assignment. The mandatory teaching assignment for professors at universities of applied sciences amounts to 18 contact hours per week, compared to eight or nine with a maximum of 12 contact hours per week at universities. At universities, there is also a variety of mid-level academic positions, which are regularly assigned to professorships or projects to support their work. This is not commonly the case at universities of applied sciences.

As a result, universities have a higher degree of impact on the scientific community through their structurally embedded enhanced research activities and associated reputational assignment. Accordingly, demands for a reduction of the mandatory teaching assignment to, e.g. 12 contact hours per week and the allocation of scientific staff have been made for a long time.

Thus, on the one hand, the actual relationship between universities of applied sciences and universities is at times a competitive and conflicting one in matters related to social work. On the other hand, cooperation between the two types of higher education institutions takes place in many forms and continues to develop in constructive ways. The parallel non-simultaneity of different developments in the relationship of the two types of higher education certainly creates new opportunities for cooperation, but frequently, structural limits are encountered in the form of massively unequal framework conditions, which have long lacked a sound and transparent justification.

Another specific fact in Germany is that, because of the federalism in Germany, social work education varies widely among the German states. These differences can be seen in the length of studies, the subjects and the general structure. Therefore, it is impossible to give an exact overview of the modules, subjects and structural conditions of social work education in Germany. However, many federal states have some commonalities, like the fact that most students learn about the methods of social work, communication, law, psychology, sociology, medicine and education in their studies of social work. In general, a bachelor's degree requires 180–210 ECTS points and a master's degree 90–120 ECTS points.

In many German states, dual models of social work studies have been developed to add more practical experience to the theoretical studies. In such programmes, students study and work at the same time.

The faculties of social work are highly self-organised in the Department of Social Work (FBTS: *Fachbereichstag Soziale Arbeit*) throughout Germany. The FBTS is the official national representative of the departments and faculties of social work at state-owned and ecclesiastical universities in [the Federal Republic of] Germany. As a superordinate, collegiate organ of academic self-administration, it combines the professional, organisational and educational activities of around 80 locations or members.

One of the outstanding results of the work of the FBTS is the development and continuation of the Qualifications Framework for Social Work (*Qualifikationsrahmens Soziale Arbeit* – QR SozArb) as a national framework for education in social work in Germany. The QR SozArb is a subject-specific reference framework for social work, which was clarified once again in 2016, in contrast to other disciplines and professions, by including the definition of social work. It consistently follows the emphasis on competence introduced in the Bologna Process. After continual updates, it is now in its sixth version since 2016 and is characterised particularly by its focus on higher education. In the preamble, the Qualifications Framework for Social Work refers to the international definition of social work, putting the national competence descriptions into an international context. The QR SozArb describes, in terms of competence development, the ability to use reflective and innovative thinking and acting, including occupational and professional field-related research. As an important development of a specific competence of social work, the ability to generate knowledge and innovation is differentiated using scientific methods in the field of social work. Social, technical, methodological and personnel skills in combination with an ethically reflective attitude promote innovation in subject-specific contexts of the profession of social work, in science as well as in practice. They are organised in a disciplinary, interdisciplinary or transdisciplinary manner (cf. Schäfer and Bartosch 2016: 2–16).

General skills and professional characteristics in social work are subdivided according to the pattern shown in Fig. 1.

Figure 1 shows different levels of social professions from college to doctorate by separating them from the reference disciplines and presenting specific social work skills.

The development of this Qualifications Framework for Social Work is very important for current discourse on the social work profession – although its objectives are not implemented throughout Germany – because it abolishes the logic of the reference disciplines, like psychology or sociology, and presents social work as

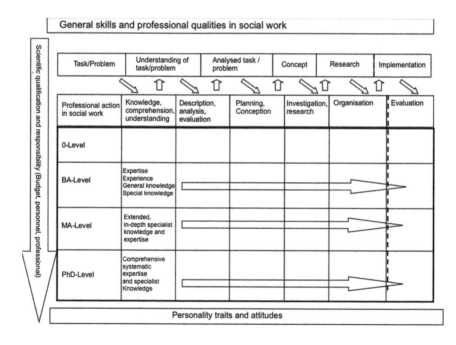

Fig. 1 Qualifications Framework for Social Work (reprinted with permission from Schäfer and Bartosch 2016: 18)

an independent profession which is clearly delimited from other disciplines. Consequently, on several occasions the Qualifications Framework has played an important role in educational policy discussions, e.g. in disputes over the state's recognition and in negotiations concerning laws for the acknowledgement of social professions, and as a reference point of the examination of the qualitative requirements for a degree programme in the accreditation procedure.

Another important framework for social work training was presented by the aforementioned DGSA. Its Core Curriculum of Social Work outlines the central contents of the study of social work. The Core Curriculum and the Qualifications Framework do not compete with but complement each other. Another major and significant actor in social work is the German Professional Association for Social Work (DBSH: *Deutscher Berufsverband für Soziale Arbeit*) – the professional association representing social work and a member of the IFSW. The initial agreement on a general definition of social work by the FBTS, together with the DGSA and DBSH, was closely based on the global definition of social work (cf. IFSW 2014; Schäfer 2017). This contributes to the emphasis on internationalisation and Europeanisation and, accordingly, professional exchange and international importance of social work.

All three organisations, the FBTS, the DGSA and the DBSH, are engaged in close cooperation and exchange to advance the science, education and profession in Germany in the context of self-organisation and self-advocacy.

5 Current Developments and Challenges for Social Work Education

Following completion of their studies, German social workers tend to face many challenges stemming from the current state of social work and social work education in Germany.

The advanced modernisation of life and global changes in the economy and politics have placed social work in a new situation in the twenty-first century. An upheaval and realignments in the relationship between public and private responsibility have taken place under the concept of an "activating welfare state". Globalisation and digitisation have permeated and changed the environment inhabited by the recipients of social services and affect the identity of social work and its future viability.

The maxim "promote and demand" refers to a concept of reorientation in social policy in which the state relies on more initiatives, self-responsibility and shared responsibility of citizens in coping with social problems. The task of the activating welfare state is primarily seen as empowering members of society through supportive framework conditions and leading them to perceive their concerns as their own responsibility. In the field of social work, this means moving from the principle of "help for self-help" to that of "guidance to self-guidance" (Wendt 2017b: 360).

This development has become especially apparent in labour market policy and in unemployment assistance. The ability to work, job placements and employment became the benchmark for successful assistance. Progress in this area is driven by neoliberal policies that aim at privatising previously public areas and services and thus subjecting them to market laws.

Here, a view of human nature is propagated which is diametrically opposed to social work: in its radical manifestation of neoliberalism, each individual is declared to be a self-responsible creator of his life according to the hegemonic ideology of "every man is the architect of his own fortune". Detached from structural factors, life becomes an individual project, and a lack of motivation and flexibility is interpreted as poor competence in self-discipline.

The emancipatory function of social work for all people, but especially for those living in disadvantaged situations, is thus called into question as well. The actions of social work run the risk of no longer focusing on one's own expertise but on the criteria of economic efficiency. In this framing, the necessary and meaningful debate about effectiveness, efficiency and evaluation threatens social work's independence.

All of this is happening in a society that has brought considerable wealth to the greater part but where inequalities are increasing (see earlier discussion). The poverty of single mothers with children, the inadequate and unfavourable conditions of immigrants, and emergencies in health care are in contrast to visible private wealth. Not being able to take part in the prosperity of the "two-thirds society" that has benefited from the recovery means misery also in the sense that many people have lost all hope.

To make matters worse, the fear of social decline has also reached the middle classes in Germany. It is no coincidence that the political parties in Germany claiming to represent a "suspended" minority are gaining popularity, and, while formally demanding more democracy, they are working incognito and de facto on its very demolition.

The dangers of intensifying social and societal processes of tension and division are also evident in the context of digitisation: the end of privacy, social alienation, threats to human dignity, machine-controlled communication and manipulation are among the risks of using new information technologies. At the same time, however, high hopes for more social participation and equal opportunities are linked to digitisation, such as nurturing social relationships and access to knowledge, education and social discourse. Digitisation permeates the worlds of social service recipients and the action contexts of social work. Social work is thus required to steer the use and significance of the new media in line with their values.

With these political, economic and social developments in Germany, the profession of social work attempts to cope with the new challenges and with problems with the profession itself. Between 2020 and 2025, children's services alone will experience a shortage of around 125,000 social workers (AGJ 2018: 5); this does not include the shortage of social workers in other areas of social work. This lack of qualified staff, in combination with the increasing demands of specific social problems, means that the profession will face particularly difficult challenges (DBSH 2019).

In addition, social work in Germany is underappreciated in society, which is one of the reasons why social work is ever striving to develop its own scientific background, social work science. Currently there is extensive discussion under way about social work science itself and the extent to which it is a science. Some experts say that there should be less science in a practice-based profession, arguing that theoretical matters would not face real problems in practice, as if they were two different worlds (Engelke et al. 2016: 19), while others see the opportunities arising from a scientifically based profession which can treat the subject area of social work – avoiding social problems and coping with them – by presenting the findings of research for practical action (Engelke et al. 2016: 20). They assert that practice backed up by science could go a long way towards addressing the challenges faced by a performance- and science-based society, but many discrepancies exist between the theory and practice of social work (Engelke et al. 2016: 19ff). Thus, much work remains to be done until all areas of social work – science, practice and education – recognise and appreciate the others' competence.

Another important challenge is globalisation, with its global economic relations and deregulated movement of capital worldwide, which contributes to deepening inequalities on both national and international levels. People's reactions to globalisation range from cross-border refugee movements to dramatic individual disturbances. On all levels, political, civilian, national and international, these challenges need to be addressed in cooperation with the different actors in order to distribute more equitably the benefits of border crossing and mobility. These challenges shift professional social action into a broad and fundamentally changed frame of reference, because global problems need a global solution.

In contrast to this important development, social work and social work education in Germany are still seen as a national profession in most cases. Thus, for example, help for refugees is a global topic and should be organised at least at the European level, but in fact every country – or sometimes every German state –focuses exclusively on its own little horizon.

However, important steps have recently been taken in German social work and social work education towards international and global orientations:

In 2019, the first German *Handbook of International Social Work* (Wagner et al. 2018) was published, and the first UAS have started teaching social work from an international perspective, including international literature, with the aim of conveying international professional skills and intercultural competence (Laging et al. 2013: 89).

However, the international and global focus remains very limited, and in order to be prepared for current developments and problems in times of globalisation, German social work and social work education should expand to an international and global level.

In the last few years, with the increase in complexity of many social problems, have witnessed important developments in interdisciplinary cooperation. In some fields of social work, workers from many different professions are collaborating; for example, in the field of drugs and addiction, social workers work together with experts from medicine, psychology and psychotherapy. However, social work science is focused on its own professional development. Therefore, one big challenge for the future will be to find solutions, not only to internal conflicts in the further professional development of German social work, but also the challenge of needing to focus outside the profession itself as well as inside, in order to continue being part of interdisciplinary settings.

In conclusion, as has been the case throughout the history of social work and social work education, new challenges must be managed in the face of social, political, economic and global changes. The self-discovery of the social work profession is not yet complete. A balance must be found between practice and theory and between the profession's standing in the national welfare state and in its international orientation. In addition, other challenges demand attention as well, like social inequalities in society at the national, European and global levels, the sensible use of digital media and sound social work education. This would empower and prepare students for current challenges, following important approaches like participation and inclusion with service user involvement in education and research (Laging and Heidenreich 2019), identifying and addressing structural causes (national, European and global contexts) of individual life situations, without misjudging existing resources and resilience or sinking into over-identification and pity, while purposefully promoting an interest in and commitment to social work at the level of political influence on social conditions.

References

AGJ. (2018). *Dem wachsenden Fachkräftebedarf richtig begegnen! Entwicklung einer Gesamtstrategie zur Personalentwicklung mit verantwortungsvollem Weitblick- Positionspapier der Arbeitsgemeinschaft für Kinder- und Jugendhilfe – AGJ* [The right way to meet the growing need for skilled workers! Development of an overall strategy for personnel development with a responsible foresight – position paper of the Working Group for Child and Youth Welfare – AGJ]. https://www.agj.de/fileadmin/files/positionen/2018/Dem_wachsenden_Fachkr%C3%A4ftebedarf_richtig_begegnen.pdf. Accessed 27 Feb 2020.

Aner, K., & Hammerschmidt, P. (2018). *Arbeitsfelder und Organisationen der Sozialen Arbeit* [Work areas and organisations of social work]. Wiesbaden: Springer VS Verlag.

BAGFW. (2018). *Gesamtstatistik 2016. Einrichtungen und Dienste der Freien Wohlfahrtspflege* [Overall statistics 2016. Institutions and services of voluntary welfare]. Berlin: Bundesarbeitsgemeinschaft der Freien Wohlfahrtspflege e. V. Retrieved from https://www.bagfw.de/veroeffentlichungen/publikationen/gesamtstatistiken. Accessed 26 Feb 2020.

Belardi, N. (2017). Von der Einzelfallhilfe zum Case-Management. In D. Kreft, & C. W. Müller (Eds.), *Methodenlehre in der Sozialen Arbeit* [Methodology in social work] (p. 69–78). München: UTB.

DBSH. (2019). *Quo vadis "Soziale Arbeit"*. DBSH Neuigkeiten 6/2019. Retrieved from https://www.dbsh.de/service-presse/newsletter-und-social-media/newsletter-2019.html. Accessed 27 Feb 2020.

Engelke, E., Spatscheck, C., & Borrmann, S. (2016). *Die Wissenschaft Soziale Arbeit. Werdegang und Grundlagen* [The science of social work. Development and basics]. Freiburg im Breisgau: Lambertus.

Esping-Andersen, G. (1990). *The three worlds of welfare capitalism*. Princeton: Princeton University Press.

Hammerschmidt, P., Weber, S., & Seidenstücker, B. (2017). *Soziale Arbeit – die Geschichte.* [Social work – The history]. Opladen/ Toronto: Barbara Budrich.

Hering, S., & Münchmeier, R. (2014). *Geschichte der Sozialen Arbeit* [History of social work]. Weinheim/ Basel: Beltz Juventa.

Hinte, W. (2017). Von der Gemeinwesenarbeit zum sozialräumlichen Handeln. In D. Kreft, & C. W. Müller (Eds.), *Methodenlehre in der Sozialen Arbeit* [Methodology in social work] (pp.88–98). München: UTB.

IFSW. (2014). *Global definition of social work*. Retrieved from: https://www.ifsw.org/what-is-social-work/global-definition-of-social-work/. Accessed 24 Feb 2020.

Kreft, D., & Müller, C. W. (2017). Grundlagen für das methodische Handeln. In D. Kreft, & C. W. Müller (Eds.), *Methodenlehre in der Sozialen Arbeit* [Methodology in social work] (pp. 12–25). München: UTB.

Laging, M., & Heidenreich, T. (2019). Towards a conceptual framework of service user involvement in social work education: Empowerment and educational perspectives. *Journal of Social Work Education, 55*(1), 1–12.

Laging, M., Waldenhof, B., & Zöller, U. (2013). Internationale Berufsfähigkeit in der Sozialen Arbeit [International professional skills in social work]. *Neue Praxis aktuell. Zeitschrift für Sozialarbeit, Sozialpädagogik und Sozialpolitik, 1*(2013), 88–97.

Michl, W. (2017). Erlebnispädagogik. In D. Kreft, & C. W. Müller (Ed.), *Methodenlehre in der Sozialen Arbeit* [Methodology in social work] (pp. 126–129). München: UTB.

Müller, C. W. (2017). Gruppenpädagogik (Social Group Work) und die Folgen. In D. Kreft, & C. W. Müller (Eds.), *Methodenlehre in der Sozialen Arbeit* [Methodology in social work] (pp. 79–87). München: UTB.

Otto, H.U., Thiersch, H., Treptow, R., & Ziegler, H. (2018). *Handbuch Soziale Arbeit – Grundlagen der Sozialarbeit und Sozialpädagogik* [Handbook of social work – Basics of social work and social pedagogy]. München: Ernst Reinhardt Verlag.

Puhl, R. (2017). Öffentlichkeitsarbeit. In D. Kreft, & C. W. Müller (Eds.), *Methodenlehre in der Sozialen Arbeit* [Methodology in social work] (pp. 157–160). München: UTB.

Schäfer, P. (2017). Kompetenzen für die soziale Praxis – Von den Lehrplänen zum Qualifikationsrahmen Soziale Arbeit (QR SozArb) [Skills for social practice – From curricula to social work qualifications framework]. In P. Schäfer, O. Burkova, H. Hoffmann, M. Laging, & L. Stock (Eds.), *100 Jahre Fachbereichstag Soziale Arbeit. Vergangenheit deuten, Gegenwart verstehen, Zukunft gestalten* (pp. 107–136). Opladen/Berlin/Toronto: Verlag Barbara Budrich.

Schäfer, P., & Bartosch, U. (2016). *Qualifikationsrahmen Soziale Arbeit – Version 6.0*. Retrieved from https://www.fbts-ev.de/qualifikationsrahmen-soziale-arbeit. Accessed 7 June 2021.

Statistisches Bundesamt (Destatis). (2019). *Pressemitteilung Nr. 419 vom 30. Oktober 2019* [Press release No. 419 from October 30, 2019]. https://www.destatis.de/DE/Presse/Pressemitteilungen/2019/10/PD19_419_639.html. Accessed 24 Feb 2020.

Statistisches Bundesamt (Destatis). (2020). *Bildung und Kultur. Studierende an Hochschulen, Fachserie 11 Reihe 4.1.* [Education and culture. Students at universities]. Retrieved from https://www.destatis.de/DE/Themen/Gesellschaft-Umwelt/Bildung-Forschung-Kultur/Hochschulen/_inhalt.html#sprg233706. Accessed 24 Feb 2020.

Thole, W. (2012). *Grundriss Soziale Arbeit – Ein einführendes Handbuch* [Social work outline – An introductory handbook]. Wiesbaden: Springer VS.

Wagner, L., Lutz, R., Rehklau, C., & Ross, F. (2018). *Handbuch Internationale Soziale Arbeit. Dimensionen – Konflikte – Positionen* [Handbook of international social work. Dimensions – Conflicts – Positions]. Weinheim/Basel: Beltz Juventa.

Wendt, W. R. (2017a). *Geschichte der Sozialen Arbeit 1. Die Gesellschaft vor der sozialen Frage 1750 bis 1900* [History of social work 1. Society before the social issue 1750–1900]. Wiesbaden: Springer VS.

Wendt, W. R. (2017b). *Geschichte der Sozialen Arbeit 2. Die Profession im Wandel ihrer Verhältnisse* [History of social work 2. The profession in its changing circumstances]. Wiesbaden: Springer VS.

Social Work Education in Italy: Backwards and Forwards in the Establishment of the Social Work Discipline

Teresa Bertotti

1 Development of Social Work in Italy

Social work in Italy fully developed about half a century later than in other European countries (Campanini and Frost 2004) at the end of World War II, after the fall of fascism. It was linked to the need for reconstruction in the aftermath of the war and prompted by the organisations engaged in the administration of international aid, received by the United Nations Relief and Rehabilitation Administration (UNRRA) and Managed by the AAI (Italian Administration of International Aids). The creation of the professional figure of a social worker was envisaged in collaboration with a group of enlightened Italians already engaged in earlier pioneering experiences in social work and social actions (Campanini 2007; Fargion 2008; Stefani 2012). In 1946, under the patronage of the new Italian government, these persons organised a conference at Tremezzo, near Lake Como, that was attended by people of both Catholic and secular backgrounds. This conference outlined the main characteristics of social workers and signalled the origin of Italian social work. Largely inspired by the values and ideals of the Italian resistance, social work was depicted as a profession that could contribute to democratisation through an emphasis on active participation and self-determination (Fiorentino Busnelli 2002).

As in other European countries, some roots of Italian social work can also be found earlier, at a 'pre-professional stage', in the activities of women philanthropists at the end of the nineteenth century, as well as in the early years of fascism, in connection with the development of a centralised overarching system of assistance aimed at controlling families and developing demographic growth responding to the ideology of the dictatorship.

T. Bertotti (✉)
Department of Sociology and Social Research, University of Trento, Trento, Italy
e-mail: teresa.bertotti@unitn.it

© Springer Nature Switzerland AG 2021 111
M. Laging, N. Žganec (eds.), *Social Work Education in Europe*,
European Social Work Education and Practice,
https://doi.org/10.1007/978-3-030-69701-3_6

After Tremezzo, social work developed as a profession mostly thanks to the many schools which were established in the post-war period; these were influenced by Anglophone or foreign scholars in a top-down fashion, rather than by social workers involved in the practice, as was the case in other countries (Fargion 2008). Instead of a top-down mode, for others the profession developed in a dialectic interplay between emerging social problems and the approaches adopted to respond to them, culturally and through social policies (Pieroni and Dal Pra Ponticelli 2005; Neve 2008; Sgroi 2001). As E. Neve (2008) points out, the evolution of social work in Italy can be divided into different stages, related to changes in social problems and social policies. Here we identify two main stages:

- a first period corresponding to the development of the Italian welfare system, from the post-war period to the 1990s, which included the establishment of the welfare state, the golden age of the Italian welfare system and its transformation towards a welfare mix model with managerial policies;
- a second period, starting from the end of the twentieth century and up to the present, which encompassed the economic crisis, the recession, austerity measures and the establishment of various forms of welfare systems.

1.1 Post-War Period and the Golden Age of the Italian Welfare System: A Mixed Paradigm

In the immediate post-war period, the Italian welfare system largely maintained many features of the fascist system of welfare. State centralised and public, the welfare system was characterised by a prevailing approach of social defence and moral control, in which social protection was provided according to specific categories of people or needs. Provided by an array of national centralised bodies, institutionalisation and material supports were the main provisions provided, dedicated to specific categories. Social work interventions were anchored only to the cure of evident and ascertained needs (Campanini 2007:108) without any focus on preventive work. Bound by this approach, social workers operated mainly with individual casework, about which knowledge was disseminated by schools of social work, mainly influenced by knowledge coming from the US. Calls for more incisive interventions to counteract the widespread levels of poverty and unemployment, as witnessed by two famous parliamentary enquiries, went unheeded. Later, when the economic boom of the 1960s created massive migration flows, both from the South to the North of Italy and internationally, with the related problems of the integration of immigrants, family disruption and increasing youth problems, modest initiatives in community work were also launched (Sgroi 2001).

The limitations inherent in such approaches to social work led to severe criticism in the late 1960s, highly influenced by the student and workers' movements and protests that spread throughout society at that time. The need to modernise society as a whole culminated in reforms both in civil life (such as the legalisation of divorce and abortion), in public administration and in the welfare system. Some powers were decentralised from the state to the regions, national bodies were dismantled, and social services were reorganised on a local basis, becoming closer to citizens and under the control of local elected bodies. (Law 616/1977)

Following the ideal types proposed by Esping-Andersen (1990), the Italian welfare system represents a mixed model. It was included in the Christian democratic welfare regime, marked by a conservative – corporatist system of social service provision (Bode 2003). However, during the 1970s, Italy started to adopt a welfare regime which was more inspired by the social democratic model adopted in northern countries, with a more universalistic character. In 1978 the National Health Service (*Servizio Sanitario Nazionale*) was established, creating an administrative structure composed of three tiers: the central government, responsible for planning and financing through compulsory contributions and taxes, regional governments, responsible for local planning and organisation, and local governments. At this level an infrastructure of local units was created so as to provide social and health services on a local basis.

A movement towards 'de-institutionalisation' – championing the closure of large institutions which hosted adults or children, following the 'antipsychiatry movement' led by Franco Basaglia – characterised the development of social and health services together with demands for democratisation.

Social work then became engaged in the promotion of changes at the political level and in the search for new forms of intervention and alternative care, such as foster care and small residential units. The idea of social assistance underwent change, and a vision of direct involvement and active participation of citizens was promoted, with a new role for social workers that was closer to advocacy and promoting changes and participation rather than pure assistance to individuals. For instance, in the 1970s, the role of social workers was considered to be too compliant with the system. During a famous conference held in Rimini in 1971, participants rejected the role of *rammendatrici dal dialogo facile*, that is of those whose work entails "carrying out repairs through facile conversations": they did not want to act as mere stopgaps at the individual level whilst dealing with situations which were in fact the result of social contradictions internal to the capitalist system – itself considered democratic in name only (Mulazzoni et al. 1971).

In the early 1980s, during the development of the public welfare system, social workers increasingly worked in local services, in the new services dedicated to family counselling, mental health, drug addiction (developed as part of the health system) and in services managed by municipalities, devoted to first access and generalist social work. Especially in the health sector, services were provided by multiprofessional teams; on such teams, social workers were engaged in several activities with individuals, groups and communities. Social workers were also employed at ministries, mainly the ministry of Justice, to provide social support to prison inmates and young offenders. Therefore, social work was represented in different services and institutions, mainly in the public sector.

As in other European countries, the Italian welfare system also enjoyed its 'golden age' during this period. Social policies grew strongly in terms of expenditure, generosity and coverage, bringing the Italian situation close to the average of other Western European countries in the 1970s (Ascoli and Pavolini 2015). Nevertheless, in the 1990s the Italian welfare model presents four specificities that distinguish Italy in the European context: a mixed paradigm, a particularistic/clientelist nature, a dual and fragmented model of functioning, and a familistic approach (Ascoli and Pavolini 2015: 2). The mixed paradigm means that "different forms of operational logics were adopted in the different policy sectors: a strictly corporatist approach in pensions, and unemployment policies, a universalistic approach in health and education and a scant development of social assistance and social care" (Ascoli and Pavolini 2015: 3). The 'particularistic/clientelist' refers to the prevalence of welfare provisions based on money transfers rather than services, associated with a low level of state presence ('stateness') that serves as the basis for political exchanges and clientelism (Paci 1989). The third Italian specificity is dualism and fragmentation related both to the divide between those who are stably enrolled in the labour market, with a rather good level of income and social protection and those who are outside the labour market or precariously employed, with no income protection (Ferrera 2005). The final specifically Italian feature is 'familism', meaning that families have a strong role in the provision of welfare and assume a wide range of caring responsibilities, mainly women (Naldini and Saraceno 2008). However, unlike other conservative–corporatist welfare states, such as Germany and Austria, whose fiscal policies promote the male breadwinner model and the role of women as carers, in Italy, familism has been largely unsupported (Saraceno and Keck 2010).

Referring to the typology proposed by Esping-Andersen (1990), the Italian welfare model can be classified as a mix between the liberal and the corporatist conservative welfare regime. However, in the late 1990s some scholars, including Ferrera (1996), argued that in addition to the Esping-Andersen models, there is a new welfare model called the Southern Europe/Mediterranean (SE/M), which included Spain, Portugal, Greece and Italy. In this model, the family is a significant key component of the welfare system but is largely unsupported and the familistic culture justifies a residual role for policy. Patronage and clientelism, coupled with the strong role of the Church, as well as widespread inequalities are other common features of the SE/M countries (Leitner 2003).

The public welfare state started to decline in the late 1980s – the so-called 'silver age' of the Italian welfare state (Ferrera 2008) – due to a realisation of both the fiscal unsustainability of the welfare state and the need to involve other actors in the provision of services. Laws to facilitate the activity of voluntary associations, cooperatives and third sector organisations were passed, leading to a welfare mix system of service provision. Trends to introduce forms of privatisation according to a 'quasi-market' logic increased in the 1990s, starting with the health sector, reformed through turning local health units into 'semi-public agencies' detached from local authorities. The system of service provision increasingly became a mix of public and private organisations, with an infusion of managerial policies under neoliberal notions regarding the benefits of competition.

1.2   Social Reform in 2000, the Recognition of Social Work and the Neoliberal Turn in the Early Twenty-First Century

The reform of the national system of social assistance, ratified in 2000 (Law 328/2000), confirmed the aforementioned trend. The reform established the principle of subsidiarity, in the 'vertical perspective', which means that higher levels of the state should intervene only when the lower levels fail to achieve their aims, and in the horizontal, meaning that all social components are entitled to, and called to contribute to, welfare provisions. Law 328/2000 also established that minimal levels of assistance should be guaranteed all over the country and that all state funding should be managed through a unified National Fund for Social Policies (FNPS), overcoming the previous distinction in categories of beneficiaries. The FNPS is funded and managed locally, through the formulation of 3-year social plans, in a collaborative and negotiated process. The reform also recalled the principle of solidarity and recognised strong roles for families and communities, thereby confirming the familistic character of the Italian welfare system (Aspalter 2011; Ferrera 1996).

The reform also provided a strong role for professional social work that was defined as 'a minimum essential level of provision' that should be guaranteed in all municipalities (art. 22); this implies a more complex role for social workers. They are asked not only to work with clients but also to act as the nearest point of contact between citizens and the public administration; in addition, they are asked to build networks at different levels: with individuals, groups, and families. In an increasingly fragmented system, they are asked to identify the needs of individuals and families and to define care plans, as well as to connect and support the integration of services that are part of different areas of the health and social system. With the process of externalisation, social workers employed in municipalities are also asked to coordinate and evaluate services offered by accredited organisations. Additionally, they are asked to contribute to and participate in the definition of local social plans and the management of social services (Facchini 2010; Facchini and Lorenz 2013).

In fact, the economic crisis that hit Italy and other countries in 2008 had a huge impact both on the need for social protection and on social work. The increased levels of poverty and unemployment and the concurrent reduction of resources available to respond to these needs (because of the austerity measures which were adopted) created a highly critical and ongoing situation. Unlike in other European countries, the Italian reaction to the economic crisis was distinguished by a greater involvement of non-profit organisations (e.g. charity groups, social co-operatives, foundations, non-profit organisations) than of profit organisations, adopting what has been defined as the negotiation model (Ranci and Ascoli 2002) or social market of services.

The crisis was managed through the introduction of neoliberal policies, accompanied by the rhetoric of a need for a 'common effort' and 'sharing the pain' (Garrett and Bertotti 2017). For social workers, this resulted in precarisation and low salaries, leading to the development of sharp tensions between social workers and their employing organisations, as well as to professional interventions being limited to mere gatekeeping and the provision of sometimes severely reduced resources. Social workers thus felt 'under siege', overworked and oppressed in their management of emergencies, and they were often exposed to violence, as evidenced by a recent study (Sicora and Rosina 2019).

The following decade, up to the present, has been marked by the struggle to overcome the consequences of the economic crisis, with minimal levels of growth. The general trend is towards a global restructuring of social services with a general withdrawal of the state from the direct management of public services (Martinelli et al. 2017). Welfare is, therefore, characterised by a plurality of welfare systems, at both the financial and the implementation level of social provision, thus broadening the number of actors replacing the role of the state. Myriad initiatives in all sectors are characterised by a contamination between different domains, calling for participation and innovation in the design and implementation of policies often in a rhetorical mode by the newly emerging actors and ways of conceiving problems and solutions. According to Bifulco, this multiplicity often engenders issues related to scaling up from the particular to a more general policy (2017).

2   Main Areas of Social Work in Italy

2.1   A Registered and Self-Regulated Profession

Over the decades, Italian social work gained formal recognition as a profession. The formal process started in the 1980s with the standardisation of social work education and the formal recognition of the academic title as the basis for the qualification of social worker. It continued up to 1993, when the full legal recognition of the professional title was achieved, with the approval of the 84/1993 act "Regulations of the Profession of Social Worker and Constitution of the Professional Register" ('*Ordinamento della professione di assistente sociale e istituzione dell'albo professionale*'). The first article of this law recognises that 'the social worker works with technical and professional autonomy and judgement in all phases of prevention, support and recuperation of individuals, families, groups and communities in need and distress', that social workers can 'conduct teaching and training activities, (…) coordinate and direct social services (…) contribute to the organisation and programming of social policies' (Art. 1 Law 84/1993). The law also establishes the creation of a national register, with compulsory registration in order for one to be allowed to work as a social worker. Furthermore, registration is conditional upon passing a special state-run examination, in addition to the degree awarded by a university.

In contrast with other European experiences where access to the social work register is managed by mixed committees (Orme and Rennie 2006), the Italian register is self-regulated, which means that the *Consiglio* is elected from and by social workers. The elected president and counsellors are officially appointed by the government (Ministry of Justice). The profession is also regulated by means of a professional code of ethics whereby violations are judged by a disciplinary committee, also elected by members.

In 1993 the order of social work was established, with a national council as well as regional ones, one each for the twenty Italian regions. In 1998 the first code of ethics was approved; it was further reviewed in 2009, and in 2020 a third revision of the code was approved. In 2012, engaging in continuing professional development was also made compulsory for all practitioners, through a system of credits.

The establishment of the professional order helped to create a sense of identity in the profession (Fargion 2008) with an effort to define specific competences and boundaries, especially in relation to other cognate professions (Abbott 1988).

At the same time, the professional qualification of psychologist was also established, and very recently (in 2018) social educators (comparable to German social pedagogues) obtained the right to establish a register.

2.2 Constantly Increasing, Engaged in Different Domains, with Growing Levels of Precarity

According to data from 2018, there are currently 44,000 registered social workers (CNOAS 2018), and this number showing a continually increasing trend. For instance, in 1999, there were 27,000 social workers (Eiss 2001: 32) showing an increase of about 60% in the number of social workers over approximately 20 years.

As for areas of employment, they have changed over time, as shown in Table 1. The first data collected after the establishment of the national register confirmed the prevailing nature of Italian social work as politically engaged work, carried out in public agencies, with social workers acting and representing themselves as 'civil servants' (Sgroi 2001; Sicora and Kolar 2015; Fazzi and Rosignoli 2020). The study carried out by CENSIS (1999) with 1000 social workers reported that more than 74% work in the public sector, with 39.5% employed in municipalities and 34.6% in health services.

A similar sample survey carried out 10 years later, in 2008, by Facchini (2010), provides further evidence of this trend, albeit with some meaningful differences.

Table 1 Trend of social workers employed in local public services (percentages reported by different studies)

Year	Municipalities	Health services	Total local public services
1999[a]	39.50	34.60	74.10
2008[b]	45.50	24.40	69.90
2018[c]	26.20	15.30	41.50

[a]CENSIS (1999) – sample survey, 1000 social workers interviewed
[b]Facchini, C. (Ed.) (2010) – sample survey, 1000 social workers interviewed
[c]CNOAS (2018) – data from national register regarding 39,000 social workers

The data still show a prevalence of social workers employed in the public sector (69.9%) with an increase in those working for municipalities (45.5%) and a decrease in those employed in the health sector (24.4%, −10% of respondents compared to 1998), thus demonstrating both the impact of the implementation of the social services reform as well as the trend of expelling social workers from health services. The study also reveals the move towards mixed forms of welfare: the number of social workers employed in the third sector (as social co-operatives) and other semi-private bodies and charities increased to 18% of respondents (Facchini and Lorenz 2013; Bertotti 2014).

The most recent data gathered by CNOAS provides further evidence of these trends. The number of social workers employed in municipalities dropped to 26.2% and the number of those employed in health services to 15.3%, whilst the number of those employed in the third sector and similar services increased to 29%[1] (CNOAS 2018).

These numbers clearly show the profound changes which occurred over the 30-year period: a massive downsizing of public welfare and the establishment of a mixed system of management of welfare services. This started with cuts in health services and an initial increase in the number of social workers employed in munici-palities. This movement came to an abrupt halt after 2008, when the Italian govern-ment adopted austerity measures and was forced to respect the stability pact, which stopped new recruitment and imposed cuts on social spending (Bordogna and Neri 2014). Such changes were followed by further outsourcing of public services to the non-profit sector as well as by the direct involvement of other subjects, such as bank foundations and private enterprises, in the provision of welfare services (Ferrera and Maino 2015).

Furthermore, social workers' functions are changing: the CENSIS survey reported that 58.1% of their time is devoted to professional interventions with cli-ents and 15.5% to frontline work consisting of 'filtering and orientation'. Only 11.3% are engaged in the management and coordination of services (EISS 2001). In the 2008 study, direct work with or for service users still predominates, taking up on average 40% of all of social workers' time, but less than was found by the CENSIS study. Moreover, on average 12%–15% of professionals' working time is devoted to administrative work and documentation (Facchini and Lorenz 2013), as a conse-quence of the introduction of systems of evaluation and need to 'prove accountabil-ity' which are typical of managerial policies (Banks 2011).

Such increasing precarity persists to the present day. The traditional view of a social worker safeguarded by stable employment in public services is true only of the old generation. A recent national study on employment opportunities for social work graduates from 2006 to 2012 showed that 45% of those employed in public services have temporary contracts. Moreover, the first place of employment is no longer the public sector: newly qualified social workers find their first jobs mainly

---

[1] Data refers to statistics collected by the CNOAS during the mandatory registration procedures for continuous education of professionals. They refer 91% of the social workers registered.

in the third sector, often with a limited number of hours and poorly paid. In addition, the average time needed to find a first job is longer, and there is an increasing discrepancy between a person's qualifications and the professional tasks they are given (Niero et al. 2015).

According to some scholars, this trend can be interpreted as an aspiration to create an 'austerity social worker', whose precarious contract and low recognition imbue them with low expectations about their career and social roles (Garrett and Bertotti 2017). Rather than being an agent of change, this is a professional figure who appears 'encouraged to be politically docile, viewing budgeting and the rationing of services to clients as paramount' (p. 37).

3 Current Model of Education for Social Work: Within the University in a Weak Position

Social work education plays a central role in providing social workers with the necessary competences to cope with and manage the changes occurring in social problems and welfare systems. Today Italian social work education is embedded in an academic context and provided at universities, considering that Italy does not have the dual system of polytechnics and academic universities which is common in other European countries.

3.1 Brief History and Development of Knowledge

The development of social work education in Italy can be seen as divided into a pre-academic and an academic period, with a transitional stage, thus leading to three different phases.

(i) The pre-academic phase started with the Tremezzo conference in 1946 and lasted until the 1980s.

As mentioned earlier, it was prompted by the need to provide the country with personnel able to support the management of post-war aid and the renewal of the Italian system of assistance, after the fascist dictatorship. Although some roots can also be found earlier – for instance, during the fascist period a school in Rome trained the 'fascist social worker' – the first school of social work was organised in Milan, in 1944. It was established under the patronage of a Catholic body, and was directed by Odile Vallin, a young antifascist French social worker (Campanini 2015). Subsequently, many other schools opened, under the patronage of private organisations – both Catholic and secular. They were inspired by democratic values and social work principles, such as respect for human beings and the personalisation of interventions, made explicit during the Tremezzo conference (Stefani 2012).

From the 1940s to the 1960s, social work schools grew in number, prompted by the patronage of many different bodies and adopting different organisations of curricula and subjects taught. Such social work schools were, despite their heterogeneity, for the most part characterised by 3-year courses, small groups of students, and strong connections with practice (Campanini 2007). The diploma awarded by these schools was a vocational title, recognised only at a local level, as social work was not officially recognised as a profession. The teaching body was mainly composed of professional social workers with longstanding experience in practice, joined by teachers from other disciplines. The subjects taught were at first influenced by knowledge derived mainly from the United States; the traditional distinction between methods of casework, group work and community work was therefore adopted.

Later, a process of what may be termed 'indigenisation' of Italian social work knowledge developed. For instance, albeit modestly, broader attention to community development started to be part of social work curricula during the 1960s, alongside individual casework (Sgroi 2001; Giraldo and Riefolo 1996). These changes were first prompted by increasing social problems linked to the massive internal migration from Southern to Northern Italy during the 'economic boom' of the 1960s (Neve 2008) and further emphasised later as a result of the 1968 social movements. Such factors led to ongoing debates within professional and teachers' associations: alongside the critique of casework and other models inspired by US authors considered too 'technical and detached from the context' (Campanini 2007), new forms of original theorisation developed. A representative example of Italian 'indigenisation' is the definition of the 'unitarian process', which outlines a unique method that can be adopted in all social work interventions without differentiating between casework, group work or community work, which is considered an Italian peculiarity (Fargion 2008; Ferrario 1996). A multidisciplinary approach to social work was also developed, theorising social work as a 'discipline of synthesis' (Bianchi et al. 1988) which further draws on other psychological and social sciences to best identify the causes of problems.

First the *Coordinamento delle Scuole di Servizio sociale* (social work school network) and, later, the social work teachers' association (AIDOSS, *Associazione Italiana Docenti di Servizio Sociale*) played a decisive role in this process, allowing space for sharing and debate. In this way it contributed to establishing a basis for the scientific community of social work (Campanini and Frost 2004).

(ii) The late 1970s–1980s saw the transitional phase of approaching university and entering academia through the back door. The increasing need for social workers and the struggle of the profession to be formally recognised prompted the opening of the first public curricula in social work attached to universities as vocational schools, in Italy called schools with special purposes. These schools, also created for other professions, nursing and physiotherapy for example, were part of the university system but enjoyed a 'lower status', including shorter curricula (3 years instead of the 4 or 5 years needed for normal degrees at the time) and awarded a *diploma* instead of a *degree*. They provided 3-year courses, with various social work subjects taught by teachers with professional backgrounds.

In 1983, social work education was regulated at the national level, and the Schools for Special Purposes were recognised as the only valid path to becoming a social worker, thus laying the foundations for the juridical recognition of the social work profession, which occurred 10 years later, in 1993. Already established private schools which already offered 3-year courses and good standards (such as in Milan, or Rome) were rapidly incorporated into the universities, and many schools for social workers were opened. The teaching staff and the structure of the educational programmes were retained, as were the connections to practice and the employment of teachers with professional backgrounds.

The provision of social work qualifications within the university system of higher education was widely discussed in the late 1980s. Teachers and students at that time were worried that academisation might result in neglecting the links to practice and losing the field's specificity. There was also concern that new training would entail greater distance from social services and a reduction in opportunities for field placements, as well as the added fear that academic endeavours might focus on less research and theories that were relevant for social work. Despite this debate, social work education fully entered the university system in 2001.

(iii) The full acceptance of social work education within university higher education followed the regulations established by the Bologna Process, adopted in Italy in 1999 which established the three levels of degrees (B.A./M.A./PhD) for all faculties. For social work this resulted in a 3-year bachelor's degree in Social Work and a 2-year master's degree in Planning and Management of Politics and Social Services, later renamed Social Work and Social Policies (Campanini 2020). As a consequence, the National Board of Social Workers established two levels of the professional title and two different sections of the national register: Social Worker (B.A.) and Specialised Social Worke' (M.A.).

The concerns of pre-academic schools as regards this transition were partly justified, as the advantages gained through the stronger social recognition attendant on being awarded a degree in fact resulted in several clear losses, for instance concerning the specificity of specialised social work teachings and a weaker and more peripheral role of social work teachers, as will be further discussed in what follows.

Moreover, in 2010 a major reform of the higher education system was implemented (the Gelmini reform – L. 240/2010), as well as discussed and critiqued. Among other relevant aspects, the reform introduced strict new criteria for the establishment, organisation and governance of faculties and research departments, and it provided broader autonomy to each university in defining the curricula, as well as in staff recruitment policies. It confirmed the requirement for a national qualification based on the discipline to which the subject is related. Furthermore, – in accordance with neoliberal and managerial principles, it established a national system of ranking and evaluation as well as budgetary cuts. The impact of such factors on social work education is becoming more and more apparent at several levels, from the pressure to reduce costs to the increase in the number of enrolled students.

3.2   Current Situation

Because Italy does not have a dual system of higher education, as mentioned earlier, social work is currently included in the higher education university system just as almost all other higher education vocational courses. Other similar vocational programmes, such as for educators, nurses, rehabilitation therapists and so forth, have gradually entered higher education, following similar pathways.

In 2018, 36 bachelor-level and 35 master-level courses in social work were offered by 98 Italian universities. The number of courses has decreased over the last few years: for example, in 2014 there were 44 bachelor's courses, a consequence of the new criteria established by the Gelmini reform. As regards the number of students who enrol every year, this is almost stable, with approximately 1300 students enrolled in the first year of B.A. programmes nationally. Only some courses (B.A.) have limited access, and the number of students ranges from 60 to 120.

3.2.1   Curriculum Structure

The structure of all curricula is underpinned by the system of credits according to the Bologna Process and each course should respect a set of minimal requirements established by the Ministry of Education, the MIUR (*Ministero dell'Istruzione Università e Ricerca*) in the choice of subjects taught.

According to these requirements, for the bachelor's degree in social work, out of the total 180 credits, the MIUR defines the standard for 108 credits, leaving the remaining 72 credits to the discretion of each university. For the bachelor's degree in social work the MIUR also established that a minimum of 15 credits should be allocated to social work disciplines – quite a low number compared to other subjects. In fact, other mandatory credits are for sociology-related subjects (24 credits), psychology (21), law (12 credits); 12 credits are allocated to other disciplines such as economics, politics, history, anthropological and pedagogical studies, and 6 credits to medical science. The B.A. curriculum also includes a mandatory field practice that represents at least 18 credits.

A similar structure is established for master's courses, which require 120 credits in total. Here, social work is not even mentioned as a minimum requirement: mandatory teachings again include sociology, law, psychology, social policies, economics and other subjects such as anthropology and philosophy; 10 credits are assigned to fieldwork placements. The picture of the minimal requirements provided by MIUR provides clear evidence of the peripheral position given to social work subjects, and since the beginning, the professional association of Italian social work teachers has expressed its deep dissatisfaction with this (Campanini 2020).

Beyond the minimal requirements established by the ministry, each university is free to plan its specific curricula, shaping programmes according to their vision and to respond to local needs and use the remaining credits and resources as they think best. This can lead some universities to give higher priority to social work and others to merely meet the minimum requirements. Important decisions are thus taken at the local level, and the composition of social work curricula is influenced by power plays within universities as well as by the influence of pre-existing social work schools. Moreover, with the increased autonomy granted by the 2010 reform, both the diversification of curricula across the country and the variety in teacher recruitment are even higher.

AIDOSS Study

For this reason, in 2015, the Italian Association of Social Work Teachers (AIDOSS) carried out a study aimed at mapping the situation, both as regards the social work subjects taught and the recruitment of social work teachers.[2] The data provided evidence of the peripheral status of social work subjects in the new system.

In fact, at the time of the study (2013), 38 universities (out of 100 in Italy) offered 42 bachelor's-level and 38 master's-level courses in social work. For each B.A., the study counted the total number of credits given and the number of credits related to social work subjects. Social work subjects include the principles and foundations of social work, methods and techniques of social work (usually given at different levels), organisation of social services, several workshops and tutoring for practice training. The study reported that 42 bachelor's courses gave 7560 credits in total, with 851 credits related to social work subjects, or 11.25%, hence with only an increase of 3% compared to ministerial standards. When adding credits allotted to field practice (881), the total percentage reaches 23% (+ 4.6% compared to the ministerial standards).

The graph in Fig. 1 shows a comparison with other disciplines and gives clear evidence of the relative unimportance attributed to social work disciplines. It also

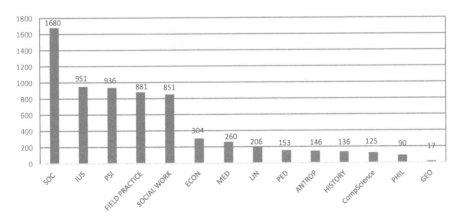

Fig. 1 Number of credits per discipline in 42 social work bachelor's programmes (2013) – AIDOSS study (AIDOSS 2015; Bertotti and Musso 2015)

---

[2] The research was carried out by Dr Gaspare Musso and the scientific supervision of the AIDOSS board and presented at the EASSW Conference in Milan in 2015 (Bertotti and Musso 2015).

shows the prominence given to sociology (1680 credits, 22.2%), followed by juridical and psychological disciplines.

A later study carried out in 2018, which calculated how many courses in social
work are provided in social work bachelor's programmes, obtained a similar finding
(Fazzi and Rosignoli 2020). Such choices clearly indicate the lack of importance
attributed to social work subjects in educational programmes because such subjects
are perceived as being of secondary importance in comparison to the main subjects
taught, like sociology and psychology. Such a lack of importance is further com-
pounded by the precarious position of social work educators themselves.

3.2.2   Teaching Staff

The transition from schools of special purposes to universities partly failed to provide Italy with an already experienced teaching body (Campanini 2015). In fact,
also because of the lack of specific indications from the MIUR, social work teachers
from schools of special purposes have not been included in the academic body as in
other countries, for example Sweden, where professional teachers were widely
employed when social work became a university subject.

The AIDOSS study provided clear evidence of this situation examining the conditions of social work educators in relation to teachers' professional background
and their employment position.

In 2013, the study determined that in the 42 social work bachelor's courses there
were 164 courses on social work subjects taught by 141 teachers. The majority of
these teachers (108, or 76%) come from professional backgrounds and 33 teachers
do not. This means that 23% of courses dedicated to the basic disciplines of social
work were taught by educators who do not have the professional title.

Moreover, the data provided evidence of the precarious position of teachers with
professional backgrounds. Among the 108 social work teachers, 97 (90%) were
employed using the weakest form of contract provided by universities: a temporary
contract, renewed every year, with a yearly fixed number of teaching hours – moreover hours which are usually insufficient to carry out the required tasks; these positions are also poorly paid. The study reported that in 2013 only 11 teachers with
professional backgrounds were in full-time employment at universities: 7 as
researchers, 3 as associate professors and only 1 as full professor. Conversely, the
situation of the remaining 33 teachers who teach social work subjects without having the professional title is much more stable: only 9 have temporary contracts,
whilst 13 are researchers, 6 are associate professors and 5 are full professors.

In the 5 years since 2013, the picture has changed only slightly. The survey carried out in 2018 (Fazzi and Rosignoli 2020) highlights two sets of contrasting data:
firstly, a weak trend in the stabilisation of social work teachers with professional
backgrounds (with the number of permanent positions increased from 11 to 16);
secondly, a decrease in the total number of teachers teaching social work subjects
(from 141 of the AIDOSS study to 120) and an increase in teachers teaching social

work subjects without having the professional title (from 23% of the AIDOSS study to 33%).

Beyond the debate about the need for social work educators to have professional experience, the AIDOSS study also showed that almost 70% of the social work teaching body is precariously employed, thus negatively impacting any opportunities to contribute to the elaboration of the corpus of disciplinary knowledge. This is because, although such teachers are highly motivated, their engagement is characterised by a lack of continuity and a lack of time. In fact, because of their low (often derisive) salaries, they are unavoidably engaged in other professional activities or are retired. They therefore have little time to participate in planning educational activities or to devote to studying or participating in research projects carried out at universities. That means that, despite the advantage of having a large professional component in the teaching staff, these instructors have reduced (or null) influence on the overall programme and development of the discipline.

3.2.3   Subjects Taught and Teaching Methodologies

As for the body of knowledge taught, from the picture painted in the preceding discussion, it is clear that sociology (and other disciplines) have a relevant role in educating social workers in Italy. This would not represent a serious problem per se because the need for an integrated and multidisciplinary approach is commonly recognised by social work educators, as mentioned earlier. However, what appears to be of serious concern is the compartmentalisation of teaching and the tendency to provide knowledge to social work students in discrete blocks. In fact, probably as a consequence of the weakness of the social work discipline, it seems difficult for experts from other disciplines to recognise the specificity of social work and, consequently, to adapt their contents to social work. Moreover, there is a lack of explicit connection between such teachings and social work, thus favouring a fragmentation of knowledge which is detrimental to the multidisciplinary approach which underpins social work (Bertotti and Riva 2014).

The reduced space available for social work also hampers the introduction of new subjects and topics, itself necessary to keep updating the body of knowledge available to new social workers. Hence, the main topics are still related to such traditional teachings as principles and foundations of social work, which usually include history, ethics and organisation of the profession, and methods and techniques of social work, which include various theoretical approaches and the three methods of casework, group work and community work. More current subjects, such as human rights, critical social work, advanced ethics, research in social work, and green social work, are almost totally excluded or left to the individual initiative of the lone teacher or university.

Over time, some attempts to innovate have spread, thanks to renewed connections with the European context and to efforts made by the AIDOSS, which until 2015 regularly organised seminars (called 'schools') based on collaborative work among teachers and the sharing of international experiences (Campanini 2020). For instance, a more decisive use of active teaching methodologies was discussed by Rizzo (2012) and Bertotti (2012), methods to increase reflexivity and learning from errors by Sicora (2017), and more active learning by Fazzi (2016). The involvement of service users in education is also developing, thanks to the University of Piemonte Orientale, which carried out the first Italian structured project, in connection with other European universities (Ramon et al. 2019), or the various experiences in other schools (Cabiati 2016). Additionally, research studies on social work pedagogies are slowly developing (Bertotti and Riva 2014). The University of Trento significantly reformed the structure of its curricula, increasing the amount of credits taught in social work by professors with long-term contracts. The extent of these reforms is quite unique in Italy.

Another oft-discussed issue is the lack of an approach which may further foster the development of professional competences. According to Campanini (2015), this is evident from a brief examination of currently used teaching methods. In fact, despite the inputs provided both by the Bologna Process and by the so-called tuning methodology, in Italy teaching methods still tend to rely on outmoded transmissive lectures, which highlight teachers' rather than students' roles. Similarly, evaluation approaches favour traditional oral or written examinations rather than assessing students' competences and critical thinking abilities. Furthermore, efforts to support students' acquisition of competences are often hampered by organisational factors, such as the high number of students accepted into courses and the lack of trained teachers.

One important issue is the field placement that is, in Italy as elsewhere, the 'signature mark' of social work education (Wayne et al. 2010), and providing adequate internships is central in vocational training. Field work and supervision were 'hot topics' discussed during the transition to higher education, with concerns that standards adopted by the former schools could not be maintained within universities. As mentioned earlier, the minimal number of hours dedicated to work placement is worth 18 credits out of 180 in the bachelor's and 10 out of 120 credits in the master's programme. Generally speaking, the organisation of field placements mandates that students should spend a certain number of hours in a workplace, under the supervision of an experienced professional. In addition, a university tutor (usually a professional social worker employed by the university) is responsible for ensuring the connection of the traineeship to the student's curriculum and to a social work professor (in charge of disciplinary teachings), so as to strengthen the connection between theoretical input and practice (Dellavalle 2011).

The implementation of field practice is very demanding for universities, which face specific costs as well as significant organisational hardships as regards finding training sites deemed suitable for students and experienced field instructors with sufficient time to dedicate to students. Factors such as the reduction in resources for social services, increased workloads, the introduction of managerial policies, and devaluing the contribution made by practice training have all had an impact on locating suitable field placements and on the availability of field instructors (Fazzi 2019). Moreover, the number of students who enrol every year represents an added difficulty. In order to deal with these difficulties, different forms of internship have been tested, for example involving locations where a social worker is not present, group work and other innovative approaches with discussed outcomes (Dellavalle and Rocca 2017; Fazzi and Rosignoli 2014).

The organisation of placements may vary widely across the country beyond ministerial requirements as regards the number of field placement hours, the supervision guaranteed by the university, and the support students receive. A study carried out by the CNOAS (*Consiglio Nazionale Assistenti Sociali*) found that in 2014/2015, 2 universities provided less than 300 h of field placement in the 3 years, 21 provided between 300 and 500 h, and 9 provided between 500 and 700 h (CNOAS 2015). Additionally, such data show the high degree of heterogeneity that characterises the Italian education system, following the same geographic disparity between North and South seen in the welfare system, which is a further source of concern.

3.3 Academisation, Development of Social Work Knowledge and Research

The foregoing data indicate that the academisation of social work in Italy is far from being consolidated and from providing the profession with the necessary foundations for reinforcing its distinctive knowledge and public recognition, founded on the higher quality of its professional actions. In fact, the establishment of social work as an academic discipline should include the creation of independent departments of social work, research centres which guarantee the development of research opportunities, doctorates, scientific journals and publications (Hojers and Dellgran 2016). In Italy this development is encountering several obstacles.

Firstly, as already mentioned, social work is not recognised as an independent discipline but as a branch of sociology. This lack of recognition, already evident when social work started to be taught at universities, has since worsened. In particular, the regulations established by the Gelmini reform in 2010 made the process of recognition of social work as a discipline even more difficult. The creation of departments (a unique structure merging the two previous structures dedicated to teaching and to research activities), with greater autonomy and an obligation to a minimum number of professors, redesigned the overall structure of departments and the academic powers within and outside the scientific community.

Because of the small number of tenured social work professors in higher education – rarely more than one or two at a university – they work in conditions of comparative isolation. This makes it difficult to create the critical mass that would enable them to become visible and to wield influence (Fazzi and Rosignoli 2020). Academic social workers are therefore engaged at each university in building alliances with other disciplines, with ambivalent outcomes such as increased interest in social work on the one hand and the risk of losing its specificity on the other. The reform also established a system of national qualifications for recruitment and career steps, based on each discipline. Because social work is part of sociology, this means that the qualification is evaluated by a commission composed of sociologists who may be unfamiliar with social work specificities.

Secondly, the reform also introduced a stricter system of national evaluation and university rankings, articulated according to several dimensions, such as teaching courses and the scientific production of professors. While with regard to the former – social work teaching courses – evaluations are very positive, in regard to the latter – the scientific output of social work professors – evaluations remain fairly negative. A recent study (Fazzi and Rosignoli 2020) showed that tenured social workers at universities have a relatively low profile in ranked scientific journals. Although in the last 5 years the number of articles in prestigious international journals has increased, the total number of publications remains low in comparison to the output of scientific communities in other countries and in other related disciplines such as sociology.

Thirdly, the renewal of the academic body is slow. Again Fazzi and Rosignoli (2020) stress that not only is there a dearth of social work teachers, but their average age is 50, 55 for associate professors. Indeed, in Italy the usual sequence to renew the academic body, which progresses through doctorates, post-doc fellowships, junior and senior researcher positions leading to associate and full professor positions, is uneven and fragmented. A meaningful example is given by PhD programmes in social work. These started in the 1990s, with a few universities creating social work programmes within other PhD courses, which were activated according to local decisions. A specific social work doctorate was established only a year ago. Nevertheless, in recent years several social workers have obtained their PhDs: Campanini (2020) counted more than 80 social workers who received their PhD, but very few were able to embark on academic careers. Many of them returned to their professional activities, without receiving particular recognition for their efforts.

In consequence, Italian social work research lags behind many other countries. The low number of teachers employed at universities and their isolation have made it very difficult to develop and sustain research projects which could enhance the knowledge base and feedback into teaching content (Campanini 2015). There are also difficulties to overcome in creating social work research centres and in developing connections between social workers with PhDs. Nevertheless, in the last decade some research projects have been carried out and resulted in publications, such as a study on social worker training (Bressan et al. 2011) and one on the impact of managerialism on professionalisation (Tousin and Dellavalle 2017). Additionally, some joint international studies involving Italian and foreign universities have focused on various topics such as migration, decision-making, policy practices and others (Campanini 2020). Lastly, several national inter-university research projects co-financed by MIUR were carried out with the involvement of academic social workers (Lazzari 2008; Facchini 2010; Bifulco and Facchini 2013). The most recent was approved in 2019 and is ongoing at the time of this writing. It deals with the representation of parenting and has social work academics serving both as principal investigator and as local coordinators.[3]

A relevant impulse in the development of social work research comes from contact with international contexts, for example through the conferences of European associations and networks, such as the European Social Work Research Association (ESWRA), International Social Work and Society Academy (TISSA), and European Association of Schools of Social Work (EASSW). Italian social work scholars are active participants in these associations have served on their boards and are becoming members of the editorial boards of international journals.

The Italian society for social work research (SOCISS – *Società Italiana di Servizio Sociale*) was created in 2015 as a transformation of the previous Association for Italian Teachers in Social Work (AIDOSS). Since 2017 SOCISS has committed to organising biannual conferences on social work research and providing the journal *La Rivista di Servizio Sociale* with what it needs to publish scientific articles and studies.

The professional order has also decided to support research and has established the *Fondazione assistenti sociali*, or Social Workers Foundation. The foundation has recently supported some national research projects, such as the project on aggressions against social workers, violations of the ethical code, and the role of social workers in child protection. The involvement of social work academics in these studies is central.

4   Critical Analysis and Challenges Ahead

Within this picture, it is not easy to give a clear answer to the question whether the Italian social work education system is able to respond to current challenges. The answer may vary across Italy because of the high degree of heterogeneity of the structures and the quality of programmes adopted at each university.

However, according to university student evaluations, regularly collected through the national system by the inter-university consortium Almalaurea (2019), social work courses show a higher level of satisfaction compared to other courses (+5% to 10%). The already mentioned study on occupation (Tognetti 2015) shows that students and recent graduates consider their training largely adequate in providing them with the necessary competences to meet the challenges of social work practice and changes in the welfare system. Surprisingly, such feedback is consistent regardless of changes in the cohorts of graduates or region. Regarding the subjects taught, students and recent graduates appreciate subjects related to professional practice and apprenticeship above all, but even theoretical subjects, such as social policies and understanding of social phenomena, are considered relevant and appropriate,

---

[3] "CoPInG – Constructions of parenting on insecure grounds. What role for social work." The principal investigator is S. Fargion from the University of Trento (https://www.cogsci.unitn.it/en/896/coping-constructions-of-parenting-on-insecure-grounds-what-role-for-social-work?)

though to a lesser extent (Facchini and Respi 2015). Again, regarding the subjects taught, a comparative qualitative study analysing the feeling of readiness for practice in Italy, Sweden and England provides similar appreciation for practice education, as well as a great deal of ambivalence on theory. Moreover, high value is attributed to self-reflection and personal growth (Frost et al. 2013).

However, this generally positive assessment on the part of students is not shared by social work scholars, who believe that Italian social work education is inadequate and requires fundamental reform (Campanini 2020; Facchini and Tonon Giraldo 2013; Fazzi and Rosignoli 2020). Mainly because of the structure of credits, which gives low priority to social work, and because of the characteristics of social work professors, Italian social work education far from measuring up to the standards set by the IASSW–AIETS in 2004. As for content, alongside good preparation in the analysis of social policies, there is a lack of critical capacity and an inability on students' part to apply their knowledge in enacting policy practices (Campanini 2020; Fargion et al. 2015). The lack of subjects such as human rights, social justice, research, advanced courses in ethics and critical thinking is of great concern, and it is considered a threat to the preparedness of future social workers. Moreover, teaching such 'life' skills as the ability to react, resilience and creativity is deemed necessary in a complex and constantly changing world (Fazzi and Rosignoli 2020).

There is a real risk that practitioners' professional ideals and identity, carefully cultivated during university study, will clash with the precariousness, bureaucratisation and insufficiencies found in the workplace. Welfare institutions implicitly demand that practitioners limit their activities to the simple application of rules and behave as 'welfare officers' rather than as social workers as agents of change. The risk of deprofessionalisation is real (Spolander et al. 2014) and is accompanied by the danger that newly qualified social workers will be cornered into a defensive attitude. Additionally, in the absence of guaranteed and meaningful opportunities for keeping up awareness and critical thinking, they risk becoming compliant with the system, adopting populist or neoliberal positions that are spreading around Europe (Garrett 2017; Fazzi 2015). Lastly, practitioners are being increasingly exposed to dramatic contradictions as they are asked to behave ethically in an increasingly unethical world (Weinberg and Banks 2019).

Moreover, competition with other professionals is increasing in Italy as elsewhere. In the arena of welfare and social services, several actors are emerging who are new to the field. Professionals such as urban planners, social economists, lawyers and social mediators have an increasing presence, alongside more traditional professions of educators, psychologists and sociologists. These new actors present themselves as innovators, implicitly claiming to be more creative and competent than traditional social workers, who – conversely – are described as bureaucrats and unfit for innovation. Although the presence of these new figures is felt as positive and enriching, it implies the risk of diluting the specificity of social work in the rhetoric and fashionable discourses of innovation. To withstand this competition, it is important to deepen knowledge of the specific values of social work and of social work research that may demonstrate its effectiveness and ability to make a difference. Boosting the research area is therefore a way to support social work's specificity so that other features and boundaries can be drawn (Abbott 1988).

Between innovation and continuity, Italian social work finds itself in need of redesigning the cultural project of the profession. This could be done in the presence of a strong professional and scientific community; however, the constraining factors mentioned earlier, social work's weak professional recognition and its low level of academisation, are hampering this process.

Thus far, the strengthening of social work can take place through an expansion of alliances, at different levels, in the academic and professional worlds. In academia, a possible way is through building alliances and collaborating with other disciplines. At issue is the extent to which social work will be considered a subject of study in itself, worthy of being a specific field of research and theorisation, somehow detached from the profession, and therefore becoming the core of the discipline. It could thus become an object of interest for other disciplines, avoiding the perception of social work as merely a field of colonisation and alternatively viewing it as a disciplinary field with its own consistency and dignity.

Another important line of alliance is with the professional community, in particular with the professional order. The CNOAS (National Council of Social Workers) has a specific interest in training professionals and is responsible for contributing to professional qualification standards, and it should be consulted in the formulation of educational programmes.

Moreover, the CNOAS frequently issues public statements in relation to news and events involving human rights and other political topics of social interest or in relation to social policy interventions. It has thus made visible the profession's commitment to emerging social issues and contributed to the redefinition of social work identity (Sicora and Citroni 2019).

Good reasons for an alliance with the social work profession are also linked to the large array of small-scale research projects developed in the field of practice in the different social services, which seems to be a feature specific to the Italian context (Fargion 2018). This variety was also apparent during two conferences on social work research in 2017 and 2019 where several papers were presented witnessing quite widespread collaborations between practitioners and academics, including those with temporary contracts and PhD students. The conferences demonstrated the possibility of an alliance, as well as the will and the effort to emphasise the vital link between theory and practice.

Lastly, the link with the international context plays a crucial role in this process. In Italy, this link has manifested itself on several occasions. For instance, since 2010, universities have begun to actively participate in World Social Work Day celebrations, in a trend that increasingly involves social work professionals. The link with the international perspective provides a meaningful connection with other ways of understanding social work and knowledge of other ways to develop and has fostered a renewed sense of belonging to a wider professional and scientific community, at global levels but also providing new meanings at local levels (Lorenz 2005; Gray 2019). Several international conferences have been organised, such as the EASSW conference in Milan in 2015, and the ESWRA conference in Bolzano in 2014; in 2020 the global conference of the IASSW ICSW was planned to be held in Rimini. Although difficulties still exist as regards the internationalisation of curricula, connecting with the international context is a powerful lever for strengthening knowledge and awareness of the disciplinary and professional identity of social work.

References

Abbott, A. (1988). *The systems of professions*. Chicago: University of Chicago Press.

AIDOSS. (2015). (Associazione Italiana Docenti di Servizio Sociale) – *Primo Censimento Corsi di studio in servizio sociale* [First census of social work courses in Italy]. Presented at 2014 AIDOSS summer school. Internal materials. https://logintest.webnode.com/products/a2014-autumn-school-Roma. Accessed 27 Aug 2020.

Almalaurea. (2019). *XXI survey on graduates' employment status*. https://www.almalaurea.it/en/universita/indagini/laureati/occupazione. Accessed Jan 2020.

Ascoli, U., & Pavolini, E. (Eds.). (2015). *The Italian welfare state in a European perspective: A comparative analysis*. Bristol: Policy Press.

Ascoli, U., & Ranci, C. (Eds.). (2002). *Dilemmas of the welfare mix. The new structure of welfare in an era of privatization*. New York: Kluwer-Plenum.

Aspalter, C. (2011). The development of ideal-typical welfare regime theory. *International Social Work, 54*(6), 735–750.

Banks, S. (2011). Ethics in an age of austerity: Social work and the evolving new public management. *Journal of Social Intervention: Theory and Practice, 20*(2), 5–23.

Bertotti, T. (2012). Specificità e proposte per una nuova didattica del servizio sociale [Specificities and proposals for a new pedagogy of social work]. *Rassegna di Servizio Sociale, 4*, 105–127.

Bertotti, T. (2014). Il servizio sociale negli anni della crisi : riduzione delle risorse e impatto sulla professione [Social work in the years of the crisis: resource reduction and impact on the profession]. *Autonomie Locali e Servizi Sociali, 3*, 491–510.

Bertotti, T., & Musso, G. (2015). Process of academization of social work in Italy. Obstacles and opportunities. In *Abstract of the 2015 EASSW (European Association Schools of Social Work) Conference*, University of Milano Bicocca, Milan, 29 June – 2 July 2015.

Bertotti, T., & Riva, V. (2014). L'apprendimento dal tirocinio: circolarità tra teoria e pratica secondo gli studenti di servizio sociale. Presentazione di un'indagine pilota. [Learning from field practice in social work: Results from a pilot study]. *Rassegna Di Servizio Sociale, 3–4*(14), 32–47.

Bianchi, E., Cavallone, A. M., Dal Fra Ponticelli, M., De Sandre, I., & Gius, E. (1988). *Il lavoro sociale professionale tra soggetti e istituzioni* [Professional social work between subjects and institutions]. Milano: Franco Angeli.

Bifulco, L. (2017). *Social policies and public action*. New York: Routledge.

Bifulco, L., & Facchini, C. (Eds.) (2013). *Partecipazione sociale e competenze. Il ruolo delle Professioni nei Piani di Zona* [Social participation and competences. The role of the professions in the local social plans]. Milano: Franco Angeli.

Bode, I. (2003). The welfare state in Germany. In C. Aspalter (Ed.), *Welfare capitalism around the world* (pp. 157–178). Hong Kong: Casa Verde.

Bordogna, L., & Neri, S. (2014). Austerity policies, social dialogue and public services in Italian local government. *Transfer: European Review of Labour and Research, 20*(3), 357–371.

Bressan, F., Pedrazza, M., & Neve, E. (2011). *Il percorso formativo dell'assistente sociale. Autovalutazione e benessere professionale* [The educational path of social workers. Self evaluation and professional wellbeing]. Milano: Franco Angeli.

Cabiati, E. (2016). Teaching and learning: An exchange of knowledge in the university among students, service users, and professors. *European Journal of Social Work, 19*(2), 247–262.

Campanini, A. (2007). Introduction: Educating social workers in the context of Europe. In E. Frost & M. J. Freitas (Eds.), *Social work education in Europe*. Roma: Carocci Editore.

Campanini, M. (2015). Social work education in Italy. History and the present scenario. *The Indian Journal of Social Work, 76*(1), 57–74.

Campanini, A. M. (2020). Social work education in Italy: Lights and shadows. In S. M. Sajid, R. Baikady, C. Sheng-Li, & H. Sakaguchi (Eds.), *The Palgrave handbook of global social work education*. London: Palgrave Macmillan.

Campanini, A., & Frost, E. (Eds.). (2004). *European social work. Commonalities and differences*. Rome: Carocci.

CENSIS (Ed.). (1999). *Essere protagonisti del futuro. Scenari di sviluppo per il ruolo di assistente sociale [Protagonist of the future. Developments for the role of social workers]*. Roma: Fondazione Censis.

CNOAS. (2015). *Data from internal survey carried out during the field stage of V. Di Legge*, student of the Master's course of University of Roma 3. Supervisor dr. N. Bartolomei.

CNOAS. (2018). *Notiziario Ordine Assistenti Sociali n.1/2018*. https://cnoas.org/notiziario/, newsletter of the National council of Social workers. Accessed Jan 2020.

Dellavalle, M. (2011). *Il tirocinio nella formazione al servizio sociale* [Field practice in social work training]. Roma: Carocci.

Dellavalle, M., & Rocca, V. (2017). Sperimentare nuovi percorsi di servizio sociale attraverso il tirocinio [Discovering new paths of social work through internships]. *Prospettive sociali e sanitarie, 4*, 21–25.

EISS. (2001). *Rapporto sulla situazione del servizio sociale* [Report on social work in Italy] (pp. 23–46). Roma: Tipigraf.

Esping-Andersen, G. (1990). *The three worlds of welfare capitalism*. Princeton: Princeton University Press.

Facchini, C. (Ed.) (2010). *Tra impegno e professione. Gli assistenti sociali come soggetti del welfare* [From engagement to profession: Social workers as welfare actors]. Bologna: Il Mulino.

Facchini, C., & Lorenz, W. (2013). Between differences and common features: The work of social workers in Italy. *International Social Work, 56*(4), 439–454.

Facchini, C., & Respi, C. (2015). La valutazione del percorso formativo: una diffusa positività con qualche ombre [The evaluation of the educational path: Widespread positivity with some shadows]. In M. Tognetti (Ed.), *Voglio fare l'assistente sociale* (pp. 274–289). Milano: Franco Angeli.

Facchini, C., & Tonon Giraldo, S. (2013). The university training of social workers: Elements of innovation, positive and critical aspects in the case of Italy. *The British Journal of Social Work, 43*(4), 667–684.

Fargion, S. (2008). Reflections on social work's identity: International themes in Italian practitioners' representation of social work. *International Social Work, 51*(2), 206–219.

Fargion, S. (2018). Social work promoting participation: reflections on policy practice in Italy. *European Journal of Social Work, 21*(4), 559–571. https://doi.org/10.1080/1369145 7.2017.1320528

Fargion, S., Frei, S., & Lorenz, W. (Eds.) (2015). *L'intervento sociale tra gestione del rischio e partecipazione* [Social intervention between risk management and participation]. Roma: Carocci.

Fazzi, L. (2015). Exclusionary populism, xenophobia and social work in Italy. *International Social Work, 58*(4), 595–605.

Fazzi, L. (2016). Are we educating creative professionals? The results of some experiments on the education of social work students in Italy. *Social Work Education, 1*, 89–99.

Fazzi, L. (2019). Why it's still worth it: Continuing to supervise trainee students in a period of crisis in Italy. *European Journal of Social Work, 23*, 826. https://doi.org/10.1080/13691457.201 9.1656172.

Fazzi, L., & Rosignoli, A. (2014). Reversing the perspective: When the supervisors learn from their trainees. *British Journal of Social Work, 46*(1), 1–18.

Fazzi, L., & Rosignoli, A. (2020). Social work education in Italy: Problems and perspectives. In S. M. Sajid, R. Baikady, C. Sheng-Li, & H. Sakaguchi (Eds.), *The Palgrave handbook of global social work education*. London: Palgrave Macmillan.

Ferrario, F. (1996). *Le dimensioni dell'intervento sociale* [Dimensions of social intervention]. Roma: NIS.

Ferrera, M. (1996). The southern model of welfare in social Europe. *Journal of European Social Policy, 6*(1), 17–37.

Ferrera, M. (2005). *The boundaries of welfare: European integration and the new spatial politics of social protection*. Oxford: Oxford University Press.

Ferrera, M. (2008). The European welfare state: Golden achievements, silver prospects. *West European Politics, 31*(1–2), 82–107.

Ferrera, M., & Maino, F. (2015). Conclusioni: bilancio e prospettive [Conclusions: Overview and perspectives]. In F. Maino, & M. Ferrera (Eds.), *Secondo Rapporto sul secondo welfare in Italia 2015* [Second report of second welfare in Italy] (pp. 365–382). Torino: Centro di Ricerca e Documentazione Luigi Einaudi.

Fiorentino Busnelli, E. (2002). Principi e Valori Fondanti per la professione: le prospettive degli anni 44/50 [Founding principles and values of the profession: The outlook of the years 44/50]. *Quaderni della rivista di Servizio Sociale, 17*, 11–21.

Frost, E., Hojer, S., & Campanini, A. (2013). Readiness for practice: Social work students' perspectives in England, Italy, and Sweden. *European Journal of Social Work, 16*(3), 327–343.

Garrett, P. M. (2017). *Welfare words. Critical social work and social policy*. London: Sage.

Garrett, P. M., & Bertotti, T. F. (2017). Social work and the politics of 'austerity': Ireland and Italy. *European Journal of Social Work, 20*(1), 29–41. https://doi.org/10.1080/13691457.2016.1185698. Accessed 27 Aug 2020.

Giraldo, S., & Riefolo, E. (Eds.) (1996). *Il servizio sociale esperienza e costruzione del sapere* [Social work as experience and knowledge construction]. Milano: Franco Angeli.

Gray, M. (2019). 'Think globally and locally': A new agenda for international social work education'. In I. Taylor, M. Bogo, M. Lefevre, & B. Teater (Eds.), *Routledge international handbook of social work education* (pp. 3–14). New York: Routledge.

Hojers, S., & Dellgran, P. (2016). The academisation of social work: Sweden – A case study. In I. Taylor et al. (Eds.), *Routledge international handbook of social work education* (pp. 51–56). New York: Routledge.

Lazzari, F. (2008). *Servizio sociale trifocale. Le azioni e gli attori delle nuove politiche sociali* [Three focal social work. Actions and agents of the new social policies]. Milano: Franco Angeli.

Leitner, S. (2003). Varieties of familialism: The caring function of the family in comparative perspective. *European Societies, 5*(4), 353–375.

Lorenz, W. (2005). Social work and a new social order challenging neo-liberalism erosion of solidarity. *Social Work and Society, 3*(1), 93–101.

Martinelli, F., Anttonen, A., & Mätzke, M. (Eds.). (2017). *Social services disrupted. Changes, challenges and policy implications for Europe in times of austerity*. Cheltenham: Edward Elgar Publishers.

Mulazzoni, L., Tentoni, R., & Zanaboni, L. (1971). Le rammendatrici dal dialogo facile [The easy dialogue menders]. *Inchiesta, 3*, 65–67.

Naldini, M., & Saraceno, C. (2008). Social and family policies in Italy: Not totally frozen but far from structural reforms. *Social Policy and Administration, 42*(7), 733–748.

Neve, E. (2008). *Il servizio sociale. Fondamenti e cultura di una professione [Social work. Culture and foundation of a profession]*. Roma: Carocci.

Niero, M., Rossi, P., & Tognetti, M. (2015). Professione e forza lavoro [Profession and workforce]. In M. Tognetti (Ed.), *Voglio fare l'assistente sociale. Formazione e occupazione dei laureati in Servizio sociale in tempi di crisi e discontinuità*. Milano: Franco Angeli.

Orme, J., & Rennie, G. (2006). The role of registration in ensuring ethical practice. *International Social Work, 49*(3), 333–344.

Paci, M. (1989). Public and private in the Italian welfare system. In P. M. Lange, S. Berger, & M. Regini (Eds.), *State, market and social regulation: New PERSPECTIVES in Italy* (pp. 217–234). Cambridge: Cambridge University press.

Pieroni, G., & Dal Pra Ponticelli, M. (2005). *Introduzione al servizio sociale* [Introduction to social work]. Roma: Carocci.

Ramon, S., Grodofsky, M. M., Allegri, E., & Rafaelic, A. (2019). Service users' involvement in social work education: Focus on social change projects. *Social Work Education, 38*(1), 89–102.

Ranci, C., & Ascoli, U. (2002). *Dilemmas of the welfare mix. The new structure of welfare in an era of privatization*. New York: Kluwer/Plenum Publishers.

Rizzo, A. M. (2012). Una riflessione sugli approcci teorici che sottendono i metodi di insegnamento [Considerations on the theoretical approaches underlying teaching methods]. *Rassegna di Servizio Sociale, 4*, 99–104.

Saraceno, C., & Keck, W. (2010). Can we identify intergenerational policy regimes in Europe? *European Societies, 12*(5), 675–696.

Sgroi. (2001). Introduzione: il servizio sociale come professione [Introduction: Social work as a profession]. In *EISS Rapporto sulla situazione del servizio sociale* (pp. 23–46). Roma: Tipigraf.

Sicora, A. (2017). *Reflective practice and learning from mistakes in social work*. Bristol: Policy Press.

Sicora, A., & Citroni, G. (2019). One, not one, or one hundred thousand? Voices of social workers in international comparison. *European Journal of Social Work*, 1–11. https://doi.org/10.108 0/13691457.2019.1605979.

Sicora, A., & Kolar, E. (Eds.) (2015). Social Work around the world. Colors and shapes in a complex mosaic. Special issue of the Quaderni del CSAL Centro studi America Latina (*Journal of Center for Latin American Studies*) VII, 13, ISSN 2035-6633.

Sicora A., & Rosina, B. (Eds.) (2019). *La violenza contro gli assistenti sociali in Italia* [Violence against social workers in Italy]. Milano: Franco Angeli.

Sicora, A., Nothdurfter, U., Rosina, B., & Sanfelici, M. (2018). *Service user violence against social workers in Italy: Prevalence and characteristics of the phenomenon*. Presentation at 8th European Conference for Social Work Research, Edinburgh, UK, April 2018.

Spolander, G., Engelbrecht, L., Martin, L., Strydom, M., Pervova, I., Marjanen, P., et al. (2014). The implications of neoliberalism for social work: Reflections from a six-country international research collaboration. *International Social Work, 57*(4), 301–312.

Stefani, M. (Ed.) (2012). *Le origini del servizio sociale italiano. Tremezzo: un evento fondativo del 1946* [The origin of Italian social work. Tremezzo: The founding event of 1946]. Roma: Viella.

Tognetti, M. (Ed.) (2015). *Voglio fare l'assistente sociale. Formazione e occupazione dei laureati in Servizio sociale in tempi di crisi e discontinuità* [I want to be social worker. Training and employment of social work graduates in times of crisis and discontinuity]. Milano: Franco Angeli.

Tousijn, W., & Dellavalle, M. (2017). *Logica professionale e logica manageriale. una ricerca sulle professioni sociali* [Professional and managerial logic. A research on social professions]. Bologna: Il mulino.

Wayne, J., Raskin, M., & Bogo, M. (2010). Field education as the signature pedagogy of social work education. *Journal of Social Work Education, 46*(3), 327–339. https://doi.org/10.5175/ JSWE.2010.200900043.

Weinberg, M., & Banks, S. (2019). Practising ethically in unethical times: Everyday resistance in social work. *Ethics and Social Welfare, 13*, 361. https://doi.org/10.1080/17496535.201 9.1597141.

Challenges for Social Work Education in Croatia: Lessons from a Post-socialist Context

Ana Opačić and Nino Žganec

1 Introduction

The twentieth century was the century of changes and a dramatically rapid transformation of political, value and social systems in general. These changes are particularly evident in the former socialist countries that have gone through political, institutional and economic transformations. Moreover, countries of the former Socialist Federal Republic (SFR) of Yugoslavia had experience of war. As a profession, social work was always in a dynamic relation with its internal assumptions and external social and state influence. This dynamic reflected on the educational system, but also, without a doubt, on the practice system. However, these changes on both sides were not necessarily coherent. Initially, social work was a mechanism of the welfare state, but later, in the early 1970s, this connection was challenged, and the educational system became more oriented towards raising its scientific ground and delivering some insight on how society functions (Parton 2000). There was a need to separate state administration from social work, and these tendencies have remained in place to this day because there is not enough space for professional creativity, self-reflexivity and autonomy (Dominelli 1996). It seems that changes were faster integrated within the educational system than within social work practice. Significant improvements in education started in the 1980s and were followed by an improvement in social workers' status in general (Karger and Stoesz 2003). New teaching methods were introduced in education, including technological improvements, more creative learning processes and more intense student involvement with a critical thinking approach (Agbim and Ozanne 2007). On the other hand, the educational system continues to deal with obvious changes that occurred in the field, specifically regarding budget cuts, crises and lower professional

A. Opačić (✉) · N. Žganec
Faculty of Law, Department of Social Work, University of Zagreb, Zagreb, Croatia
e-mail: ana.opacic@pravo.hr; nzganec@pravo.hr

© Springer Nature Switzerland AG 2021
M. Laging, N. Žganec (eds.), *Social Work Education in Europe*,
European Social Work Education and Practice,
https://doi.org/10.1007/978-3-030-69701-3_7

standards (Jarman-Rohde et al. 1997). With this in mind, it is reasonable to raise the issue of the relationship between the educational system and social work practice in the context of social changes.

Given the experience evident in the former Yugoslavia, specifically in Croatia, we might say that the education of social workers in the context of turbulent social change has two traits: first, it is a factor of the reproduction of the practice system, and second, it is the protagonist of the production of a new system. We will try to demonstrate these traits by describing the three stages that social work education went through. Finally, we will attempt to answer the question of what this double role of the educational system means for social work practice. In conclusion, a model is proposed that precisely captures the transformation from one role to another.

2   Process of Professional Social Work Development in Croatia

2.1   Synergy Between Education and State Intervention

The beginnings of social work education in the former Yugoslavia were closely connected to governmental intervention. Social work has been primarily a state-based and organised activity, and education served to create a profile of civil servants that were needed at the time.

The early twentieth century (until the end of World War II) brought a lot of social problems to cities – poverty, alcoholism, close association of illness with social deprivation, and the breakdown of family protection with a large number of abandoned and abused children (Majdak 2006). The fundamental interest of society was focused on its young people and children who grew up in poor families or were unprotected due to poverty, economic crisis or emigration (Puljiz 2008). The Croatian population was largely rural, but the beginnings of civil life opened the door to modern developments, including social protection (Puljiz 2006). Social deprivation was identified as a factor of the general health condition, and very soon social activity was associated with the concept of social medicine (Puljiz 2008). Religious and other civic organisations working on a voluntary basis were especially significant in providing social protection (Puljiz 2008). Their activities were based on well-educated individuals sensitive to social problems (Ajduković and Branica 2006). Initially, state interventions were insignificant, but the severity of social problems was such that the state began to develop institutions to organise a care system and assisted former amateur attempts at professionalisation. Thus, there was an attempt to introduce education for social workers by means of the Order of the Governor of the Kingdom of Croatia and Slavonia from 1920 upon the establishment of the Royal Social School in Zagreb. The authority of the state is so dominant that it formulates the purpose of education, the pedagogical approach, and the method of recruiting participants among experienced practitioners, and it provides scholarships and accommodations for poor students (Regulation of the Vice-Roy (Ban) of the Kingdom of Croatia and Slavonia of 6 December 1920, No. 26819 on the foundation of the Royal Social School in Zagreb). At these early stages, social work was already defined as an activity that has practical and theoretical foundations, as well as an epistemologically interdisciplinary ground (pedagogy, social policy), and a specific set of educational content for the social protection of only two groups: mothers and children (with developmental disabilities, without parental care, with behavioural disorders). However, in these early stages, social work was also defined as having an administrative character, and participants had to learn accounting and statistics. The beginnings of professional social work and education were predominantly characterised by the commitment and involvement of women, and to this day social work in Croatia remains a so-called female profession. Unfortunately, the first school for social workers was not established, since with the Vidovdan Constitution and with Croatia joining the Kingdom of Serbs, Croats and Slovenians, this act, like many others, became null and void. Instead of social workers, temporary social protection was provided by nurses (Ajduković and Branica 2006).

2.2   Period After World War II

The period after World War II brought dramatic political and social change. First of all, Croatia became part of the socialist system, and this fact largely characterised its further development. The socialist government was legitimised precisely by expressing interest in addressing social problems and by the vision of a classless society in which the standard of living of deprived groups would improve (Puljiz 2006). The key mechanism for this was the socialisation of the means of production, and the socialist government adopted a series of measures to accelerate industrial development with its attacks on the agricultural system (Puljiz 2006). In the first stage of socialist rule (1945–1953), bureaucracy was a leading force, instead of professional practices, and government administrative mechanisms led to the implementation of radical measures involving the nationalisation of natural resources, agricultural reform and price regulation, while local authorities were to see to the needs of the primary victims of war, young people and people with disabilities (Puljiz 2006). However, local areas experienced a dearth of educated professionals, and those who were educated prospered rapidly and eventually migrated to more developed areas. This resulted in a situation in which there was insufficient professional support to address social problems. After 1953, political power was modernised by opening up to the West and maintaining peaceful relations with the Eastern Bloc. The awareness that a good educational structure was a prerequisite for the social development started to grow, as did the notion that the task of solving social problems must be assigned to educated individuals (Puljiz 2006). Also, the awareness that a socialist society was essentially not a conflict-free society and that social problems could not be solved solely by economic growth started to mature (Puljiz 2006). On the one hand, the state developed a social welfare system (social care homes and centres for social work), and on the other, it gave impetus to the development of education. Educational programmes were designed according to the profile of professionals that the system demands.

In this period, the social welfare regime began to develop. Although Yugoslavia was not listed in Esping-Andersen's typology, it had many characteristics of a conservative regime with dominant public security mechanisms connected with employment status (Esping-Andersen 1990). The only exception was the fact that subsidiarity was not strongly promoted. Instead the state would immediately assume responsibility for the most vulnerable sections of the population, which resulted in the development of large residential complexes.

The first systematic social work education appears in the 1950s. In 1952 in Zagreb, the College of Social Work was established, becoming the first of its kind in South-East Europe. Colleges were also established in other centres of SFR Yugoslavia in the 1950s and 1960s (Zaviršek 2008). Three forces played a role in establishing an educational system: prominent local individuals, foreign experts and the government (Bresler 2002). The synergy between the political establishment and education was also evident in the fact that the first students were part of the communist regime, and teachers were often involved in political processes (Zaviršek 2008). The establishment of the College of Social Work was an indicator of the push for decentralisation and democratisation in Yugoslavia (Ajduković 2002). The focus at the national level was reflected in the college curriculum, which in education and in publishing predominantly included topics regarding youth with behavioural disorders, followed by persons with disabilities (especially resulting from war-time activities), and social work in the economy in connection with the fact that the protection of labourers was one of the dominant issues in socialist countries (Švenda Radeljak 2006). Work with children and adolescents was so advanced that the field witnessed the beginnings of research activities, particularly through the Institute for Research on Neglected and Abused Children, professional literature, and legislation (Majdak 2006). This remains one of the most popular topics in current social work. Synergy between education and state-level decision-making was also reflected in the fact that the state managed enrolment in the college and prescribed the profile of staff needed in the civil service.

In terms of organisation, social work education was supported by an established association of social workers. In addition, the level of professional knowledge was raised through the establishment of a fund for research and literature, and teamwork was promoted (Bresler 2002). Social work is accepted as a broadly applicable profession that must find its place in social, health, economic and other organisations according to national regulations, and additional training must be provided to experts on a continual basis (Vlada Narodne Republike Hrvatske 2002).

What content was covered within the curriculum? First of all, social work has a wide interdisciplinary basis. There was a set of general knowledge from certain social sciences, such as economics, pedagogy, sociology, the fundamentals of legal science, the theory of the state, psychology, and social medicine. Taking into account the socialist context, historical materialism was also taught. Another group of courses referred to vocational subjects, including general ones like social security, organisation of social services, and concern for social standards, and specific ones, such as working with people with disabilities, social work in industry, and social work in institutions for children. However, a third group of subjects consisted of items that were related to the development of professional administrative work in an administrative context, and skills such as typing, shorthand, administration management and budget management were taught (Bresler 2002). A similar proportion of these content units remained in the curriculum until 1970, with the addition of an introduction to social policy, which was included in the curriculum in 1961, and community social work and research methodology, included in 1966 (Bresler 2002).

In conclusion, it can be said that in the first stage of social work education, the educational system was compatible with the state social welfare system, and it was supposed to reproduce it in an ideological, organisational and methodical way. However, these links seemed to weaken in the years that followed, which would continue in the third stage of educational development.

2.3   Separation of State and Academic Influence on Education

The 1970s were in Yugoslavia, as in many other places around the world, times of economic and social crisis. Socialist Yugoslavia experienced its limitations under a tremendous debt burden, a return of previously emigrated populations from crisis-affected countries, and the realisation amongst citizens that the state cannot protect their rights in the proclaimed manner, and this created an atmosphere of unrest and discontent (Puljiz 2008). On the other hand, the desire to strengthen the development of social workers' education became obvious, and social work education started to diverge from just fulfilling state requirements. It is at this stage education began to diverge from practice. Specifically, in 1972 a system of higher education for social workers was introduced whereby social work took shape as an interdisciplinary profession, reflected in the fact that courses were organised at several faculties. However, according to the curricula from 1970 until the end of the 1980s (Bresler 2002), the lack of specific courses focused on specific areas of social work and stronger involvement of other social sciences as in, for example, sociology – family sociology, industrial sociology, sociology of the village or psychology – developmental psychology, personality psychology, and industrial psychology. The teaching of basic socialist ideas was also maintained: the fundamentals of Marxism, the Yugoslav political system, and, later, as part of the theory and practice of self-government. On the one hand, this approach raised the "ambition" of social work regarding the development of an epistemological basis distinct from the technical approach (Ajduković 2002), which was evident in the increased involvement of students in research and counselling work (Kljajić 2002). This approach truly advanced the interdisciplinary approach in the profession (including economics, law, medicine, sociology, psychology) (Kljajić 2002). However, the shift from the areas particular to social work began to raise questions about the authentic nature of the role and characteristics of social work (Martinović 1987; Halmi 2000). On the other hand, based on agreements among faculties and the state (Kljajić 2002), the state expected a lot from social work: professional analytical work, research work, the development of social policy measures, the evaluation of activities and the development of preventive and curative programmes in individual cases, groups and communities. On the other hand, positivistic – diagnostic approach and teamwork are considered as key features of the social work profession. This raises the question of how this general knowledge might develop specific expertise that will respond to these requests. Also, it must be said that some demands remain hard to meet, such as taking part in the adoption of social policy measures or evaluating practice.

These issues were somehow resolved in the 1980s when the authenticity of social work identity was developed through the introduction of specific methodical areas: social work with individuals, families, groups and communities, as well as through the scientific and theoretical foundations of social work (Magdalenić 2002). Also, the diversity of issues that social work is engaged in expanded. Alongside traditional areas, such as family issues, a shift occurred towards various marginal groups, e.g. persons with mental disorders, particularly in connection with addiction problems (Magdalenić 2002). This direction of development will remain visible in the coming years with the integration of new pro-European paradigms.

3 Current Social Work in Croatia and Its Reflection in a Transitioning Society

One of the most turbulent periods in the socialist camp occurred in the late 1980s and the early 1990s. This was a time of war, economic transition, and the construction of separate state systems and, later, of the involvement in the Europeanisation process. At the normative level, Croatian society has integrated the idea of greater civil liberties and the development of a private market economy (Puljiz 2008). Also, at the normative level, the idea of social partnership is promoted, as is the development of a mixed welfare policy involving family support, local communities, nongovernmental organisations (NGOs), government measures and the private sector. These ideas will find their place in the curriculum related to social policy. On the other hand, a stronger influence is being exerted by the World Bank and International Monetary Fund, which advocate the transition of health, pension and the welfare system to the privatisation of some activities, while influential European bodies promote greater decentralisation (Puljiz 2008). Also, various socially affected or socially excluded groups seeking social protection are recognised (United Nations Development Programme 2006).

The actual context in relation to such ideas was that in Croatia during the war years, crisis care measures were almost exclusively provided to war-affected populations, especially persons with disabilities, refugees and displaced persons (Puljiz

2008). Since 1996, Croatian society has been dealing with the consequences war and there has been an awareness that the sense of social security, social equality and employment (inherent in a socialist society) has been lost (Zrinščak 2003). During the war years the importance of NGOs grew, particularly international NGOs, under whose influence civil society continues to evolve (Bežovan 2008). The work of NGOs introduced some new methods, such as counselling, group work (Knežević 1996) and, later, project management techniques and organisational management. Different social groups also became more visible through civil society activities (e.g. chronically ill people, ethnic minorities, asylum seekers). This new focus led to changes in topics covered as part of social work education and to a more psycho-social orientation, while other, more structurally oriented, approaches, such as social work in communities and international social work, have found their space in recent years. The psychosocial approach still attracts a lot of students' attention, as counselling is one of the most popular areas in social work (Acker 2004).

However, apart from this field of practice, the fact is that the majority of social work is still connected to tradition and the social welfare system in Croatia continues to nurture the system built in the socialist period. Social work in Croatia is mostly connected to public institutions, and the majority of social workers are employed in the public social care sector. Based on recent data, there are 1148 social workers in social welfare centres and 329 in social care homes (Ministry for Demography, Family, Youth and Social Policy 2018). Currently the Croatian chamber of social workers has 2410 members, which suggests that approximately 60% of social workers are employed in the public social care sector. Research done by Matković et al. (2015) on employment after completing social care studies shows that the first jobs graduates find are in social welfare centres (29%), social care homes (24%) or civil society organisations (19%). Also, current employment for the majority of social workers who completed their education between 2004 and 2010 was in social welfare centres (30.8%), social care homes (22.1%), NGOs (13.9%) and local or regional government (12.5%). Only 12.2% of social workers work in other sectors (justice, health, education), while 8.5% work completely outside the profession (Matković et al. 2015). Employment in the public social care sector demands a certain type of professional activity, particularly the obligation to act in accordance with the regulations and legal requirements and to follow an increasing number of prescribed procedures. This is why new social workers find legal courses more useful for their work placement than many other courses in core social work methods, with the exception of casework (Matković et al. 2015).

Keeping in mind the considerable concentration of social workers employed in public social care and the fact that many ambitious and complex reforms were terminated as a consequence of changes in political structures and decisions (Žganec 2008), we have a situation of significant inconsistency between social work practice and social work education.

4 Current Model of Education of Social Work in Croatia

Social work education continues the trend that began in the 1980s towards strengthening specific areas of theories, research methodologies and practices. On the other hand, the gap between theory and what is commonly considered the practice of social work in society seems still significant. The reason for that may lie precisely in the idea that education should be a lever for the production of a new system of practice, not the reproduction of old ones. As mentioned earlier, NGOs and foreign organisations played an important part in the introduction of new ideas and topics. The key idea in planning the new curriculum was not restricted to what exists right now, but what are the desired achievements of social work practice in the future (Ajduković 2003). In addition to the profession, in the aftermath of the 1990s there was a tendency to grant social work recognition as a scientific field which emerged in 2000, followed by the establishment of postgraduate education in 2002.

Current social work education consists of university bachelor's studies (4 years at the University of Zagreb, 3 years at the University of Osijek) and master's studies (1 year, only at the University of Zagreb). At the University of Zagreb, students can take one of two master's-level studies, in social work or social policy, which is only separate on the master's level. At the University of Zagreb, students can enrol in doctoral studies in social work and social policy (3 years) or one of many postgraduate specialist studies (2 years, in supervision, family mediation, community development, social policy, or psychosocial approach). During their bachelor's and master's studies, students complete a total of 330 h of field practice (210 at the bachelor's and 120 at the master's level), which is considered insufficient from both the teachers' and the students' perspectives. The level of academisation is quite high; social work is recognised as a scientific discipline, the studies are at university level, and all lecturers must earn a professorial title (assistant professor, associate professor or full professor).

Still, three areas compose the educational content of the programme, but in slightly altered proportions: a general introduction to closely related social sciences is retained, such as law particularly economics, sociology, psychology and criminology. Social medicine, which has been related to social work since its beginnings, was removed from the group of obligatory courses. This might be linked to an attempt to shift away from positivistic diagnostics and the so-called medical model of social work and introduce new postmodern perspectives (Urbanc 2006). However, the medical approach has been integrated with social work since its beginnings, and the shift is hard to carry out in practice. Some courses of successful organisation management remain part of the programme, but to a lesser extent, such as the organisation of social services and management in social work (the managerial approach is sometimes favoured, but in the context of social work in Croatia it has not yet taken the form of managerialism, which is a concept widely discussed in current social work), foreign languages, informatics and statistics. Clearly, courses which are part of the authentic body of social work knowledge and practice are being strengthened: general topics, such as social work theory, research methodology, and basic methodological work with individuals, groups, communities and families; specific social issues, e.g. social work with the elderly, people with disabilities, drug addicts, young people; or particular skills like strategic planning, consulting and interpersonal communication. A growing number of elective courses promote social work in other, currently more marginal, areas (in the penal system, health care, labour and employment, crisis management, system of education), new skills or expanding familiar concepts (such as preventive services, human rights, civil society development, using creative methods and techniques of drama, spirituality, conflict resolution, ethics, history, social work and service users' perspectives). The educational system is becoming manifestly dualistic; on one hand there is social work, and on the other more separate areas of study like social policy. Unfortunately, experts who graduated from social policy studies still are not recognised enough on the labour market. As for an integrated undergraduate degree, there is an enhanced body of common knowledge in general social policy, at the European and national levels, and at the graduate and postgraduate levels, social work and social policy are completely separate. In keeping with European trends, ideas of social partnership, mixed social policy, decentralisation and active policy towards final users are promulgated. Graduate degrees are intended more as a means to deepen learned content, and new courses have been introduced recently, such as integrative social work, palliative care, multiculturalism and international social work. At the postgraduate level there are two clear directions for profiling educational content. One is more micro orientated towards the development of psychosocial work and includes studies such as the psychosocial approach in social work, family mediation and supervision. The other one is more focused on the macro and structural level with an eye towards social development, and it includes studies of social policy and social community development.

A further expansion of the educational content can be expected. However, what is definitely evident is a different approach in education, not only in content. Social work in Croatia strongly promotes the theoretical postmodern paradigm emphasising the subjective experiences of both social workers and service users. This is reflected in the teaching process. In the last 10 years, there have been improvements in field practice, ensuring both supervision and evaluation (Ajduković 2003). Supervision and evaluation are promoted as an essential part of the professional culture and behaviour, but without stronger implementation in practice. Furthermore, more interactive work with students is promoted, which means that it is necessary to reach a more favourable student/teacher ratio. There are ongoing efforts to enhance students' self-reflection on personal characteristics in the context of professional development (Ajduković 2003). One of the new approaches is attributing greater significance to service users' perspective in education, research and practice. This idea still has its opponents among teachers who are not yet familiar enough with the idea. Furthermore, service users do not have enough experience of active participation in issues directly connected to them as a result of the socialist legacy (Čekić Bašić 2009; Skokandić and Urbanc 2009).

The Croatian educational system has been greatly enriched by foreign perspectivess since many contributors have come from abroad, mainly the United States,

Germany, the Netherlands and Sweden. These connections continue to develop (Ajduković 2003), and many new ideas have been introduced as a result of this influence. Since foreigners have made contributions, field practice emerged, mostly in the non-governmental sector. Core social work practice remained the same, with little modification. However, some topics ought to be included in the curriculum and become part of the general educational approach. Nonetheless, topics such as action research and evaluation or the de-institutionalisation and decentralisation of the welfare system are on neither the practical nor educational agenda. Action and evaluation research is close to the idea of evidence-based practice that had been widely elaborated in social work (Howard et al. 2003; Edmond et al. 2006) but never existed in these areas. It would also be necessary to introduce other perspectives, such as international, globalised and ecological perspectives (Edwards 2011) and perspectives critical of current social disparities (Finn and Jacobson 2003).

5   Critical Reflections on Social Work Education in Croatia

The experience of social work education in Croatia accurately reflects the transformation from playing its role in the reproduction of what existed towards the production of new social work practice in society (Fig. 1).

The idea of social work evolved through the education system from what was originally conceived of as practical social work. The evolution of social work education was not proportionally followed by the evolution of social work in the field, resulting in the existence of a dual system of practice. One, which is predominant, is in the jurisdiction of the state, and many believe that legislation stipulates what social work is and that the role of social workers within the state system consists in implementing it. On the other hand, there is social work in the field, which has not yet been sufficiently developed and which, mainly through civil society organisations, legitimises this conceptual shift. Furthermore, there are not enough coherent links between the educational system and the dominant system of state practice, or between the two systems of practice.

What can we learn from this experience?

First of all, two roles of social work education can be distinguished:

The first role is to reproduce the current practice, especially when the educational system is closely connected to the authority on social work practice in society (usually the state government).

The second role is to produce new practices, which could emerge as a consequence of new ideological influences, recognition of social change, and new methodological and epistemic achievements.

If the role of education changes faster than practice, the dual system can be expected to continue without harmonisation of practices in the field, with both having social legitimacy, and a discrepancy between education and practical work. New achievements in the ideological and technical sense and recognised social changes can give legitimacy to new educational programmes and, consequently, to new

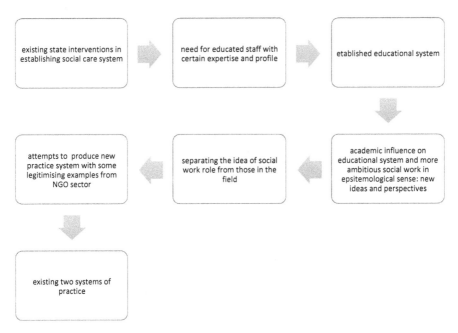

Fig. 1 Process of transformation of the role of social work education

practices of social work. However, it is also likely that the formerly dominant practices will be upheld based on the will of their enforcer (in this case the government), the habitual patterns of social workers' activities, and public expectations vis-à-vis social work. The education of social workers cannot escape from its central position, i.e. being in between field work practice and social and theoretical changes (Fig. 2).

This is particularly obvious in the twenty-first century, where permanent social change are visible in population migration, the impact of inter-cultural diversity and economic instability. However, it is necessary to ensure the educational system is critically oriented towards both field practice and these wider social changes.

If education indeed has as its function to reproduce social work practice, it is necessary to constantly evaluate the effectiveness of these practices and implement changes within educational programmes in order to improve field practices (changes from within).

On the other hand, if the education system plays a role in the production of new practices by introducing new ideas and views on social life and the role of social workers (and if these changes do not emerge from the practice field, but from external factors), then it is important that the education system develop a way of monitoring field experts and their adaptability to changes which occur in the epistemological sense, in order to keep practice safe from being trapped and isolated from its professional basis, or left to other agents, e.g. government to profile the profession. That would mean that it is necessary to determine whether new ideas are acceptable for existing providers of social work in the field and assess the likelihood that these

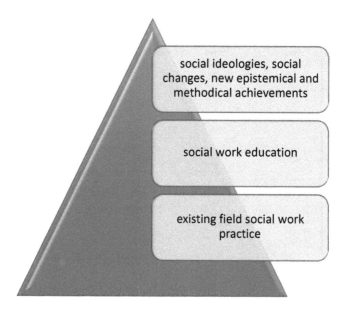

Fig. 2 Social work education, internal practice and external influence

changes will be implemented. It would also be necessary to examine existing obstacles and find ways to overcome them.

Over the last two decades, social work in Croatia has become more visible in the public as well as the political arena. The social welfare sector, the main field of employment for social workers, launched its reform in early 2000, and social workers played an important role in the process. At that time, the Croatian government issued a document entitled "Strategy for the Reform of the System of Social Assistance and Social Care" (Puljiz and Žganec 2002). Based on this document, other strategies were later developed aiming to improve the sector of social care, which is largely seen as social workers' main field of activity. Among different stakeholders, social work academics were frequently included in the preparation of reform activities. This fact contributed to the higher level of connectivity between social work practitioners and academics. It also contributed to a better understanding of the mission of social work and its role in society.

As noted earlier, during this time period, social work came to be recognised as a scientific field. This was made possible not only by solid argumentation about the discipline but also by a certain amount of professional influence gained by social work academics in the public sphere.

The continual process of improving social work study programmes at different levels shows a slow but clear trend towards the further academisation of the main social work subjects but also contributes to the changing perception of social workers. Social workers are becoming a stronger professional community which had been especially visible at the time of the first discussions about the need for social work as a regulated profession. In 2011 legislation on social work was adopted by the Croatian parliament and came into force in 2012. Thanks to this law it was possible to establish a chamber of social workers, a professional organisation whose main mission is to protect and advocate for the interests of social workers as well as to develop the profession of social work in general. The role of the professional association – the Croatian association of social workers – should also be recognized, especially with regard to the organisation of national social work conferences. The conferences are organised regularly on an annual basis and bring together social work practitioners, academics, service users and politicians. With the help of the media, these conferences enable the voices of social workers to be heard by the wider public.

In the last 10 years, social workers' education was further enriched by European perspectives. Members of the academic staff started extensive collaborations with European teams, Erasmus-supported student exchanges have grown in popularity, the import of European concepts, regulations and schemes have been happening much faster and there are some initiatives to develop the national qualification framework for social work based on the European qualification framework. However, all these connections brought to light severe conceptual and legal differences between the Croatian system and the European one when it comes to education in social work. Social work education in Croatia finds itself in the middle of a rigid and conservative social care system, which is the dominant employer of social workers, as opposed to an almost *laissez-faire* approach when it comes to social work education in many European countries. This once again poses serious questions about social work education as a determinant of the social work identity and vice versa, and finding an appropriate balance will be a challenge in the foreseeable future.

The current model of social work education in Croatia faces various challenges, some of which were discussed earlier in this chapter. The existing model of social work studies established according to the Bologna Process, which is divided between a general social work programme at the undergraduate level and specialist programmes at the master's level, should be challenged with new demands derived from a permanently changing environment. Social work education should find a proper balance between discovering adequate solutions regarding what social work practice currently needs and opening new areas of professional development in the future. In some ways openness towards a permanent reform of the social work syllabus is needed to be able to react in a timely manner to identified needs and changes in the profession.

Finally, given that the social work profession must constantly watch over the changing reality in which it operates, the educational system should develop mechanisms for communication, with both external and internal factors. These dynamic connections should serve as a channel enabling ongoing review and keeping in touch with practitioners who need to remain beneficiaries of the educational system throughout their careers.

References

Acker, G. (2004). Role expectations of social work students. *The Journal of Baccalaureate Social Work, 10*(1), 95–104.

Agbim, K., & Ozanne, E. (2007). Social work educators in a changing higher education context: Looking Back and looking forward 1982–2005. *Australian Social Work, 60*(1), 68–82.

Ajduković, M. (2002). Razvoj obrazovanja socijalnih radnika u Hrvatskoj. In M. Ajduković (Ed.), *50 godina studija za socijalni rad 1952.–2002* [50 years of the School of Social Work 1952.–2002] (pp. 9–13). Zagreb: Faculty of Law, University of Zagreb.

Ajduković, M. (2003). The education of social workers: What next? *Annual of Social Work, 10*(1), 5–20.

Ajduković, M., & Branica, V. (2006). Beginnings of social work in Croatia between two world wars. *Annual of Social Work, 13*(1), 29–45.

Bežovan, G. (2008). Civilno društvo i kombinirana socijalna politika. In V. Puljiz (Ed.), *Socijalna politika Hrvatske* [Croatian Social Policy] (pp. 391–436). Zagreb: Faculty of Law, University of Zagreb.

Bresler, K. (2002). Kako je došlo do osnutka Društva socijalnih radnika Narodne Republike Hrvatske? In M. Ajduković (Ed.), *50 godina studija za socijalni rad 1952–2002* [50 years of the School of Social Work 1952–2002] (pp. 16–18). Zagreb: Faculty of Law, University of Zagreb.

Čekić Bašić, S. (2009). Service user involvement in social work practice, education and research in Bosnia-Herzegovina. *Annual of Social Work, 16*(2), 241–257.

Dominelli, L. (1996). Deprofessionalizing social work: Anti-oppressive practice, competencies and postmodernism. *British Journal of Social Work, 26*(2), 153–175.

Edmond, T., Megivern, D., Williams, C., Rochman, E., & Howard, M. (2006). Integrating Evidence-Based Practice and Social Work Field Education. *Journal of Social Work Education, 42*(2), 377–396.

Edwards, B. L. (2011). Social work education and global issues: Implications for social work practice. *Education, 131*(3), 580–586.

Esping-Andersen, G. (1990). *The three worlds of welfare capitalism*. Princeton: Princeton University Press.

Finn, J. L., & Jacobson, M. (2003). Just practice: Steps toward a new social work paradigm. *Journal of Social Work Education, 39*(1), 57–78.

Halmi, A. (2000). Is there really a chance for the establishment of a practical theory of social work? *Annual of Social Work, 7*(1), 35–56.

Howard, M. O., McMillen, C. J., & Pollio, D. E. (2003). Teaching evidence-based practice: Toward a new paradigm for social work education. *Research on Social Work Practice, 13*(2), 234–259.

Jarman-Rohde, L., McFall, J. A., Kolar, P., & Strom, G. (1997). The changing context of social work practice: Implications and recommendations for social work educators. *Journal of Social Work Education, 33*(1), 29–46.

Karger, H. J., & Stoesz, D. (2003). The growth of social work education programs, 1985–1999: Its impact on economic and educational factors related to the profession of social work. *Journal of Social Work Education, 39*(2), 279–295.

Kljajić, S. (2002). Međufakultetski (Interfakultetski) studij za socijalni rad Sveučilišta u Zagrebu. In M. Ajduković (Ed.), *50 godina studija za socijalni rad 1952–2002* [50 years of the School of Social Work 1952–2002] (pp. 51–76). Zagreb: Faculty of Law, University of Zagreb.

Knežević, M. (1996). The concept of "Social" in social work. *Croatian Journal of Social Policy, 3*(1), 17–24.

Magdalenić, I. (2002). Studij socijalnog rada u sklopu Pravnog fakulteta u Zagrebu tijekom osamdesetih godina dvadesetog stoljeća. In M. Ajduković (Ed.), *50 godina studija za socijalni rad 1952–2002* [50 years of the School of Social Work 1952–2002] (pp. 77–87). Zagreb: Faculty of Law, University of Zagreb.

Majdak, M. (2006). Snapshots from the history of social work with children and young people who have grown up in high-risk circumstances. *Annual of Social Work, 13*(1), 85–100.

Martinović, M. (1987). *Znanstvene osnove socijalnog rada* [Scientific basis of social work]. Zagreb: Narodne novine.

Matković, T. et al. (2015). *Zapošljivost i razvoj karijere osoba koje su diplomirale na Studijskom centru socijalnog rada Pravnog fakulteta Sveučilišta u Zagrebu između 2004 i 2010. godine* [Employability and career development of social workers who graduated from the Faculty of Law of the University of Zagreb between 2004 and 2010]. Resource document CROSBI Croatian Scientific Bibliography. https://www.bib.irb.hr/891830. Accessed 28 Feb 2020.

Ministarstvo za demografiju, obitelj, mlade i socijalnu politiku. (2018). *Godišnje statističko izvješće o zaposlenicama u ustanovama socijalne skrbi u 2018. godini* [Annual report on employees in social care institutions in 2018]. https://mdomsp.gov.hr/pristup-informacijama/statisticka-izvjesca-1765/statisticka-izvjesca-za-2018-godinu/10185. Accessed 28 Feb 2020.

Parton, N. (2000). Some thoughts on the relationship between theory and practice in and for social work. *British Journal of Social Work, 30*(4), 449–463.

Puljiz, V. (2006). Social policy and social activities in Croatia in the period from 1900 until 1960. *Annual of Social Work, 13*(1), 7–28.

Puljiz, V. (2008). Socijalna politika Hrvatske. In V. Puljiz (Ed.), *Socijalna politika Hrvatske* [Croatian social policy] (pp. 1–72). Zagreb: Faculty of Law, University of Zagreb.

Puljiz, V., & Žganec, N. (2002). *Strategija reformiranja sustava socijalne pomoći i socijalne skrbi* [Strategy for the reform of social assistance and of the welfare system]. Zagreb: Ured za strategiju razvitka Republike Hrvatske.

Skokandić, S., & Urbanc, K. (2009). Participation of service users in social work education – Teachers' perspective. *Annual of Social Work, 16*(2), 327–354.

Švenda Radeljak, K. (2006). Journal social work – The first decade (1960-1969). *Annual of Social Work, 13*(1), 115–132.

The Regulation of the Vice-Roy (Ban) of the Kingdom of Croatia and Slavonia from December 6, 1920 No. 26819 about the foundation of the Royal Social School in Zagreb. Available at *Annual of Social Work*, 2006, 13(1), 165–171.

United Nations Development Programme. (2006). *Unplugged: Faces of social exclusion in Croatia*. Zagreb: United Nations Development Programme (UNDP). in Croatia.

Urbanc, K. (2006). Medical, social or Neomedical approach to the Care for the Disabled. *Annual of Social Work, 12*(2), 321–333.

Vlada Narodne Republike Hrvatske (2002). Uredba o osnivanju Više stručne škole za socijalne radnike. In M. Ajduković (Ed.), *50 godina studija za socijalni rad 1952–2002* [50 years of the School of Social Work 1952–2002] (pp. 21–23). Zagreb: Faculty of Law, University of Zagreb.

Zaviršek, D. (2008). Socialist social work and its legacies in the countries of former Yugoslavia. In S. Bornarova (Ed.), *Contemporary developments in social protection and social work. Professionalization, deinstitutionalization and reforms* (pp. 73–86). Skopje: Faculty of Philosophy.

Žganec, N. (2008). Social welfare in Croatia – Trends of the development and reforms. *Croatian Journal of Social Policy, 15*(3), 379–339.

Zrinščak, S. (2003). Social policy in the context of thorough social transformation of post-communist countries. *Croatian Journal of Social Policy, 10*(2), 135–159.

Social Work Education in Latvia: Post-crisis Impact and Development Perspectives

Lolita Vilka and Marika Lotko

1 Introduction

The place and role of social work as a profession and as an academic discipline in the case of Latvia can only be understood in the context of social and political transformations over the last decade of the last century.

The history of social work education in Latvia is only measured over three decades. The first social work education programme was opened in 1991, which is treated as the beginning of social work as a profession.

Nowadays social work in Latvia is one of the main instruments for providing social services. But the way social work is perceived by society in today's Latvia, both by professionals themselves and by the recipients of services, largely depends on the nature of social policy acquired over the last nearly 30 years, during which the socialist system that existed until 1990 was replaced with a new social security system.

Three main stages in the formation of Latvia's social security system can be distinguished:

Stage 1, 1991–1997: This stage marks the transition to a free market economy, while creating the preconditions for the development of the social work profession;

Stage 2, 1997–2002: This is the period in which Latvia's welfare system underwent reform, which included the introduction of market principles in the provision of social assistance services (Baltā grāmata 1997);

L. Vilka (✉) · M. Lotko
Department of Welfare and Social Work, Rīga Stradiņš University, Riga, Latvia
e-mail: lolita.vilka@rsu.lv; marika.lotko@rsu.lv

© Springer Nature Switzerland AG 2021
M. Laging, N. Žganec (eds.), *Social Work Education in Europe*,
European Social Work Education and Practice,
https://doi.org/10.1007/978-3-030-69701-3_8

Stage 3: This stage includes the following steps:

2003: Improvements in the social security system and development of the wel-
    fare model corresponding to the Latvian context.
2004: Latvia's accession to the European Union.
2008–2011: Financial-economic crisis.
2012–present: Post-crisis 'remission' period.

The context in which social work and social work education has developed in
Latvia is characterised by such keywords as social transformation, change, reform,
free democratic society, social security, and well-being.

2 Process of the Development of Professional Social Work

2.1 Socioeconomic, Cultural and Political Context

In the 1990s radical political and socioeconomic changes took place in Latvia that
should be seen in the wider context of the historical events of 1989–1991.

The most important processes relate to the decay of the communist regime in the
1990s, which permanently changed future developments in Eastern Europe, including the Baltic States – Lithuania, Estonia and Latvia, which regained their national
independence in 1990. A strong rise in national self-confidence also permeated this
historic phase.

With the restoration of independence in Latvia, the transition from a centralised
management model to a democratic governance system and from a planned to a
free-market economy took place.

The shift from a planned society to a free democratic society led to a series of
social problems, such as the rapid spread of unemployment and poverty and a general decline in welfare. For example, in 1993 consumer prices increased 60 times
compared to 1990. In many sectors of the economy, the average monthly wage of
those employed was lower than the minimum wage per employee. In the last quarter
of 1992, 83% of the population received income below the value of a full subsistence product and service basket (Goša 1995).

To a certain extent, it may be considered that the emergence of social work in
Latvia was a response to some sort of 'social demand' to address the problems that
society had not faced until the country regained its independence.

In fact, in the early 1990s Latvia laid the foundations for a new state order by
reforming all areas of life. Pauloviča (1995) writes about this change: when starting
work on the reforms of the social security system, the aim was to redistribute
responsibility – from the full responsibility of the state to the responsibility of all
individuals for their own lives, living conditions and provision for family members.
This means that a person must first be treated as a personality, not as an object under
state care subjected to the power and will of others.

Regional administrative reform (Kazinovskis and Keišs 2014) took place in combination with the reform of the social welfare system in Latvia. As a result, the Law on Social Services and Social Assistance (LSSSA 2002) was adopted. The law contained significant innovations:

- separation of responsibilities of the state and local government and responsibilities in the area of social welfare;
- duty of municipalities to establish social services;
- allocation of social aid, determining clients' participation duties;
- providing social services only after assessing a client's needs;
- rendering of social services as close as possible to clients' place of residence;
- legitimisation of social work services, separation of duties and tasks of social work specialists.

At the turn of the millennium, Latvia was anticipating some very important events. The most important was Latvia's preparation for accession to the European Union. Because of this accession, slated to occur in 2004, several important documents had to be prepared and ratified in Latvia, including Latvia's Joint Memorandum on Social Inclusion. The memorandum outlines the principal challenges in relation to tackling poverty and social exclusion, presents the major policy measures taken by Latvia in light of an agreement to start translating the EU's common objectives into national policies, and identifies key policy issues for future monitoring and policy review (Joint Memorandum on Social Inclusion of Latvia 2004).

Latvia's economic growth in the period 2000–2007 exceeded that of other EU member states, reflecting, foreign financial flows and very strong demand for consumption. However, as a result of the at least partly expansive macroeconomic policy, the economy overheated (Par Latvijas 2011), and Latvian society experienced one of its most severe crises in 2008–2011.

At the time of the crisis and continuing to today, one of the biggest losses in Latvia is the decrease in population. According to data from the Central Statistics Bureau on demography, in 2011 the population of Latvia decreased by more than 30,000. Between 2012 and 2016, the population in Latvia had fallen from 2,023,825 to 1.97 million. At the same time, the poverty risk index was 19.4% in 2012, but in 2013 it increased to 21.2% (Dovladbekova and Berķe-Berga 2015).

Post-crisis social space-time (time-place) dynamics have created new contexts of social practice. Social problems and needs have also been transformed. For example, the large migration of the population in search of work outside the country has created the so-called euro-orphan problem in Latvia where parents leave the country, but their children stay behind.

The aforementioned regional administrative reform policy has also significantly changed socio-space scales, creating urban-rural, centre-peripheral accessibility and mobility issues, affecting the lifestyle and habits of citizens. This has also spurred changes to the traditional forms of and approaches to social work, responding to citizens' needs for services.

The emergence of smart technologies in people's daily lives has changed the nature of information usage, social communication and social behaviour. The use of smart technologies in connection with service availability and accessibility is also increasing in Latvia.

Transformations are also taking place in the value orientation of society.

These are just some of the small-scale but visible social changes taking place in the country, followed by certain people's life stories, which are not always stories of successful adaption to environmental changes.

2.2 Esping-Andersen's Concept of Welfare-Regime

In the context of the reform policy, the issue of a welfare model appropriate to Latvia's situation was topical and has remained relevant and at the crossroads of discussions between researchers and politicians. Ten years after the reform of the social security system was launched in the early 1990s, a 2001 conference entitled "Reform of the Welfare System in Latvia – Today and in the Future" was devoted to the evaluation of the experience of welfare reform.

At this conference academician R. Karnīte critically evaluated the achievements of the reforms: "In general, the service offered by the social welfare system (material provision) is not sufficient for a newly introduced system. Every new social survey conducted in Latvia finds an increase and deepening of poverty, and the poor layer is usually formed by people who depend on the social security system (pensioners, families with children, disabled people)" (Par mūsu labklājības reformu attīstību 2001).

The 10th International Conference (Baltic Forum 2005) paid special attention to the following questions: Can we expect a common European social standard or even a common social model in the near future? What requirements would that entail in Latvia's case? Are the principles of the Nordic welfare model (a competitive, technologically advanced economy with a large part of the public sector ensuring social equality and inclusion) also relevant for other countries, including Latvia?

An important priority was the accelerated development of the economy, which required the implementation of several important reforms and measures, a big part of which included regional administrative reforms together with reforms of public administration and administrative-territorial or local government (Kazinovskis and Keišs 2014). The aim of the reform was "to decentralise the state administration, create opportunities for the creation of an optimal municipal system, which would provide the financial, economic and social basis of local governments, allow them to independently manage, develop the necessary infrastructure, and create living conditions that are in the interests of the population" (VARAM Informatīvais ziņojums 2013).

Concerning the welfare model of Latvia, one should agree with the opinion expressed by Homko (2007) that social policy in Latvia includes tendencies of liberalism, features of the conservative model regarding labour relations and features of the social-democratic model regarding the social insurance system. Rajevska bases her ideas on Gosta Esping-Andersen's classification recognised in social sciences and characterises the social policy model of Latvia as a liberal model with some features of a conservative model and a post-communist basis (Latviete 2013).

3   Main Areas of Social Work

3.1   Professional Activities

The formation of social work as a profession has been closely related to the development of the social security system, while the development of social work education is closely related to the processes of education reform in Latvia.

There was a shortage of social workers in the early 1990s. The profession had not yet firmly established itself, and the tasks at hand were performed by a wide range of professions. The first professional social workers started working in the social service system in the period 1993–1995.

The legal recognition of social work as a profession and the establishment of a social work education institute marks one stage of development. The end of this stage can be set in 1997, when the first social work institution (SDSP Attīstība) and the professional study programme Social Work were accredited for the first time (Akreditētās augstskolas un studiju programmes 2000).

In 1997 the government approved the Social Welfare System Reform Project "Administration of the Social Assistance System – White Paper".

The white paper highlighted several social groups that needed specific service programmes and advanced forms of care:

- families with children,
- children in out-of-home care,
- the elderly,
- people with disabilities, including persons with mental disabilities.

Approval of the white paper signified that a choice had been made to decentralise the administration model of social assistance policy in Latvia. This included a long-term transition to the introduction of a new market principle in the provision of social assistance services and the gradual privatisation of state-owned enterprises and institutions (Baltā grāmata 1997).

In 1999, for the first time, a tender for public procurement was launched – 100 spots for the preparation of social workers (Welfare Ministry of Latvia 2000). Public procurement for the training of social work specialists played an important role in further development of social work education and the profession in general.

3.2   More Relevant Work Areas

In parallel to the development of the social service system in the country, the preparation of professional social workers was one of the most important areas for establishing the social worker profession in Latvia.

In Latvia, the opening of a social work study programme started as a private initiative. At that time, there was no clear idea of what a new profession referred to as "social work" in Western societies would be called in Latvia. From the point of view of the complexity of social problems, the most appropriate name for the profession at that time was "*socionom*", but ultimately the prospective professionals in Latvia were referred to as "social workers" (Vilka 2005).

The first private higher education institution – the Higher School of Social Work and Social Pedagogy Attīstība was founded and accredited in Latvia (Higher School Attīstība existed until 2014), which was entitled to issue a state-recognised diploma (Kalniņš 1995).

In 1991, by a decision of the Board of the Ministry of National Education of the Republic of Latvia, "On the Opening of the Faculty of Social Workers", the new profession was characterised as follows:

> The democratic development of modern society, overcoming the totalitarian heritage in state facilities, necessitates the development and realisation of a new social policy that focuses on human care, happiness and prosperity…The main content of professional *socionom* activity is conscious CARE for a sensible and effective organisation of human life in general, for the spiritual development and physical and moral health of the person throughout his life. The socionom contributes to a truly cultural standard of living among members of society. (Zemīte 2003)

In this vision, the new profession emerged from the idealism, largely inspired by the ideal of a period of national awakening in Latvia.

However, it would be incorrect to think that the formation of social work in Latvia has been isolated from the general tendencies of the time in the context of social work in European countries.

For example, the Baltic states, including representatives of Latvia, attended the Vienna Colloquium of the Ministers of Education and Welfare of the Eastern European Countries in November 1991, organised by the International Association of Schools of Social Work, to discuss social problems and issues in the region, national goals, the role of social work, the cadre and levels of personnel required, the content of training, and the support needed for training by government (Constable and Mehta 1994).

In the period till 1994, social work education programmes developed rapidly at various public and private universities and colleges.

The first generation of social work educators in Latvia were specialists in various fields without social work education. An important role in the education of staff and students was played by different countries – e.g. Sweden, Denmark, England, Switzerland, Germany, Israel, USA – whose guest lecturers and highly qualified specialists in social work education visited Latvia.

3.3   Triggers and Causes (Economic, Political, Cultural) of These Developments

The years of economic crisis (2008–2011) clearly marked the gap between social work before the crisis and social work after the crisis while also pointing to new challenges facing the social work profession. For social workers this was a time of professional certification.

The then president of the Latvian Association of Local and Regional Governments, A. Jaunsleinis, wrote as follows about the crisis: "In periods when life is relatively peaceful and prosperous, social work does not seem necessary. At the same time, when the welfare of a large part of society is shaken, it provides the necessary support. This was clearly manifested in the years of crisis, when social workers, through enormous and unselfish work, cushioned the consequences of rising unemployment, benefit constraints and other adverse social developments" (Jaunsleinis 2015).

To mitigate social tensions caused by the crisis, the Latvian government adopted the Social Security Network Strategy (Par Sociālās drošības tīkla stratēģiju 2010). The aim of the strategy was to develop a set of emergency safety measures whose implementation would reduce the negative social impact that has developed of (1) as a result of the global and Latvian financial and economic crisis and (2) as a result of structural reforms.

Describing the situation, the strategy recognises that the social service is currently the only place a person in a critical situation can turn to free of charge and talk about their problems. However, in 2008 social services were established in only 26.9% of local governments, while 61.9% of local governments had one social work specialist.

To prevent this situation, in 2009 a law was passed requiring that each local government establish a municipal institution – a social service. The law stipulated that no fewer than three social work specialists should be employed in the social service, at least one of the employees being a social worker in order to provide professional social services, social assistance, and the administration of social services.

The strengthening of social services is particularly important as social tensions rise during times of economic hardship. It can also have negative effects on family relationships, where a professionally educated and trained employee can often help prevent a crisis of relationships (Par Sociālās drošības tīkla stratēģiju 2010).

4   Current Model of Social Work Education

In 1991, the Law on Education stipulated that higher education must include the division of higher professional education and higher academic education (Latvijas Republikas Izglītības likums 1991). Although initially there were no clearly defined standards that would distinguish between the two branches of higher education, social work education programmes subsumed higher professional education, as is the case in Latvia today.

If we were to describe one social work education model used in Latvia, it would be difficult to find one. Social policy features in Latvia are largely reflected in the content of social work education.

However, features may be identified suggesting a hybrid model where social work, on the one hand, holds onto the "preservation of the prevailing social system also accepting restrictions on its role and function" (Ornella et al. 2016), but on the other hand, there is the need to take into account the neoliberal style of governance (Ornella et al. 2016), which is increasingly evident in the field of social services. Latvia has four so-called social work specialists: social workers, social rehabilitators, organisers of social benefits and social carers who unite professionals of different qualification levels. From the perspective of society and clients there is a lack of understanding about each of the mentioned professionals' functions and tasks. The lower educational qualification for social rehabilitators, organisers of social benefits and social carers engenders situations where social workers as professionals with their specific competences are downgraded in comparison to other social work specialists.

In the field of education, Latvia had become a participant in the Bologna Process (1999), when then Minister of Education Tatjana Koķe signed the Bologna Declaration on behalf of Latvia with 28 other European ministers.

The Bologna Process envisaged a number of reforms, introducing professional bachelor's and master's degrees, diploma supplements, credit systems, accreditation, a system of recognition of diplomas, a formal requirement for internal quality culture and other requirements (Rauhvargers 2003).

Since 2000 Latvia has been implementing the Bologna Process, significantly changing the regulatory framework for university activities. Quality requirements for the design and licensing of study programmes were established; the requirements for awarding qualification and degrees to be acquired were determined by introducing educational standards for the acquisition of academic education and the acquisition of second-level higher professional education. The education standards determined the proportion of the study programme's components.

According to the Law on Higher Education Institutions currently in force, apropos of the state-accredited study programme, the following may be obtained at higher education institutions: (1) first-level professional higher education and fourth-level professional qualification and (2) second-level professional higher education (Augstskolu likums 1995).

4.1 Length of Studies at Universities or Professional Higher Schools

The education standard requires that the total duration of the bachelor's and master's degree shall be no less than 5 years.

To understand the special features of Latvian education in social work, it should be noted that in the social work sector, four social work specialists are distinguished: social workers, social rehabilitators, social carers and social assistance organisers (Sociālo pakalpojumu un sociālās palīdzības likums 2002). Besides the professional social worker, there is another kind of educated social work professional: the charity (caritas) social worker. The only higher education institution providing education for this profession is the Latvian Christian Academy (Caritadic social work 2020).

The first and most significant difference between the four social work professionals is the level of education to be attained, and the second difference is the professional competence required, which highlights the specific work responsibilities and assignments.

Social workers in Latvia must acquire second-level professional higher education, receiving the fifth-level professional title Social Worker, while for social rehabilitators, social carers and social assistance organisers, the requirement is only first-level professional higher education.

Those who have acquired first-level professional higher education as social carers, social rehabilitators or social assistance organisers may continue their studies in bachelor's programmes to become social workers.

Regarding the situation on the labour market, those who have obtained the education of a social worker can work as any of the previously mentioned four social work professionals, while those who have acquired the first-level education cannot perform the duties of a social worker. Article 41 (Sociālo pakalpojumu un sociālās palīdzības likums 2002) of the Law on Social Services and Social Assistance states that persons who have acquired the second-level professional higher or academic education in social work or charity social work have the right to perform social work.

The need for the education of social workers is stipulated by the Law On Local Governments (Likums "Par pašvaldībām" 1994), which provides for social services and social assistance to local communities, as well as by Article 10 (Sociālo pakalpojumu un sociālās palīdzības likums 2002) of the Law on Social Services and Social Assistance. The norm stipulates that there should be at least one social worker per 1000 inhabitants.

One of the largest employers of social work is the social services of local governments, which are the ones who must implement the aforementioned norm for social services and social assistance – one social work specialist per 1000 inhabitants.

4.2   Curriculum Content and Characteristics

The current state standard for professional higher education requires that the second-level professional higher education and the fifth-level professional qualification be acquired by mastering professional bachelor's and professional master's study programmes, which are implemented after secondary education, and professional study programmes implemented by academic (bachelor's or master's) education or second-level professional higher education (MK noteikumi Nr. 512. 2014). The compulsory structure of the bachelor's programme consists of the following items:

- study courses;
- practice;
- state examination, part of which is the development and presentation of a bachelor's thesis or diploma paper (diploma project).

To work as a social worker in Latvia, it is necessary to obtain a second-level professional higher education (bachelor's or master's degree) and fifth-level professional qualification. The requirements of the professional higher education state standard are also applicable to social work education programmes in Latvia.

At the same time, work was also carried out on the establishment of the Profession's Standard for Professionals in Social Work. In Latvia, the first standard of the social work profession was approved in 2002 (Izglītības un zinātnes ministrijas gada 6. jūnijā rīkojumu Nr. 351 2002). This included a description of responsibilities and tasks, a specific factor characterising the work environment, and a description of skills and knowledge (Profession standard 2002).

Thus, the occupational standard of social workers ensured the content of education of social workers by developing study programmes according to the standard structure of second-level professional higher education.

The current Regulations on the National Standard (Noteikumi par otrā līmeņa profesionālās augstākās izglītības valsts standartu 2014) for Second-Level Professional Higher Education state that the volume of the bachelor's study programme must be at least 160 credit points and its compulsory content consists of the following items:

- general education courses worth at least 20 credit points (30 European Credit Transfer and Accumulation System (ECTS) points);
- basic theoretical courses in the field (professional field) and courses in information technology worth a minimum of 36 credit points (54 ECTS points);
- courses of professional specialisation in the field (professional field) worth at least 60 credit points (90 ECTS points);
- elective courses worth at least 6 credits (9 ECTS points);
- practice worth at least 20 credit points (30 ECTS points);
- state examination, part of which is the development and presentation of a bachelor's thesis or diploma paper (diploma project) worth at least 12 credits (18 ECTS points).

The master's programme requires at least 40 credits (60 ECTS points), and its compulsory content consists of the following items:

- study courses that provide in-depth learning of the latest achievements in the field (professional field), in both theory and practice, worth at least 5 credits (7 ECTS points);
- courses in research work, creative work, design work and management studies for at least 3 credits (4.5 ECTS points);

- practice for a minimum of 26 credits (39 ECTS points), if it is designed for graduates of a bachelor's degree programme or at least 6 credits (9 ECTS points) to acquire master's degree for graduates of the bachelor's programme;
- State examination, part of which is the writing and defence of a master's thesis or diploma paper (diploma project), for at least 20 credits (30 ECTS points).

The autonomy of universities confers the right to independently determine the content and form of their study programmes.

Since 2012 the rules on the recognition of the results of studies from previous education or professional experience have been in force in Latvia.

Recognition of competences acquired from professional experience and learning outcomes achieved during previous education allows students to acquire professional qualifications more flexibly through different educational pathways.

Students in Latvia may become social workers not only by completing a bachelor's degree programme but also a master's programme, even if the basic education or bachelor's degree was not obtained in social work. The law stipulates that professional or academic degrees may also be obtained in the master's programme in cases where basic education was acquired in another sector. Students without a basic education in social work must enter professional practice and acquire specific knowledge in social work.

For educators this is an opportunity to attract students to study more, but at the same time, it presents certain challenges.

However, employers acknowledge that those who have acquired their social worker qualifications only within the master's programme do not necessarily understand the profession, nor do they always have the necessary knowledge and skills to carry out the duties of a social worker.

4.3 Level of Academisation (Social Work as a Scientific Discipline)

The legal recognition of social work as a profession and the establishment of an institute for social work education mark one stage of the development, whose completion can be identified as 1997, when the first social work institution (SDSP Attīstība) and the professional study programme Social Work were accredited for the first time (Akreditētās augstskolas un studiju programmas 2000).

The issue of social work as representing a relationship between an academic discipline and practice, social work as a science and the status of the social work profession was first updated in the International Baltic Conference on Education Standards in Social Work held in Riga in 1996.

In the same year, social work was included in the professional register of the Republic of Latvia, and after lengthy discussions with the Latvian Science Council, social work was also included in the nomenclature of academic and scientific degrees as a sub-branch of sociology in social policy and the organisation of social work.

In 2018 (Cabinet Regulation No. 49 – Regulations on Latvian Science Sectors and Sub-sectors), amendments were made to the classification of the branches of science. According to these amendments, a branch of science called sociology and social work was created. It includes sociology, demography, anthropology, ethnology, social topics (women's and gender-related studies), social issues, family research and social work.

5   Critical Analysis of the Educational System

The current situation in the social work sector in Latvia cannot be viewed in isolation from the wider socioeconomic processes that occurred in Latvia after the economic crisis. The years of crisis clearly marked the gap between social work before the crisis and social work after the crisis, while also pointing to the new challenges facing the social work profession. Dynamic transformations are continuing in the financial, economic, educational, welfare and healthcare sectors in an effort to reduce social inequality and build a welfare model appropriate to Latvia's context.

The mood in the profession as a whole has also changed. The criterion given in the Law on Social Services and Social Assistance on the number of social work specialists in social services in relation to the number of inhabitants of a municipality (1:1000) was met only by 52% in 2011 (Guidelines for the Development of Professional Social Work 2014–2020 2013).

Despite the political commitment to increase state funding of social workers' education, the number of publicly funded spots in academic institutions for social work education was reduced by 11% in 2014 compared to 2013. At Rīga Stradiņš University alone (financed by the Ministry of Health) the number of state-funded spots in educational institutions was reduced by 31% in 2014. At the time, the exhaustion of professional capital was already evident in the social work sector. In recent years, training of specialists in the sector has been slower than required by the labour market. At the end of 2013, the number of social work specialists was still insufficient – only 64% of the required number worked in social services (Guidelines for the Development of Professional Social Work 2014–2020 2013).

The results of ex-ante research, published by the Ministry of Welfare in 2012, "Initial Impact Assessment (Ex-ante) on Planned Structural Reforms in the Field of Professional Social Work Policies", showed a number of weaknesses in the education of social workers, including:

- unwillingness of graduates of social work study programmes to perform social work;
- lack of mechanisms to ensure that social workers studying at state funded study places are attracted to the industry;

- insufficient links between education and practice, which is one of the most important parts of professional studies of social work;
- lack of cooperation between educational institutions offering social work programmes, employers, ministries, and other interested establishments;
- association of social work with practical rather than scientific activities.

This situation is influenced by the traditions of social sciences in Latvia, the classification of sciences, the lack of academic staff, and the lack of doctoral students (Gala ziņojums 2012).

Considering the situation in the social work sector described in the 2012 ex-ante study, the Ministry of Welfare started working on the social work development policy for the coming years. In 2013 the Cabinet of Ministers approved the "Guidelines for Professional Social Work 2014–2020".

The Guidelines identified several sector-specific tasks, including:

- review of state-funded allocation principles and the provision of budget funds for social work study programmes;
- promotion of co-operation between the three parties – the higher education institution that 'prepares' social workers, social services – employers, and students – potential social work professionals;
- improvement of student internship system for social work study programmes by elaborating a uniform internship regulation and setting requirements for the management of study practice for trained specialists;
- offer to waive student loans covering student fees and living expenses or pay them from the state budget (Profesionāla sociālā darba attīstības pamatnostādnes 2014.-2020.gadam 2013).

However, the situation regarding insufficient numbers of social workers in the country cannot be simply assessed.

In 2015, in relation to the refusal to launch social welfare studies at any of the Latvian higher education institutions, the Ministry of Education and Science of the Republic of Latvia reached the conclusion that the study opportunities offered in higher education institutions of Latvia in social welfare studies are not fully utilised (Par atteikumu atvērt studiju virzienu "Sociālā labklājība" sabiedrībā ar ierobežotu atbildību "Sociālo tehnoloģiju augstskola" 2015). Although social welfare studies can be recognised as a priority in the development of Latvia's economy, experts of the Inter-sectoral Coordinating Centre have warned that "if the education structure is not changed by 2020, a lack of specialists with higher education in social welfare may become evident" (Par atteikumu atvērt studiju virzienu "Sociālā labklājība" sabiedrībā ar ierobežotu atbildību "Sociālo tehnoloģiju augstskola" 2015).

This criticism is not without foundation. There is a significant disproportion in the provision of state-funded study opportunities between the first- and second-level higher education programmes in institutions educating social work specialists. Public procurement for lower-qualification specialists – social rehabilitators, social service organisers, social carers – has for a long time been higher than for social workers with second-level professional higher education.

In recent years, discussions on the competence and professional preparedness of social workers have garnered considerable attention in the country. The 2017 "Ex-ante and Ex-post Assessments of Functional Efficiency of Municipal Social Service" study suggests that in the opinion of the heads of social services, the preparedness of graduates of social work study programmes is rather poor (51%) or very poor (2%). According to one view, there is need for a new concept of social work education. At the same time, the issue of the limits of social work practice is topical. The heads of social services (83%) believe that social services are expected to fulfil duties that should not be performed within the framework of social work (Pašvaldību sociālo dienestu un sociālā darba speciālistu darbības efektivitātes novērtēšanas rezultāti un to analīze 2016).

What should social work in Latvia look like in the next decade and beyond? There is no clear answer right now.

Another study expressed the opinion that there is no unified vision on the role of social work specialists in social services at present and that currently it is very difficult to determine whether there is a vision regarding the limits of a social worker's work and functions (Sociālo dienestu vadītāju un sociālā darba speciālistu apmierinātības mērījumi un to analīze par sociālā darba praksi 2017).

Conceptually, social work in Latvia is mainly seen as micro-social work (work with individual clients, casework, work with families, or group work).

The Occupational Classifier, when comparing social work to counselling professionals, does not consider social working practices on mezzo and macro levels.

The Law on Social Services and Social Security (SPSP) defines, in substance, not the principles of social work, but the principles of providing and receiving social services and social assistance.

Social work as a professional activity is characterised by the concept of assistance, and with regard to its content it is interpreted as a service only for the purposes of the law.

The law does not include parts of the functions that social workers perform in non-governmental organisations (NGOs) or other service institutions, such as social work in hospitals or probation, for example.

The established system for purchasing social services in Latvia is increasingly shifting social work from the main employer – local government social services – to the sector of NGOs.

However, the predominant understanding of social work is that both studies and planning of social work policy focus on social work, mainly from a municipal perspective, with less focus on social work for NGOs.

Furthermore, the division of social work professionals into four categories highlights the difficulty of the public's understanding when it comes to these four types of social work professionals.

It is difficult for the public and often for professionals from different sectors to identify the differences between social work professionals. It has led to a situation where the work of a social worker is associated with the provision of material assistance to the poor or the provision of care to the elderly. Such lack of understanding affects both the prestige of social work as a profession, what the public expects from social workers, and the willingness of students to choose to study social work.

5.1   Meaning of Academisation of Social Work

The Professional Standard of social workers in Latvia gets updated. The Professional Standard is a regulatory document defining the knowledge, skills and competences of a social practitioner and describing the level of quality in practical social work. The agenda for implementation also includes the Education Development Guidelines 2021–2027 "Future Skills for Future Society" in Latvia (Pamatnostādņu projekts "Izglītības attīstības pamatnostādnes 2021.-2027.gadam "Nākotnes prasmes nākotnes sabiedrībai" 2020). In the coming years, development of the quality of higher education will be linked to skills development studies, in close cooperation with the professional sector, in order to improve the content of the relevant study programmes and align them with the development needs of the sector. This will also affect further development of social work as an academic discipline.

It will not be overvalued, arguing that in recent years the extensive introduction of information technologies in many sectors of the economy, including social services, constitutes a new culture of social relations. Referring to the vision of the modern Spanish sociologist Castells on twenty-first century trends and network society as a space of flows (Castells 2004), it can be noted that social-spatial transformations are also taking place in Latvian society, and configurations of new social relations are being formed.

Looking at social work education from the perspective of this new cultural formation, it is topical to think about what a future social worker should be. What and how, in theory and practical terms, should be learned, for example, by young people who choose to study social work in 2021/2022 but will start their own independent work in 2025 and later? It is no less important to think about how the teaching and learning strategy should change from an educational science perspective.

The widespread use of information technology (IT) designed to create new synergies between problem-based education, interdisciplinary education and digitisation.

Experience gained in the context of the COVID-19 pandemic highlighted the unpredictability of changes in normal life, including the organisation of education. Teaching audiences as a physical space "transformed" into a virtual space in a short time. IT tools and online communication have become understandable and accepted at Latvian universities in the education of social workers as well.

Although the current situation reveals many weaknesses in the social work sector, the time spent on social work in Latvia over the past three decades has not been useless but has been used to raise awareness about social work and creating the sector as a whole. A new, active and creative generation of social workers has emerged, capable of defending the fundamental values of social work.

These changes are taking place too quickly for people to respond to.

Awareness and understanding of social transformations and changes is a challenge for social work education and practitioners, social work education policy makers, employers and clients, as well as for Latvian society as a whole, and however, it can be realised by educating and learning.

References

(2000). *Akreditētās augstskolas un studiju programmas* [Accredited higher education institutions and study programmes]. https://www.vestnesis.lv/ta/id/9242. Accessed 3 July 2019.

(1995). *Augstskolu likums* [The Law on higher education]. https://likumi.lv/doc. php?id=37967&version_date=26.12.2000. Accessed 3 July 2019.

(1997). *Baltā grāmata. Latvija: sociālās labklājības sistēmas reformu projekts Sociālās palīdzības sistēmas administrēšana* [White Paper. Latvia: Social welfare system reform project. Administration of the social assistance system] (pp. 10). www.lm.gov.lv/upload/normativie_akti/baltagramata.doc. Accessed 3 July 2019.

(2005). Baltic Forum. http://www.balticforum.org/produkti/2005-gads/. Accessed 3 July 2019.

Castells, M. (2004). *The network society. A cross-cultural perspective.* Cheltenham/Northampton: Edward Elgar Publishing Limited. http://socium.ge/downloads/komunikaciisteoria/eng/Castells%20Manuel%20The%20Network%20Society.pdf. Accessed 12 Oct 2020.

Constable, R., & Mehta, V. (1994). *Education for social work in Eastern Europe: Changing horizons.* Chicago: Lyceum books.

(1994). *Deklarāciju par nodomiem sadarboties augstākās izglītības kvalitātes novērtēšanā Baltijas valstīs* [Declaration of intentions to cooperate in the quality assessment of higher education in the Baltic States].

Dovladbekova, I., & Berķe-Berga, A. (2015). *Ekonomiskās krīzes sekas: Latvijas iedzīvotāju novērtējums* [Consequences of the economic crisis: Assessment of the population of Latvia]. Conference paper presented on March 26–27, 2015. https://www.rsu.lv/sites/default/files/imce/Zin%C4%81tnes%20departaments/zinatniskas_konferences/2015/8sekcija/ekonomiskas_krizes_sekas.pdf. Accessed 3 July 2019.

(2012). *Gala ziņojums (t.sk. rekomendācijas) Par profesionāla sociālā darba attīstības veicināšanu* [Final report (including recommendations) on promoting the development of professional social work]. https://www.mk.gov.lv/sites/default/files/editor/07122012_gala_zinojums.pdf. Accessed 3 July 2019.

Goša, Z. (1995). *Sociālas problēmas Latvijā. Dzīves jautājumi. Zinātniski metodisks rakstu krājums* [Social problems in Latvia. Issues of life. Scientific methodical inventory] (pp. 28–29). I. Riga: SDSPA "Attīstība".

(2002). *Izglītības un zinātnes ministrijas gada 6. Jūnijā rīkojumu Nr. 351* [Order no. 351, Ministry of Education and Science].

Homko, I. (2007). *Sociālās drošības garantijas.* Latvijas Brīvo arodbiedrību savienība. Rīga

Jaunsleinis, A. (2015). *Sociālā darba attīstība un tā nozīme. Zināšanu pārnese sociālā darba praksē: var pazīt pēc darbiem* [The development of social work and its importance: Knowledge transfer in social working practice: Can be recognised by work]. http://www.lm.gov.lv/upload/lm_istenotie_projekti/2/nr1_zinasasanu_parnese_sept_2015.pdf. Accessed 3 July 2019.

(2004). Joint memorandum on social inclusion of Latvia. Brussels, 18 December 2003. https://www.vestnesis.lv/wwwraksti//2004/106/B106/SOC_IEKL_MEMOR_AN.PDF. Accessed 3 July 2019.

Kalniņš, A. (1995). *Izglītības vadības un reformu demokratizācija Latvijā* [Democratisation of education management and reforms in Latvia]. *Latvijas Vēstnesis 76*, 359. https://www.vestnesis.lv/ta/id/27208. Accessed 4 Apr 2019.

(2020). *Karitatīvais sociālais darbs* [Charitative social work]. http://www.niid.lv/niid_search/program/192?qy&level_1=7. Accessed 1 Feb 2020.

Kazinovskis, A., & Keišs, S. (2014). *Reģionālā attīstība Latvijā administratīvi teritoriālās reformas norises gaita, problēmas, risinājumi* [Regional development in Latvia in the course of the administratively territorial reform, problems, solutions] (pp. 167). Riga: Vītola izdevniecība.

(1991). *Latvijas Republikas Izglītības likums* [Education Law of the Republic of Latvia]. https://m.likumi.lv/doc.php?id=67960. Accessed 3 July 2019.

Latviete, I. (2013). *European social fund financing in the welfare sector in Latvia.* PhD thesis for scientific degree of Dr. Oec. http://llufb.llu.lv/dissertation-summary/regional-economics/Ilze_Latviete_promocijas_d_kopsavilkums_2013_LLU_EF.pdf. Accessed 3 July 2019.

(2014). *Latvijas Republikas Labklājības ministrija. Augstākās izglītības padomei. Par valsts budžeta vietu finansējumu un sadalījumu 2015.gadam* [Ministry of Welfare of the Republic of Latvia. For the Council of Higher Education. On the financing and distribution of public budget site for 2015]. Documents, 04.11.2014. Nr.35-1-04/2249.

(2000). *Latvijas Republikas Labklājības ministrija. Sociālais ziņojums* [Social report. Ministry of Welfare of the Republic of Latvia]. From http://www.lm.gov.lv/upload/socialais_zinojums/soczin_par1999_lat.pdf. Accessed 3 July 2019.

(1994). Likums *"Par pašvaldībām"* [The law "On Local Governments"]. https://likumi.lv/doc.php?id=57255. Accessed 25 June 2019.

Ornella, A., Spolander, G., & Engelbrecht, L. K. (2016). The global social work definition: Ontology, implications and challenges. *Journal of Social Work.* http://journals.sagepub.com/doi/abs/10.1177/1468017316654606. Accessed 3 July 2019.

(2005). *Ministru kabineta rīkojums Nr. 413. Par Profesionāla sociālā darba attīstības programmu 2005.-2011.gadam* [Cabinet Order No. 413 on the programme for the development of professional social work 2005–2011]. https://likumi.lv/ta/id/111596-par-profesionala-sociala-darba-attistibas-programmu-2005-2011-gadam. Accessed 3 July 2019.

(1996). *Metodiskie norādījumi augstskolu un to studiju programmu novērtēšanai* [Guidelines for the evaluation of the programmes of universities and their studies]. https://www.vestnesis.lv/ta/id/204498-metodiskie-noradijumi-augstskolu-un-to-studiju-programmu-novertesanai. Accessed 3 July 2019.

(2014). *MK noteikumi Nr. 512. Noteikumi par otrā līmeņa profesionālās augstākās izglītības valsts standartu* [Cabinet Rule No. 512 Regulations regarding the State Standard od second-level vocational higher education]. https://likumi.lv/doc.php?id=268761. Accessed 3 July 2019.

(2014). *Noteikumi par otrā līmeņa profesionālās augstākās izglītības valsts standartu* [Rules on the national standard for second-level vocational higher education]. https://likumi.lv/doc.php?id=268761. Accessed 3 July 2019.

(2020). *Pamatnostādņu projekts "Izglītības attīstības pamatnostādnes 2021.-2027.gadam 'Nākotnes prasmes nākotnes sabiedrībai'"* [Draft guidelines "Education Development Guidelines for 2021–2027 'Future Skills for Future Society'"]. Riga. http://tap.mk.gov.lv/lv/mk/tap/?pid=40492545. Accessed 12 Oct 2020.

(2015). *Par atteikumu atvērt studiju virzienu "Sociālā labklājība" sabiedrībā ar ierobežotu atbildību* [On the refusal to open the course of "Social Welfare" studies]. Sociālo tehnoloģiju augstskola. *Latvijas Vēstnesis, 77* (5395) https://www.izm.gov.lv/images/licencesana/24042015/4.pdf. Accessed 21 Apr 2019.

(2011). Par Latvijas 2011. Gada valsts reformu programmu un ar ko sniedz Padomes atzinumu par Latvijas atjaunināto konverģences programmu 2011.–2014. gadam [On Latvia's 2011 national reform programme and delivering a Council opinion on Latvia's updated convergence programme for 2011–2014. Official Journal of the European Union]. *Eiropas Savienības Oficiālais Vēstnesis.* (2011/C 215/03). http://eur-lex.europa.eu/LexUriServ/LexUriServ.do?uri=OJ:C:2011:215:0008:0009:LV:PDF. Accessed 3 July 2019.

(2010). *Par Sociālās drošības tīkla stratēģiju. Ministru kabineta rīkojums Nr. 490* [Cabinet Order No. 490 On the strategy of the Social Security Network]. https://likumi.lv/doc. php?id=215386. Accessed 3 July 2019.

(2001). Par mūsu labklājības reformu attīstību [On the development of our welfare reforms]. *Latvijas Vēstnesis*. Laidiens: 25.10.2001., Nr. 153 (2540). https://www.vestnesis.lv/ta/ id/54995. Accessed 3 July 2019.

Pauloviča, I. (1995). Sociālās reformas un sociālo vērtību izmaiņas sabiedrībā [Social reforms and changes in social values]. In *Dzīves jautājumi. Zinātniski metodisks rakstu krājums I* (pp. 35–36). Riga: SDSPA "Attīstība".

(2016). *Pašvaldību sociālo dienestu un sociālā darba speciālistu darbības efektivitātes novērtēšanas rezultāti un to analīze* [Results of evaluating the effectiveness of the activities of local government social services and social work specialists and the analysis]. Gala ziņojums. http://www. lm.gov.lv/upload/projekts/faili/5_gala_zinojums_saskanots.pdf. Accessed 3 July 2019.

(2013). *Profesionāla sociālā darba attīstības pamatnostādnes 2014.-2020.gadam* [Guidelines for the development of vocational social work 2014–2020] (pp. 12). http://www.lm.gov.lv/ upload/tiesibu_aktu_projekti_2/iesibu_aktu_projekti_3/lmpamatn_140613_sd.pdf. Accessed 3 July 2019.

(2002). *Profesijas standarts. Sociālais darbinieks* [Professional standard. Social worker]. https:// visc.gov.lv/profizglitiba/dokumenti/standarti/ps0079.pdf. Accessed 3 July 2019.

Rauhvargers, A. (2003). *Latvija Boloņas procesā*. Ziņojums par Latvijas augstākās izglītības reform gaitu, virzoties uz Eiropas vienoto augstākās izglītības telpu [Latvia in the Bologna Process. Report on the progress of Latvia's higher education reform towards the European Single Higher Education Area]. https://www.lu.lv/materiali/biblioteka/es/pilnieteksti/izglitiba/ Latvija%20Bolonas%20procesa%20-%20Zinojums%20par%20Latvijas%20augstakas% 20izglitibas%20reformu%20gaitu,%20virzoties%20uz%20Eiropas.pdf. Accessed 3 July 2019.

(2017). *Sociālo dienestu vadītāju un sociālā darba speciālistu apmierinātības mērījumi un to analīze par sociālā darba praksi* [Measurements of the satisfaction of social service leaders and social work professionals and the analysis of social work practices] (pp. 260). http://www. lm.gov.lv/upload/projekts/faili/3_soc_darba_spec_zinojums_saskanots.pdf

(2002). *Sociālo pakalpojumu un sociālās palīdzības likums* [The Law on Social Services and Social Assistance]. https://likumi.lv/doc.php?id=68488. Accessed 3 July 2019.

(2013). *VARAM Informatīvais ziņojums "Administratīvi teritoriālās reformas izvērtējums"* [Informative report "Assessment of the Administrative Territorial Reform"]. Riga. http://tap. mk.gov.lv/lv/mk/tap/?pid=40278571&mode=mk&date=2013-03-26. Accessed 3 July 2019.

Vilka, L. (2005). *Sociālā darba profesijas attīstības specifika Latvijā. „Sociālo zinātņu attīstības tendences Eiropas Savienības paplašināšanās kontekstā" materiāli* [Special features of the development of the social work profession in Latvia. Materials for the development of social sciences in the context of the extension of the European Union] (pp 150–160). Riga: RSU.

Zemīte, Ē. (2003). *Sociālā darba pamati. Pielikums Nr.5. LR Tautas izglītības ministrijas Kolēģijas lēmums Nr.4. 1991* [The basics of social work. Annex 5. Decision No. 4 of the College of the Ministry of People's Education]. 16.aprīlī. Riga: SDSP "Attīstība".

Reconstruction of Social Work Education in the Netherlands

Raymond Kloppenburg and Peter Hendriks

1 Developments in Society and the Social Domain

1.1 Socioeconomic, Cultural and Political Context

On 1 January 2018, the Netherlands had close to 17.2 million inhabitants. In 2017 more people immigrated to the country than left. The population grew by a hundred thousand in 2017. A few demographic developments in the densely populated Dutch society can be highlighted, with major impacts on the social work profession and social work education. The two most important are the ageing of the population and the increasing numbers of inhabitants with roots abroad, either because they were born there or because their parents came from another country. As in many European countries, urbanisation in the Netherlands is increasing, especially in the western part of the country and the four big cities (Amsterdam, Rotterdam, The Hague and Utrecht). In rural areas the population is shrinking. Urban areas remain relatively young due to the continuous influx of young people, who often stay after finding a partner and starting a family (CBS 2017).

Historically, a small country like the Netherlands has always been strongly connected to and dependent on other countries. It always has been heavily dependent on foreign markets for its economy. The economy of the Netherlands was the 17th largest in the world in 2019 according to the World Bank and the International Monetary Fund. Its GDP per capita was estimated at roughly € 44,052 in fiscal year 2017/2018, which makes it one of the highest-earning nations in the world. Between 1996 and 2000, the annual gross domestic product (GDP) averaged over 4%, well above the European average of 2.5% at the time. The Dutch economy was hit considerably hard by the financial crisis of 2007 and the ensuing European

R. Kloppenburg (✉) · P. Hendriks
HU University of Applied Sciences, Utrecht, The Netherlands
e-mail: Raymond.Kloppenburg@hu.nl; Peter.Hendriks@hu.nl

© Springer Nature Switzerland AG 2021   171
M. Laging, N. Žganec (eds.), *Social Work Education in Europe*,
European Social Work Education and Practice,
https://doi.org/10.1007/978-3-030-69701-3_9

sovereign-debt crisis. Despite the fact that the Netherlands can be considered a rich country, 13% of households are at risk of poverty. Because of the social safety net in the Netherlands, physical survival is not an issue in the case of poverty. Rather, poverty is related to the general level of prosperity of society and means having insufficient income to realise a certain level of consumption that is considered the minimum necessary in the Netherlands (CBS 2019). Poverty is higher among certain groups of people with a migration background. Globalisation increased migration, which has had an influence on the composition of the population. For example, in Rotterdam or Amsterdam, people of more than 150 different nationalities live together. A growing group of mobile citizens live in the Netherlands temporarily because of their work. The switch from an emigration to an immigration country (for the second time since the so-called Golden Age) took place in the early 1960s. The increase in prosperity in the Netherlands reduced emigration and induced new immigration flows at the same time (Zorlu and Hartog 2001). Since World War II, immigration to the Netherlands has had three main sources. First, the de-colonisation of Indonesia and Surinam generated sizeable immigration flows, concentrated between 1949 and 1957 for the former and peaking in 1975 and 1979–1980 for the latter. Second, the post-war economic growth attracted 'guest workers' from Mediterranean countries. Next to asylum applications from refugees (20,353 according to the Immigration and Naturalisation Service: IND 2018), at the moment the main motive for non-native immigrants to settle in the Netherlands is family migration. In 2018, 23.1% of the Dutch population had a migration background, which is defined as 'those who have at least one parent born abroad' (CBS 2018).

The Netherlands has become an increasingly heterogeneous society, with a great diversity of social cultural groups, and also a society of social dividing lines. Social and cultural differences can be drawn between ethnic groups, but a deeper analysis shows that dividing lines seem to be even more determined by the level of education and social economic status. Statistics from 2019 showed that not everybody was sharing in the economic boom, which has seen GDP grow by around 2.3% in 3 years (CBS 2019). Around 3.3% of the total population is living in long-term poverty, including 117,000 children. While education attainment levels in the Netherlands are high, socioeconomic and cultural background determine school performance to a comparatively high degree. Study grants for tertiary students have been abolished and replaced by loans. With a relatively large immigrant population, the country has a well-developed integration policy. However, ethnic discrimination in the labour market is widespread, and the government has sought to discourage refugees from coming to the country (SGI-networks 2016).

The most dominant issues in Dutch politics, such as debates on the European Union, migration, the reform of the pension system, climate change, and the costs of healthcare, have a major divisive impact on the Dutch political landscape. Next to this, being Dutch has become increasingly defined as modern and progressive (such as being tolerant on homosexuality) and secular. The centrality of religion in the framing of who belongs and who does not contrasts with the situation in other countries such as the US, where religion is less contested, and impacts the meaning of identifying as Muslim in particular ways. The Netherlands is considered by some to be an extreme case in Europe because it has experienced a shift from a relative tolerance of cultural and religious diversity to harsh intolerance, expressed through culturalised notions of citizenship (Duyvendak and Tonkens 2016). Not only migrants and their offspring, but many native Dutch as well struggle to feel at home in the Netherlands. One of the questions is how to shape the public domain and its democratic values. To be accepted as full-fledged citizens, migrants need to feel at home in the Netherlands, demonstrate knowledge of supposedly Dutch traditions, practice Dutch customs and internalise so-called Dutch morality. This trend is identified as the 'culturalisation of citizenship' (ibid.). In the early 2000s, the Netherlands was one of the first countries, along with Austria, to experience the rise of anti-establishment populism. Migrants were blamed for socioeconomic deprivation, the decline of social values and feelings of insecurity, seen as a threat to Dutch culture.

1.1.1 Esping-Andersen's Concept of Welfare-Regime

From the perspective of the national government, it is relevant to point out that the Netherlands is by origin a welfare state, though the country now displays aspects of corporatism and social democracy. Esping-Andersen (1990), therefore, labelled it a hybrid welfare state. The Dutch welfare state has traditionally had paternalist features, with the strong and fortunate expected to care for the weak and disadvantaged. Indeed, the literal translation of the Dutch word for 'welfare state' is 'caring state' (verzorgingsstaat). However, while once considered an ideal worthy of pursuit, the welfare state is now contested, in part due to financial difficulties in supporting public services. This has led to the implementation of an array of efficiency and structural changes in the way services are provided to citizens. A major recent development is the previously mentioned shift of responsibilities from national to local authorities.

In the Netherlands, the state is decentralising social policies to the market, civil society and the local level, the municipalities. It is happening concomitantly in youth care, mental health care, elderly care and care for the disabled. Also, responsibility for social benefits and activation to the labour market is slated to be fully decentralised. The 'transition' in the field of social work practice in the Netherlands is often identified as a 'transformation' in which major welfare state reforms are developed and implemented, with a strong impact on the social domain and the social work professional identity. It is part of the transformation from welfare state to participatory society. The first transition concerns a development that started several decades ago and can be identified as a move towards decentralisation. The decentralisation of responsibilities for the social domain takes the form of a shift from the national to the municipal level. This shift means that the state is delegating responsibility for the implementation of social policies to the market, civil society and the local government level. Another transition relates to the process of 'deinstitutionalisation', based on the ideal of an inclusive society in which the disabled, the sick and the elderly are taken care of within mainstream society, rather than outside society in institutions. The healthy and able-bodied population is asked to help, and the advantages of inclusion into mainstream society are obvious (Hendriks 2018). It is, however, unclear whether people, such as older adults, have networks to rely on. The change in the policy of the long-term care system seems to have also caused more confused people in the streets and neglect of elderly people in nursing homes. The rising costs associated with the increasing numbers of older adults needing long-term care forced the Dutch government to change its long-term care system.

1.2   Main Work Areas of Social Work

The idea is to work with a broad generic social worker who works closely together with other professionals, like family doctors, district nurses, mental health therapists and mentors, and local police, on the one hand, and with citizens as volunteers and informal carers, on the other. Most municipalities choose to work with social teams spread over the different districts of the town or villages within the region. In a social team, professionals from different backgrounds work together to meet the needs of all kinds of people with problems in the field of social functioning (behaviour, relationships). Welfare state reforms, however, challenge the boundaries between professionals and non-professionals, such as volunteers and service users, raising issues with respect to professional identity and normativity.

Dutch social workers are employed in a wide range of fields with a large diversity of target groups in their contexts, for example, children, young people and the elderly in community centres, parenting support in families, people in debt in district teams, people with psychiatric problems or with mental disability who receive guidance on living in shelters, and people convicted of crimes whose probation is supervised. Social workers are also active in efforts to improve the quality of life in neighbourhoods through theatre, music and the visual arts. The methods used are derived from the target groups, organisations and contexts. Correspondingly, social workers focus on improving the social functioning of people in and with their environment. The work can be oriented individually or more collectively, and the focus can be on activation and participation, but also on assistance and support (Scholte et al. 2012). The degree of organisation of the social work profession in the Netherlands is relatively low compared to other countries. The professional association has professional codes of ethics for various sectors. Professional registration is a legal requirement for working in the youth care sector; social workers in the mental health sector can also be registered.

It is difficult to assess how European or international social work practice is in the Netherlands. International social work stands for a common field of action, an international body of knowledge and a professional international community. Dutch (urban) social work is one of working in a pluralistic reality in an extraordinarily diverse context. In this way, social work is acquiring more and more characteristics also found in other countries. It is for this reason that many authors prefer to speak of transnational social work (Furman et al. 2008) rather than international social work: the practice of social work transcends the nation-state, which also applies to the social problems of the people with whom social professionals work (Kloppenburg and Tirions 2020).

Only a few professionals in the Netherlands work in international agencies, like the Red Cross, UNICEF or Amnesty International. Cross-border social work can be found in the big cities where there are homeless people originating from many other European countries or where professionals work with victims of human trafficking, using different European languages and cooperating with social workers from other countries.

Internationalisation is one of the core activities of the Dutch Professional Association for Social Work (BPSW). The association is a member of the International Federation of Social Workers (IFSW), and an active exchange takes place. International cooperation consists of partnerships (twinships) with professional associations abroad, for instance in Morocco. Through exchange one gets to know the issues and solutions in the professional practice elsewhere. The exchange with Morocco provided the opportunity to study working with volunteers in both countries, dealing with poverty or establishing a professional register and professional code, to name just a few examples. There are also examples showing how a government subsidy supports social workers in developing countries in setting up a professional association. Although this kind of partnership is considered important, there is a slight preference for cooperation within Europe in view of the professionalisation of its own members. There are many similarities in policy developments with neighbouring countries such as Germany or Denmark from which one can learn.

An illustration of this is Denmark, when it dealt with the decentralisation of youth care. The Danish government had started a transition from youth care to municipalities in 2007, and this decentralisation was slated to be implemented in 2015 in the Netherlands (Weijers 2016). However, a few years earlier the reverse had taken place in neighbouring Norway, where, in 2004, out of dissatisfaction with the existing level of youth care and its fragmentation, it was decided to centralise all youth care under the direction of the national government. Comparison of these policy developments would have reasonably suggested possible impacts of such a systemic change in the Netherlands.

2 Social Work Education: Current Model and Process of Innovation

Social work education in the Netherlands is the most comprehensive area of the higher social studies (HSS) sector and the largest of all bachelor's-level studies at universities of applied sciences in the Netherlands. The HSS sector also consists of the following courses: applied psychology, pedagogy, religious pastoral work and creative therapy (translation of *Vaktherapie*). Eighteen universities of applied sciences offer one or more HSS at different locations throughout the Netherlands. Of these eighteen universities of applied sciences, ten offer a master's programme in social work. This can be a generic social work master or a specialised master's programme, for example a master's degree in community development, in forensic social work, or in health care and social work. In 2018 the bachelor's programmes of the HSS sector accepted approximately 5700 new students, of which 80% were female. In total, about 27,000 students are enrolled in higher social studies (Vereniging Hogescholen 2019). Currently 1054 students are following a master's programme in social work. The bachelor's programme comprises 240 European Credit Transfer and Accumulation System (ECTS) points in a 4-year programme, the master's programme includes 60 ECTS points and takes at least 1 year and in some cases 2 years. The bachelor's and master's programmes can be pursued on a full-time or part-time basis. The latter variant offers the possibility of combining the study programme and work. Universities of applied sciences themselves do not offer a PhD in social work. A number of research universities do offer this possibility, and recent years have seen an increasing number of social work PhDs. There are no exact numbers of PhDs available, partly because there is no precise substantive delineation of social work PhD subjects.

2.1 Brief History

Looking back in history, in 1899 the first school for social work in the Netherlands was founded in Amsterdam. The course, which had mostly women, prepared them for poverty care, family child protection and youth work (Bijlsma and Jansen 2012). Until then social work was mostly part of charity work and done by volunteers. It was accepted that education was needed for those who could work as civil servants in child protection. In 1905 children's laws (*Kinderwetten*) were implemented, in which guidelines were given about whether or not to remove children from families. However, most social workers remained largely uneducated. After World War II thousands of so-called war children (Jewish orphans, children of families who collaborated with the Nazis, children from broken families) had to be taken in and resettled, and the conviction prevailed that well-educated workers were needed. New courses and especially part-time courses in child protection (from 1947) changed this. Since then, with increasing frequency, youth care workers earned a diploma (van Lieshout 2012).

   In the mid-1950s, social work in the Netherlands expanded, and even a ministry for social work was established (*ministerie voor maatschappelijk werk*). The prevailing view was that in the post-war Netherlands, in addition to economic planning, social planning was also necessary and should be the responsibility of government (de Boois 2018). In 1968, six Dutch universities started a programme in andragogical, or adult education, sciences. The programme was dedicated to the professional social support and education of adults. The university programme only existed for a short time. As a result of the economic crisis in the early 1980s and cuts in higher education, the programme was abolished in 1983 (de Boois 2018).

This was not the case in higher vocational education, where the number of courses in the social domain was increasing. Students could choose from a wide range of courses and specialisations within them. As a result of this expansion of social studies, the connection to the labour market was not always clear. In 1990, a platform was set up by social partners, government and educational institutions with the aim of developing a qualification system that would, among other things, ensure better alignment between the qualifications of social workers and learning outcomes of vocational study programmes (Commissie Ontwikkeling Kwalificatiestelsel Zorg & Welzijn 1992). One of the important tasks of the platform was to determine which students who graduated from a social work programme would qualify for professional practice. The term qualification was an intermediary concept between person and profession. On the one hand, it defined attributes a person had to have to become a social work professional, and on the other, it defined requirements for the performance of tasks. The qualification system has led to a better match between social work education and professional profiles.

The Bologna Declaration in 1999, which focused on the harmonisation of European higher education, has brought further renewal of social work education. Schools for social work, which had been part of vocational education and training (VET), were transformed during the last 20 years into universities of applied sciences. This led to new concepts, such as the academisation of social work education, and included an increased focus on practice-based research and internationalisation. Students who entered the labour market with just a bachelor's degreecould continue their studies in a master's programme in social work.

Didactic innovations were aimed at the promotion of independent and lifelong learning, the learning of authentic practical situations and a more flexible kind of education thanks to e-learning and course-independent assessment programmes. For most social work courses, a classification of the curriculum based on scientific disciplines was replaced by a more integrated and coherent curriculum based on current professional issues. Concerning the alignment between education and social work, new innovative practices emerged. Experience has been acquired with respect to learning arrangements that involve cooperation within the triangle of education, practice and research. Also, the importance of the involvement of service users and experts by experience in education was acknowledged.

2.2 Transformation of Social Work Education After the Millennium

As in many countries, social work education in the Netherlands can be characterised by a continuous adaptation to developments in society and professional practice. These developments often take place gradually, and sometimes there are more radical transformations. The development of a generic bachelor's programme in social work education over the past decade is an example of the latter. A starting point can be marked in 2013 by a request of the association of Dutch schools for social work to an advisory committee to conduct a forward-looking exploration. The advisory committee expressed great urgency with regard to the adaptation of study programmes and advocated a qualitative leap. It recommended reinforcing the profile of the study programme and profession, improving the reflective capacity of graduates by strengthening their knowledge base and professional attitude, clarifying the structure of three graduate profiles, and improving cooperation with social work practice and research (Verkenningscommissie hoger sociaal agogisch onderwijs 2014). The same year the Dutch Health Council (Gezondheidsraad 2014) published, at the request of the State Secretary of Health, Welfare and Sport, a recommendation which stated that social work urgently needed further professionalisation based on a full-fledged knowledge-production system. Social work professionals must also expand their professional organisation and establish means of updating skills and conducting further training. The establishment of a professional register should further strengthen the professional status of social work professionals.

These recommendations prompted the Dutch association of schools of social work to launch a nationwide programme to innovate social work education. The overarching idea was presented as a metaphor of a tree with a strong common trunk and branches as light specialisations (van Ewijk 2016). This resulted in a renewed profile of Dutch social work education with generic learning outcomes, a common knowledge base and three graduation profiles for all bachelor's degree programmes (Kloppenburg et al. 2019).

2.2.1 Flexible Employability of Social Work Graduates and Registration in Professional Registers

One of the core issues in innovation is the alignment between social work education and professional practice. This is determined by the extent to which graduates of social work education (bachelor's and master's programmes) are able to start working as social workers in practice. This starting competency can be understood as direct employability or as flexible employability of graduates and has been an ongoing point of discussion between social work education and the heterogeneous social work practice in the Netherlands (Kloppenburg 2011; Witte 2015). Initial competence as direct employability means a close link between education and professional practice, enabling graduates to perform professional duties directly within a specific setting. Initial competence as flexible employability is aimed at achieving greater flexibility of employees. This flexible approach is seen as more in keeping with the rapid and unpredictable development of the labour market. To better prepare students for this, there is a greater need for a broadly based curriculum. This means that the content of vocational training must be derived from the generic characteristics of a profession and that education must pay attention to promoting the flexibility of social workers by acquiring skills that enable lifelong learning, mobility and transfer. Van Merriënboer et al. (2002) noted that in the debate on vocational education, employers of organisations prefer a more direct link between education and the labour market, focusing on the technical-instrumental qualifications necessary for the direct employability of graduates. This is visible in the social domain, where in sectors such as mental health care and youth care, voluntary or compulsory registration in a professional register imposes requirements on the study programme of students. On the other hand, within the social domain, we also see in the contact between universities and their network in practice that more broadly educated social professionals are receive plaudits from the professional field.

2.3   A New Profile of Social Work Education

As a result of the innovations of social work education, in 2017 a national social work education document (Sectoraal Advies College Hogere Sociale Studies 2017) appeared as a guide for all Dutch schools of social work. The document elaborates on aspects of the social work curricula which are carried out by all programmes. It includes a description of the generic learning outcomes, knowledge base and graduation profiles of bachelor level social work education.

2.3.1   Learning Outcomes

To align with social work practice, the following tasks of the social professional are explicitly chosen as starting points for the description of generic learning outcomes of bachelor level social work education. A distinction is made in three professional core tasks. For each of these tasks core qualifications are identified (Table 1).

2.3.2   Generic Body of Knowledge

The national document also contains a generic knowledge base that constitutes at least 50% of the programme of all courses. To develop this knowledge base, a model with seven building blocks was developed (Box 1), each of which has been elaborated into three themes and subjects falling under them (Kloppenburg et al. 2019). The generic knowledge base must be practice-based, science-based, usable and sustainable. Practice-based means a direct and strong connection of the knowledge base with professional practice. Science-based was formulated as a strong scientific grounding of the knowledge base. To be usable for students and teachers, the knowledge base should offer clarity about subjects and room for local specifications, for example, specific books or authors (Kloppenburg et al. 2019). Sustainability was deemed necessary to make sure that the knowledge base would hold in a dynamic world and was fit for knowledge accumulation.

Besides this criterion, emphasis was placed on the fact that, in addition to scientific knowledge, other knowledge sources are also relevant to professional practice and education. In general, at least three sources of professional knowledge were

Table 1 Learning outcomes of generic social work education

Core task 1 Promoting the social functioning of people and their social context.
1. Social work professionals approach people and their social contexts and allow themselves to be approached. Social work professionals are 'present'; they allow contact through different channels and capture signals.
2. Social work professionals promote the social functioning of people and their primary living environment in a methodical manner, evidence based and practice based. They do this reciprocally and in consultation, aimed at self-direction and participation. They pay attention to the safety of children and young people.
3. Social work professionals promote the social functioning of people and their networks in a methodical manner, evidence based and practice based. They do this reciprocally and in consultation. In doing so, they take into account the individual character and capacity of people and networks to act.
4. Social work professionals promote the social functioning of people and their communities in a methodical manner, evidence based and practice based. They focus on strengthening social cohesion and embedding, the development of collective arrangements, justice, legal and social cohesion, and the development of a culture of social justice equality, equity, social security, social sustainability, social innovation and promoting social policy.
Core task 2 Strengthening the organisational relationships within which social work takes place.
5. Professionals in social work conduct effective management with regard to, for example, identification, acquisition and deployment of resources and deployment of professionals in social work and other professionals involved in specific cases. They work transparently, in a results-oriented and efficient manner, and distinguish output and outcome.
6. Social work professionals contribute to interdisciplinary and inter-professional cooperation within or between (professional) networks. They do this in such a way that people, networks and communities can achieve their own objectives.
7. Social work professionals operate actively and entrepreneurially. They contribute to the progress of teamwork, communicate to team members what needs to be done, contribute to the acquisition of assignments in tenders and put subjects on the agenda of clients. They sometimes also operate as social entrepreneurs themselves.
Core task 3 Promoting one's own professionalism and the development of the profession.
8. Social work professionals learn from their experiences by always reflecting on their own professional actions. In this way, they themselves develop as professionals and they renew their professional practice as well.
9. Social work professionals have an investigative attitude. They have the ability to apply knowledge from other people's research and to do practice-based research themselves. They are able to translate the results of research into innovation in professional practice.
10. Professionals in social work make ethical considerations using (inter)national professional codes discretionary space and highlight their ethical considerations to the various parties involved. Social work professionals are critically reflective and aim for the sustainable functioning of their professional actions.

identified: (1) scientific knowledge originating from different scientific disciplines and gathered through theorisation and empirical research; (2) generalised knowledge that arises in professional practice and leads to working principles and rules; and (3) case-specific (episodic) knowledge that arises from specific professional situations and relates to events, circumstances, decisions and actions (Eraut 1994; Guile and Young 2003; Kloppenburg 2011). In addition to these three sources, the

Box 1: Generic Body of Knowledge of Dutch Social Work Education

Building Blocks and Scientific Perspectives		
	Societal Context of Social Work	
	Organization of Social Work	
Social Work Profession	Service Users of Social Work	Scientific Perspectives
	Methods of Social Work	
	Professionalization of Social Work	
	Research and Innovation of Social Work	

Kloppenburg et al. (2017), translated by authors

experiential knowledge of service users and experts is highlighted as an important fourth source of knowledge (Chiapparini 2016).

2.3.3   Graduation Profiles

In accordance with the metaphor of a tree with a firm trunk and light branches within the generic bachelor's programme, and in addition to the policy areas of the decentralisation of care and welfare, three graduation profiles were developed to enable students over the course of their studies to choose from one of the sectors of social work of their interest (Sectoraal Advies College Hogere Sociale Studies 2017). The size of each graduation profile is at least 90 of the 204 ECTS points.

- *Social work and community development and inclusive society* is located at the intersection of social and socio-cultural aspects. The focus is on the basic social infrastructure of communities. They sometimes work from an individual point of view with an eye towards collective aspects, and vice versa from a collective perspective with an eye towards individual questions and development.
- *Social work and health care* focuses mainly on supporting people with disabilities, physical disorders or disabilities, intellectual disabilities or psychological vulnerability and their immediate environment. Social work professionals support people to enable them to function optimally in society despite their disorders and limitations.
- *Social work and youth professional* focuses on young people up to 23 years of age. Professionals contribute to promoting and exploiting opportunities for young people to develop into autonomously functioning and participating adults. They concentrate on the safety of children and young people and prevent threats to their physical and psychosocial development, remove them or counteract them. In addition, they strengthen parents' parenting skills.

2.4   Ethics in Social Work Education

Social work is considered a highly normative profession, and the normative dimension of the professional activities is receiving increasing attention in social work education in the Netherlands. In all schools, analyses of ethical dilemmas, the process of ethical decision-making, the use of ethical standards, and understanding of ethical theories are part of the curriculum. Dealing with moral dilemmas, rules of engagement and the application of codes of ethics is considered very important. Future social workers must learn to see that there are also moral aspects to deal with, and they should learn to distinguish them from other aspects, such as technical, pedagogical or political perspectives. Ethical perspectives in a professional context are not primarily about knowledge of great names and underlying theories. The intended learning objective is for good social workers to be able to work ethically. Typically, what characterises professional activities is ideally the attempt to realise humanitarian values, like empowerment or social justice, in complex circumstances (de Jonge 2015). Because of its value-ridden complexity, the required expertise cannot be reduced to processes or procedures but must primarily be embedded in individual professionals and in their collective practices.

The personal values of professionals can conflict with clients, professional organisations or policy-makers, and much attention is given to how the personal and the professional are related. Students need to learn how to identify and challenge their own personal beliefs (especially in supervision) in such a way that it enables them to provide services without interference from their personal values. Values and beliefs are often implicit, and education needs to contribute to identifying them. Critical consciousness and awareness of implicit biases need to be incorporated throughout social work education. Students' own assumptions need to be confronted.

The increasing diversity of Dutch society also implies moral diversity. How can professionals deal with moral difference, where values are in conflict, and how does this impact their professional work? Professionals realise very well that values cannot be imposed because values are related to inner convictions that cannot be enforced. One of the challenges in discussing moral dilemmas in social work education is that we tend to focus on process and often neglect outcomes, while at the same time making the assumption that such a process can be guided by a universal set of deontological values shaped by the liberal tradition. These aspects become particularly problematic in a world characterised by deepening social and economic differences and inequalities and by the aggressive promotion of neoliberal values (Watson 2006).

2.5 Academisation

The higher education system in the Netherlands is currently based on a three-cycle degree system, consisting of bachelor's, master's and PhD degrees. Like many countries, the Netherlands has a binary higher education system. Research-oriented education is traditionally offered by research universities, and higher professional education is offered by universities of applied sciences. Within social work education the transition from vocational education to universities of applied sciences was characterised by the introduction of applied research aimed at improving the quality of graduates of higher professional education, at keeping education responsive and at innovating professional practice. Applied research is directly fed by questions from social work practice and education; the unique interaction between education, research and practice is characteristic of applied research. Research is often on a smaller scale, closer to practice and with shorter deadlines (Vereniging van Hogescholen 2019). Applied research is practically relevant and meets scientific (i.e. methodological and ethical) criteria that are common within the research tradition used. It aims to produce results that can be transferred to other contexts. Research activities by students in the bachelor's programme in social work are very different in nature. Students must have research capabilities that contribute to be able to better perform in social work. Andriessen (2014) gives a summary of research capabilities of students starting with an investigative attitude. This means that social work students are attentive, curious, thoughtful, critical and willing to share information. Secondly, he emphasises the ability to apply results obtained in other research. This means that social work students can locate scientific and professional literature that is relevant to the social work profession and can assess and learn from it. Last, Andriessen also mentions the ability to conduct research within the framework of professional practice. This means that social work students master the methods of data collection and analysis that are customary in carrying out social work.

2.6 Service Users, Experts by Experience

During the last 10 years, experts by experience have been increasingly involved in social work practice and education. Experts by experience use their own experiences to support service users and professionals. The Netherlands has two accredited social work programmes for experts by experience in which knowledge by experience is claimed to be equivalent to scientific and professional knowledge. Also, within regular social work programmes expertise by experience ensures a more powerful contribution of the client perspective within the programme. Since 2016, Alie Weerman has been a professor. Her research focuses on 'the recognition of experiential knowledge'. She states that people with knowledge gained from experience bring the world of clients into social work more emphatically and more sensitively (Weerman 2016). According to van Haaster et al. (2013), the training of students with experience expertise makes specific demands on social work education, such as (i) a supportive environment with committed teachers and supervisors who can build good relationships with students; (ii) teachers who, through their own experience or through their vision, have the qualities to help turn experiences into experiential knowledge and have the capability to connect well with regular teaching material; (iii) experiential expert coaches (as role models); and (iv) information to stakeholders (academic counsellors, lecturers, deans and fellow students) about the impact of psychological problems.

2.7 Internationalisation

Schools for social work in the Netherlands are accredited with regard to the existence of an international perspective in education. Internationalisation can be achieved by enabling students to carry out parts of their studies abroad (internationalisation abroad) and by adding an international dimension to the curriculum by including guest lectures, international weeks, international knowledge sources and e-learning (internationalisation at home). The extent to which internationalisation is part of the curriculum differs from one university to the next. This depends on the strategic goals of universities and the availability of expertise and of international networks (Hendriks and Kloppenburg 2016). Depending on the type of international activity, specific learning outcomes related to internationalisation are emphasised. Many schools of social work in the Netherlands look to the Belgian University College Leuven-Limburg for guidance concerning the learning outcomes of internationalisation (ICOM's) it has described. An international curriculum contributes to the development of international expertise, international involvement, intercultural sensitivity, language skills and personal growth (University College Leuven-Limburg 2019).

2.8 Instruction, Integration of Academic and Practice Learning

The dominant emphasis in instruction during the last 20 years in social work education has been on the enhancement of active, self-regulated and personalised learning in authentic learning environments. This is underpinned by a cognitivist and social constructivist conception which presupposes that knowledge development in students takes place in interaction with and under the influence of the social context of education and professional practice (Van Bommel 2013) and that students are not passive recipients of knowledge but actors who construct and internalise their personal professional knowledge (Schaap et al. 2009; Kloppenburg et al. 2019). As a consequence, in recent years, the classic idea of internship periods has given way to a more comprehensive approach to practice-oriented education in many study programmes. To this end, education is provided in so-called workshops or ateliers, inside and outside the school. These workshops are set up together with social work professionals, service users and researchers. In this context, practical issues form the starting point for learning activities of students. As a result, the sharp distinction between in-school learning and learning in internships disappears. The objective is to support in-depth learning aimed at connecting and integrating practical experiences and theoretical knowledge and self-directed learning as a means of adapting future working careers to the new requirements of professional practice (Kloppenburg 2011). In addition to the workshops/ateliers, theoretical knowledge acquisition takes place in supporting lessons. Coherence in the curriculum is achieved on the basis of overarching profession-oriented themes. Assessments are aimed at demonstrating that learning outcomes are controlled. Students are given more room to explore different learning pathways.

3   Critical Analysis of Educational System

In this chapter we presented a global overview of social developments, developments in the social domain and innovations in social work education in the Netherlands. Within this context an important question arises: To what extent is education succeeding in preparing students well by addressing the important developments within the profession? Schools for social work also raise questions about the extent to which they are able to position themselves as important stakeholders in the social field. For social work education, professional practice may be the most important starting point for the content and design of the curriculum. However, does this mean that practice plays a decisive role and education need only respond? Or does social work education also have an independent responsibility and have to make a substantial contribution to the development of practice through education and research? It seems most desirable to optimise the reciprocal interaction between practice and education. We discuss this by reiterating some of the dominant discussions in social work education and practice.

3.1   Becoming a University of Applied Sciences, Drifting Away from Practice?

Historically, Dutch social work education has its roots in vocational education and is strongly practice-oriented. This kind of professional education always existed in close connection to social work practice, with assignments, placements and research in all years of the curriculum. Most educators were practitioners, recruited from social work practice. This close connection to practice resulted in the construction of curricula that more or less followed the developments in practice, instead of relating to practice in a more critical way.

The development from Vocational Education and Training (VET) to a university of applied sciences has certainly contributed to strengthening the profile of social work education and practice. A solid knowledge base within a programme contributes to enabling graduates to underpin and justify their professional decisions and actions on the basis of scientific knowledge. It also contributes to the fact that social professionals who increasingly work in interdisciplinary collaboration with doctors, nurses, safety experts, and lawyers, as well as with volunteers and informal carers, are able to emphasise the added value of their own profession. Another assumption was that a curriculum with a stronger theoretical focus has a stronger emphasis on policy issues and the macro level in general.

However, the development of the university of applied sciences also involves risks. Too much emphasis on scientific research poses the risk that education, as an independent practice, with its own language and culture, will drift away from professional practice. This will also make it more difficult for students, instructors and practical professionals to cross the boundaries between the worlds of study and practice (Guile and Young 2003). The tendency of study programmes to focus on research in so-called high-stakes assessments at the end of a study programme does not do justice to the essence of a competent social professional and to what distinguishes vocational education from education at research universities. Especially in social work, the recognition of multiple sources of knowledge, such as the practical experience of professionals and the experiential expertise of service users, is essential. This requires a strong alignment of school, practice and research. Only this will help schools of social work to educate reflective practitioners (Schön 1983) who are capable of establishing a solid connection between practice and theory and between knowledge gained through experience and through scientific knowledge.

3.2   Does Dutch Social Work Education Neglect the Political?

Activism, in all its forms, has been notably absent in Dutch social work education and practice in recent decades. This raises questions about social work education itself but also why activism in general is not very popular in Dutch society. The country is relatively stable, and most people have it pretty good, which might be one reason why they are less willing 'to rock the boat'. This seems to be somehow in line with the weak position of trade unions in the country. According to some researchers, this can be explained by the so-called Dutch polder model, a consensus decision-making model based on the acclaimed Dutch version of consensus-based economic and social policy-making, especially dominant in the 1980s and 1990s. Others emphasise the instrumental ideas of professionalisation and the focus on the micro level of social work that do not seem to be compatible with different forms of activism. In general, criticism of new developments in Dutch social policies does not originate from the professional social work community. It took quite some time in the process of the transition to a participatory society before the first critical voices were heard. Participatory society as a strength-based approach, in which citizens need to appeal to friends, family and neighbours first (in Dutch: *mantelzorgers*) before professional support will be considered, was, however, not only an ideological choice; it was also introduced as a way to reduce the role of the state and to reduce costs. The first response from professionals and educators to this approach is in general to make it a collective responsibility to make it work, as we are all aware that the ageing of the population and growing healthcare costs have become almost unpayable. While in the welfare state some tasks are performed by professionals who get paid, in participatory society tasks are performed without being paid by others, who sometimes receive an allowance or social benefit in return. This can be considered a threat to the welfare state, but confrontations were not sought. It was the Dutch professor Margot Trappenburg (2015) who pointed out the risk that active solidarity burdens those who are already burdened. Slowly, the impact of this process became more visible. Women as primary carers and those in low paid jobs are especially burdened.

This case shows that the social work profession and education are essentially linked to the political domain and are not neutral, a point which has, in a way, been neglected. The limited attention paid to the political nature of Dutch social work education is also apparent in the almost negligible support for critical theory and critical or radical social work. Anti-racist or anti-discriminatory approaches in social work never gained a strong foothold in Dutch social work education. However, a recent manifesto signed by a large group of Dutch educators and scholars involved in social work proposed that social work needs to be re-evaluated as a human rights profession (Hartman et al. 2016). According to this manifesto, the neglect of the political can be attributed to the dominance of technical and instrumental ideas over professionalisation. The manifesto states that the social work profession and, therefore, social work education are political in essence, not neutral, as they seek to contribute to social justice and human dignity.

3.3 How Does Social Work Education Contribute to the Professional Identity?

The issue of professional identity receives a lot of attention in the social work literature, and it has been suggested that a distinct (moral) professional identity could offer support in times of transition and change. The need for a distinct identity is also expressed in claims about the character of the profession. Is the profession basically secular, a semi-profession, or a human rights profession? (de Jonge 2015) Should it be neutral and apolitical, or should the profession be activist? The boundaries separating professions are blurred, and professional roles seem less distinct. Professionals work in established and in emerging professions and increasingly collaborate as part of multiple professional teams. What are the underlying values and concepts of social work that delineate the profession, and how can these values and concepts help social workers frame their identities and situate themselves as professionals? The move from the traditional welfare state to a participatory society means that everybody must participate in providing care, which challenges the boundaries between professionals and non-professionals (such as volunteers) and service users. In addition, as a result it challenges the social work professional identity, in some cases resulting in an unwanted process of de-professionalisation. The other side of the coin is that citizens become co-producers of social work on a more equal basis. Also, in social work education, service users' knowledge needs to be taken more seriously, as has been argued for a long time already. It is in the context of transformation that professionals and the profession need to reposition and include 'non-professionals' such as volunteers in their decision-making. The social work community, including its practice, education and research, is faced with the challenge of redefining its own professional role within changing social relationships.

3.4   How International and Diverse Is Social Work Education?

A key strategy for responding to the influence of globalisation adopted by universities across the country (as elsewhere) is internationalisation, generally understood to mean the integration of an international and intercultural dimension into education. 'Internationalisation at home' touches upon everything – from the academic curriculum, to the interactions between local and international students and faculty, to the cultivation of internationally focused research topics, to innovative uses of digital technology. Most importantly, it focuses on allowing all students, not just those who are mobile, to reap the benefits of international higher education. Diversity and inclusion are currently dominant concepts in social work education. The concept of diversity is related to internationalisation at home and aims at contributing to a resilient society that is well prepared for social risks, that promotes core social values such as participation and social cohesion and that fights and prevents exclusion and inequality.

The Dutch urban population has become increasingly diverse in terms of ethnicity, culture, lifestyle and religion, as has the social work student population. How can social work education support 'new' students and professionals in social work? How can practitioners from diverse backgrounds, both secular and religious, be supported in working effectively with religious and ethnic diversity? The secular and 'Western' character of the profession and the dominant 'whiteness' of organisations are challenged. One of the challenges is the question whether the curriculum, Western and ethnocentric, needs to be adjusted to the diversity of students and to make sure that content from a variety of cultures is used. Increasing diversity among students and professionals underlines the need to recognise that professionals are not only white, not only middle-class, and not culturally neutral. In staffing and recruitment policies, universities are struggling to match this increasing diversity among staff members. Social work is a normative profession, and this means that when values are at stake, it immediately has an impact on the profession. Educators expect that increasing diversity will have a greater impact on social work education than on other professional education. Some educators respect students' choice not to work with specific service user groups (conscientious objectors) because of their religion or ideology; other educators think that a professional should never exclude any group. This also concerns the refusal to work with certain ethically complex problems, such as abortion or euthanasia, or more implicit ethical issues, such as views on homosexuality. Students question whether they need to be all-inclusive professionals, able to work with all groups and moral dilemmas. This leads to the question of the extent of the freedom social work professionals and educators have to follow their own individual beliefs in their work and to select their own target groups. In general, the position is defended '…that as long as my colleagues are willing to assist or willing to take over a service user, why should I need to help people when it's against my own personal values…' More recently, political diversity in social work education has also become a much-debated issue owing to accusations that education in general is the domain of those who are politically left-wing. Social work students (and staff) in the Netherlands are not predominantly politically left-wing, as in the early 1970s to 1980s, but how tolerant or restrictive should professional social work practice and education be with respect to diverse opinions and ideologies?

Overall, the dominant question is how to develop an empowering school culture, aimed at increasing the strength of students from diverse socio-cultural backgrounds. High priority is given to a 'sense of belonging' among ethnic-minority students, as a lack of this sense of belonging is seen as a major reason for such students' premature departure from the field. This may lead to a curriculum which is more student-oriented than profession-oriented. Another challenge is the broad freedom of choice to match students' interests. This can result in highly subjective experiences and knowledge (Hendriks 2018). Diversity itself could be avoided in this way.

References

Andriessen, D. (2014). *Praktisch relevant en methodisch grondig?* [Practically relevant and methodically thorough]. Utrecht: Utrecht Kenniscentrum Innovatie & Business.

Bijlsma. J., & Jansen, H. (2012). *Sociaal Werk in Nederland, vijfhonderd jaar verheffen en verbinden* [Social work in the Netherlands, 500 years connecting and elevating]. Bussum: Couthino.

Boois, M. de. (2018). *Discipline zonder discipline, de opkomst en opheffing van de andragologie 1950–1983* [Discipline without discipline, the rise and abolition of andragology 1950–1983]. PhD thesis. Amsterdam: University of Amsterdam.

CBS. (2017). *Statline, population; key figures 2017.* https://statline.cbs.nl/StatWeb/publication/?VW=T&DM=SLEN&PA=37296eng&LA=EN. Accessed 11 Aug 2020.

CBS. (2018). *Statistics Netherlands: Population.* https://www.cbs.nl/en-gb/background/2018/47/population. Accessed 11 Aug 2020.

CBS. (2019). *Poverty and social exclusion.* https://longreads.cbs.nl/armoede-en-sociale-uitsluiting-2019/samenvatting/. Accessed 11 Aug 2020.

Chiapparini, E. (Ed.). (2016). *The service user as a partner in social work projects and education: Concepts and evaluations of courses with a gap-mending approach in Europe.* Berlin: Barbara Budrich publishers.

Commissie Ontwikkeling Kwalificatiestelsel Zorg & Welzijn. (1992). *Kwalificatiebeleid in de sector Zorg & Welzijn* [Qualification policy in the Healthcare & Welfare sector]. Utrecht: NIZW.

de Jonge, E. (2015). *Images of the professional, sources of inspiration for professionalization.* Delft: Eburon Academic Publishers.

de Jonge, E., van Bommel, M., & Kloppenburg, R. (2018). Zicht op sociale complexiteit. Over het belang van wetenschappelijke perspectieven in sociaal werk [Overview of social complexity. On the importance of scientific perspectives in social work]. *Journal of Social Intervention Theory and Practice, 27*(4), 29–47. https://doi.org/10.18352/jsi.547. Accessed 11 Aug 2020.

Duyvendak, J. W., & Tonkens, E. (2016). Introduction: The culturalization of citizenship. In J. W. Duyvendak, P. Geschiere, & E. Tonkens (Eds.), *The culturalization of citizenship. Belonging & polarization in a globalizing world.* London: Palgrave Macmillan.

Eraut, M. (1994). *Developing professional knowledge and competence.* London/New York: Routledge Falmer.

Esping-Andersen, G. (1990). *The three worlds of welfare capitalism.* Princeton: Princeton University Press.

Furman, R., Negi, N. J., Schatz, M. C. S., & Jones, S. (2008). Transnational social work: Using a wrap-around model. *Global Networks: A Journal of Transnational Affairs, 8*(4), 496–503.

Gezondheidsraad. (2014). *Sociaal Werk op een solide basis* [Social work on a solid basis]. The Hague: Gezondheidsraad.

Guile, D., & Young, M. (2003). Transfer and transition in vocational education: Some theoretical perspectives. In T. Tuomi-Gröhn & Y. Engeström (Eds.), *School and work: New perspectives on transfer and boundary-crossing* (pp. 63–81). Amsterdam: Pergamon.

Hartman, J., Knevel, J., & Reynaert, D. (2016). *Stel mensenrechten centraal in het sociaal werk!* [Put Human rights in the heart of social work!] *Sociaal.* Net, Retrieved from https://sociaal.net/opinie/mensenrechtenberoep/

Hendriks, P. (2018). *Turkish-Dutch and Moroccan-Dutch female professionals in social work. The self-perception and positioning of young, newly-started professionals in social work.* Delft: Eburon Academic Publishers.

Hendriks, P., & Kloppenburg, R. (2016). Internationalisation of Bachelor's programmes in social work in Europe. *Journal of Social Intervention: Theory and Practice, 25*(1), 28–46.

Kloppenburg, R. (2011). *Competently assessed, content, function and quality of competence assessments in social work education.* Utrecht: University of Utrecht.

Kloppenburg, R., & Tirions, M. (2020). Professionalisering in sociaal werk vanuit een internationaal perspectief [Professionalisation in social work from an international perspective]. In M. van Pelt, R. Roose, M. Hoijtink, M. Spierts & L. Verharen (red.), *Professionalisering van sociaal werk Theorie, praktijk en debat in Nederland en Vlaanderen* (pp. 197–215). Bussum: Coutinho.

Kloppenburg, R., Bommel, M. van, & Jonge, E. de (2017). *Gemeenschappelijke kennisbasis van sociaal werk opleidingen in Nederland* [A shared knowledge base for social work education in the Netherlands]. The Hague: Vereniging Hogescholen.

Kloppenburg, R., van Bommel, M., & de Jonge, E. (2019). Developing common ground for a sustainable knowledge base for social work education in the Netherlands. *Social Work Education, 38*(1), 7–20. https://doi.org/10.1080/02615479.2018.1529154. Accessed 13 Jan 2021.

Schaap, H., de Bruijn, E., van der Schaaf, M. F., & Kirschner, P. A. (2009). Students' personal professional theories in competence-based vocational education: The construction of personal knowledge through internalisation and socialization. *Journal of Vocational Education and Training, 61,* 481–494.

Scholte, M., Sprinkhuizen, A., & Zuiderhof, M. (2012). *De generalist. De sociale professional aan de basis* [The generalist. The social professional at the base]. Houten: Bohn Stafleu van Loghum.

Schön, D. (1983). *The reflective practitioner: How professionals think in action.* New York: Basic Books.

Sector Adviescollege Hogere Sociale Studies. (2017). *Landelijk opleidingsdocument Sociaal Werk* [National document social work education]. The Hague: SWP.

SGI-networks. (2016). *Sustainable governance indicators.* http://www.sgi-network.org/2016/The_Netherlands/Social_Policies. Accessed 11 Aug 2020.

Trappenburg, M. J. (2015). Active solidarity and its discontents. *Health Care Analysis, 23*(3), 207–220.

University College Leuven-Limburg. (2019). *ICOMs Internationale competenties* [International competences]. http://www.internationalecompetenties.be/nl/icoms/. Accessed 11 Aug 2020.

van Bommel, M. (2013). *Learning knowledge for competent social work, students' learning experiences and knowledge outcomes in a constructivist bachelor's programme.* Heerlen: Open Universiteit.

van Ewijk, H. (2016). *Hollandi sotsiaaltöö liigub detsentraliseerimise suunas* [Dutch social work moving towards the decentralisation of social work]. *Sotsiaaltöö, 3,* 74–77.

Haaster, H. van, Wilken, J. P., Karbouniaris, S., & Hidajattoellah, D. (2013). *Kaderdocument ervaringsdeskundigheid* [Experimental expertise framework document]. Utrecht: Hogeschool Utrecht.

Lieshout, M. van. (2012). *Canon Sociaal Werk.* https://www.canonsociaalwerk.eu/nl/. Accessed 11 Aug 2020.

van Merriënboer, J. J. G., van der Klink, M. R., & Hendriks, M. (2002). *Competenties: van complicaties tot compromis. [Competences from complications to compromises]* Den Haag, The Netherlands: Onderwijsraad.

Vereniging Hogescholen. (2019). https://www.vereniginghogescholen.nl/sectoren/socialestudies. Accessed 11 Aug 2020.

Verkenningscommissie hoger sociaal agogisch onderwijs. (2014). *Meer van Waarde, Kwaliteitsimpuls en ontwikkelrichting voor het hoger sociaal agogisch onderwijs* [Being of more value: Quality impulse and developmental direction for social higher education]. The Hague: Vereniging Hogescholen.

Watson, V. (2006). Deep difference: Diversity, planning and ethics. *Planning Theory, 5*(1), 31–50.

Weerman, A. (2016). *Ervaringsdeskundige Zorg en Dienstverleners, Stigma, verslaving & existentiële* transformatie [Expert by experience care and service providers, stigma, addiction & existential transformation]. Utrecht: Eburon.

Weijers, G. (2016). *Transitie van de jeugdzorg: steeds gewezen op Denemarken, maar niks geleerd* [Transition in Youth care: Often drew attention on Denmark but nothing learned]. https://blog.pedagogiek.nu/blog/2016/07/25/transitie-van-de-jeugdzorg-steeds-gewezen-op-denemarken-maar-niks-geleerd/. Accessed 11 Aug 2020.

Witte, T. (2015). Koersen op de toekomst: Innoveer sociale opleidingen! [Race for the future: Innovate social work education!]. *Journal of Social Intervention: Theory and Practice, 24*(1), 71–75.

Zorlu, A., & Hartog, J. (2001). *Migration and immigrants: The case of the Netherlands. Institute for Migration and Ethnic Studies University of Amsterdam.* Amsterdam: Tinbergen Institute.

The Revival of Romanian Social Work Education and Its Prospects

Florin Lazăr

1 Historical Perspective on the Process of Professional Social Work Development

Social work in Romania began within the context of religious charitable activities of the fourteenth century, which evolved into more structured support for the poor and disadvantaged towards the late nineteenth century. With the establishment of the Romanian nation-state in the early twentieth century, social assistance was transformed from charity work into a state-organised activity (Lazăr 2015c). Established in 1929 with the support of the Bucharest Sociological School led by Dimitrie Gusti, the Christian Women's Association, and under the patronage of the Royal House, the first school of social work (Princess Ileana School of Social Work) aimed to bring social change and improve the quality of life of the most vulnerable people (Mănuilă 1936). The teaching staff of the first school of social work was composed of sociologists, lawyers, philosophers, doctors and a few graduates of US-based social work schools. Practice placements were available in Colțea Hospital, in a family community centre and in a centre for young offenders/delinquents (Mănuilă 1936; Mănoiu and Epureanu 1996). Only women could attend the school, though men were allowed to serve as assistants. Veturia Mănuilă, the first head of the school and wife of Dr Sabin Mănuilă (demographer and minister), saw social work as contributing to the building of the nation-state and was a promoter of eugenics (Bucur 1994). Xenia Costa-Foru (trained in Germany and the United States) continued the development of the school of social work as head of the department (Văcărescu

F. Lazăr (✉)
Faculty of Sociology and Social Work, Social Work Research Commission of the National College of Social Workers, University of Bucharest, Bucharest, Romania

Social Work Research Commission of the Nationall College of Social Workers, University of Bucharest, Bucharest, Romania
e-mail: florin.lazar@sas.unibuc.ro

© Springer Nature Switzerland AG 2021
M. Laging, N. Žganec (eds.), *Social Work Education in Europe*,
European Social Work Education and Practice,
https://doi.org/10.1007/978-3-030-69701-3_10

2011). The women's liberation movement is associated with their active involvement in social assistance activities and the development of social work education (Văcărescu 2014).

In 1929, the first issue of the newly established journal *Social Work: Bulletin of the Princess Ileana School of Social Work* presented the teaching staff and curricula of the School of Social Work, with courses varying from philosophy, psychology, sociology, social medicine, and law to social work methods and legislation or methods for researching of social work problems. With some of the teaching staff emigrating (Veturia and Sabin Mănuilă) or being imprisoned (e.g. Mircea Vulcănescu) by the communist regime, which was established in 1947, the School of Social Work was downgraded in 1952 from higher education to vocational training and dissolved completely in 1969 (Buzducea 2009). Social work activities were turned into administrative work, and the only forms of social interventions were large-scale residential institutions (Zamfir 1999; Lazăr 2015c).

After the fall of communist rule in 1989, social work education at the university level was re-established in 1990, together with sociology and psychology, including in faith-based faculties (e.g. Orthodox, Roman Catholic, Baptist, Pentecostal, Adventist). The first generation of social workers graduated in 1994 (Zamfir 1999). The newly created schools of social work comprised various (mainly) social scientists (e.g. sociologists, psychologists, lawyers, doctors), virtually without social workers (there were minor exceptions when one or two social work graduates from the period before the ban were employed).

To understand some of the stages in the evolution of the post-communist period, a brief overview of the social policies of the communist regime would be helpful. During the communist period, the welfare regime was a centralised/socialist one (Zamfir and Zamfir 1995), with universal health care, education, housing services and work-related benefits (including a comprehensive pension system, full-employment policies or family-oriented social policies). Some policy domains such as unemployment, poverty and disability were neglected for ideological reasons, whilst an aggressive pro-natalist policy (i.e. virtually prohibiting abortion) was promoted starting in 1966 to boost the labour force and economic growth (Zamfir 1999; Bucur and Miroiu 2018).

As Cătălin Zamfir (1999) states, the social policies of the post-communist period started with a restoration stage when some of the perceived injustices of the old regime were "repaired": abortion became possible, the ban on imported goods was lifted, property rights were restored (e.g. for houses, land), political detainees were released, and benefits were introduced for opponents of the communist regime (imprisoned for political reasons) or in the 1989 revolution. In the following years, new social policies were implemented for people with disabilities (in 1992) and for the unemployed (in 1991), and welfare benefits for the poor were introduced (in 1995). In the first few years after 1990, social work activities were mostly charitable, provided by international organisations as well as individuals moved by the poor conditions in residential institutions for abandoned children. Once the first generation of social workers graduated in 1994, services started to diversify, although they were mainly provided by non-governmental organisations (NGOs).

One of the first comparative studies of welfare states to include Romania and former communist countries was developed by Bob Deacon (1993), who, based on general indicators, included Romania in a group of 'post-communist conservative-corporatist' welfare regimes/states. Although Deacon's typology has the merit of being a pioneering work, it lacked the theoretical complexity and adequacy of indicators. Later on, the same author underlined the role of international organisations in shaping the social policies in the former communist countries of Eastern Europe (Deacon 2000).

When compared with the welfare regimes described by Gosta Esping-Andersen (1990), Romanian scholars suggested a hybrid/mixed welfare regime with a general shift towards the liberal model from a predominantly conservative type (Preda 2002) or closer to the Southern/Latin Rim developing welfare regimes (Lazăr 2000) previously identified by Stephan Liebfried (1993) and Maurizio Ferrera (1996). The communist legacy was still evident in the early years after 1990 in the provision of insurance-based benefits and the high coverage of the pension system (Preda 2002; Lazăr 2000). Only in 1995 was the first law on the provision of a cash social benefit (in Ro. *Ajutor social*) for the poor enacted, but due to high inflation, its value became almost 'insignificant', and very few people actually availed themselves of it (Pop 2002). During the transition years, the family took over many responsibilities in providing welfare to the individual, from ensuring access to education for children and the costs of continuing to higher education, care for children (as grandparents) and the elderly to subsistence agriculture when unemployment and inflation peaked in a very short time (Preda 2002). The clientelist nature of some Latin Rim welfare regimes was also found in Romania (Lazăr 2000), for instance in the provision of significant unemployment insurance or specific benefits in key industrial areas or with strong union movements (e.g. mining, transport, health care). Fenger (2007) considers that in Central and Eastern Europe the welfare regimes gradually changed from a socialist type towards a (neo)liberal/hybrid welfare regime, Romania being part of a developing welfare state (together with Moldova and Georgia). Haggard and Kaufman (2008) undertook a thorough analysis of 'neglected'/less researched countries of Latin America, Eastern Europe and East Asia and concluded that Romania and Bulgaria were somehow different from their Eastern European neighbours in that they were less developed and experienced more socioeconomic 'relapses' during the transition from the socialist welfare regime. In a literature review of research on the welfare states in Central and Eastern Europe (CEE), Adăscăliţei (2012) points out that these welfare states share many similarities, although more research is needed to highlight and understand their differences. He suggests that Western typologies (e.g. Esping-Andersen's classical typology) do not fully capture the roles played by specific cultural, historical, political and social factors in the current configuration of welfare states.

2 Contemporary Social Work in Romania – State of the Art

In the early 1990s, before the first generation of social work graduates entered the labour market, most social work activities were charitable and directed towards children (especially children with disabilities) in large residential institutions supported by international donors and volunteers (Lazăr 2015c). Due to the special attention given to the living conditions and rights of children in public care, the field of child protection benefited the most from international funds and became the most developed area of social work practice (Dickens and Sarghi 2000). Whilst the first (post-communist) law on the national social work system was enacted in 2001 (Law No. 705), the law on the status of social workers 466/2004 led to the establishment of the National College of Social Workers (NCSW) and introduced registration requirements for social workers. Overall, the practice of social work in Romania is largely a combination of case management with some administrative work. These combinations differ by area of practice. The most developed area is child protection, which has been based explicitly on case management principles since 2006, when case management was legally recognised as the main approach in child protection services (Ordinance No. 288/2006; Cojocaru and Cojocaru 2008). Each case of a child in need/at risk of having his/her rights violated/broken has a case manager and a case responsible. Usually a case manager is a social worker or another professional with at least 5 years of practice experience in child protection and a university degree in social sciences. With the reform of social work services from 2004 to 2005, which united in a single institution at the county level services for adults and children, case management was considered a viable option in other areas too (e.g. services for drug users).

In social work with people with disabilities, there is a higher trend/tendency towards a more administrative approach, most people being required each year to renew their disability paperwork (for some cases, with life-time disability, the renewal is made every 2 years). In theory, this annual renewal is meant to ensure a better adaptation/individualisation of the services required for a person's social integration/rehabilitation. In fact, in many cases the services proposed in the rehabilitation plan are not fully implemented/carried out or monitored or even available in the area/locality (Lazăr 2009).

Recent surveys (Lazăr 2015a; Lazăr et al. 2016) reveal that 75% of registered social workers are working in public services, mostly in child protection services, with the elderly, people with disabilities in local social services and in health social work (either in hospital settings or community organisations/services). The General Directorates for Social Work and Child Protection (GDSWCP) at the county level (in Romania there are 41 counties and 6 districts of Bucharest) are the main employers of social workers, while NGOs attract about a fifth of registered social workers. Social workers are least represented in central administration, the social economy, penal justice and migrant-related work (Lazăr et al. 2016: 45–48). Of a total of about 8500 social workers registered in the National Register of Social Workers (in December 2018), a small proportion had opened private practice offices (in

December 2018 there were about 100 private practice cabinets/offices). Almost half of social workers have an M.A. in Social Work (48%), whilst about 5% have a PhD (Lazăr et al. 2016). Although in Romania 45% of the population live in rural areas (National Institute of Statistics 2013), only 11% of registered social workers are active in rural communities, revealing big rural–urban discrepancies/inequities (Lazăr et al. 2016). Some research suggests that qualified social workers represent a minority within the social work system (about a third of public employees), at least in local public services (Lazăr 2015b).

Social work services in Romania evolved from being provided mainly by NGOs in the 1990s to a predominantly public provision after 2000. This situation can be a consequence of an expansion of the type of services/activities to respond to increasing needs/vulnerabilities and newly discovered types of clients (e.g. children with migrant parents, residential care for dependent elderly, foster care, homeless people, drug users), but also due to fewer funding opportunities for NGOs (especially after Romania joined the EU in 2007). A reform strategy of the social assistance system for 2011–2013 focused almost exclusively on cash benefits aiming to reduce already low social assistance spending and reduce error and fraud. Only recently (Ministry of Labour, Family, Social Protection and Elderly 2015) has the balance changed to increase the role of social services compared with the provision of cash benefits, which had prevailed. Although in 2016 Romania met the 2020 EU national target to lift 585,000 people out of poverty, Eurostat data (2019a) revealed that Romania still has one of the highest rates in the EU of people living at risk of poverty or social exclusion (about a third of the population in 2018), especially among children (the highest percentage in the EU zone in 2018, at 37.9%). Moreover, in Romania, employment does not remove the risk of poverty, since more than one in six employees are still at risk of poverty, almost double the EU average (Eurostat 2019b). With a minimum income guarantee (MIG) scheme in place since 2001 and several other measures aimed at alleviating poverty, social policies tend to target the poorest of the poor, which is a sign of the neoliberal turn (Dale and Fabri 2018).

To fight poverty and social exclusion by providing basic integrated social services (health, education and social assistance), recent measures promote the creation of community teams composed of a social worker, a community nurse and a school mediator (Order No. 393/630/4236/2017). Also, in line with the national strategy to fight poverty 2015–2020, several EU-funded projects have been implemented by the Ministry of Labour and Social Justice to increase the number of rural and small communities employing at least one social worker, to provide integrated social services and dismantle the last few large-scale residential care institutions for children (see Ministry of Labour's website). At the end of 2018 the placement of any child under the age of 7 in a residential institution was forbidden, with the goal of preventing the negative consequences of institutionalisation and encouraging care in foster families and small family-type institutions. This measure continued a previous regulation (in 2004 the age limit was set at 2 years old, increased to 3 years old in 2014) which emerged after a longitudinal study (see Bucharest Early Intervention Project) had revealed the negative consequences of institutional care in early childhood (Nelson et al. 2007).

3   Current Model of Education of Social Work in Romania

As mentioned earlier, social work education was re-established in 1990 at the University of Bucharest and the Babes-Bolyai University of Cluj, and in 1991 at the Alexandru Ioan Cuza University in Iaşi, initially as post-high school (vocational) education, but transformed into university-level education in 1992 (when a social work school was also created at the West University of Timişoara) with 4 years of study. Later on, social work schools were established/created at other universities as well (e.g. Alba Iulia, Arad, Bacău, Baia Mare, Braşov, Constanţa, Craiova, Oradea, Piteşti, Petroşani, Reşiţa, Sibiu, Suceava and Târgovişte). It is worth mentioning that as early as 1991–1992 at some of these public universities social work programmes were also created at theology faculties (Orthodox, Roman Catholic, Greek Catholic, Baptist, Reform, and Pentecostal). This specific situation was, on the one hand, a measure aimed at compensating for the oppression of religion during the communist regime and, on the other hand, reveals the importance of religion and of different churches/confessions in the post-communist period. Courses devoted specifically to social work were attended by students of both secular and religious departments within the same university (e.g. University of Bucharest). Initially, the teaching staff was composed mainly of social scientists (sociologists, psychologists, law graduates/lawyers) and doctors (psychiatrists, geriatricians, paediatricians), whilst some international/foreign tutors/teachers were involved (e.g. from the United Kingdom, United States, the Netherlands) based on specific projects (e.g. European projects such as Tempus and Erasmus, but also intervention projects with NGOs or Fulbright scholars) and collaborations. For instance, some British and Dutch influences are to be found at the University of Bucharest (Zamfir and Zamfir 1995), from Ireland at Braşov (Walsh et al. 2005), from the US at Cluj-Napoca, from the UK and US at Timişoara (Goian 2013) and from France at Iaşi. Collaborations with universities from neighbouring countries such as Hungary were also important, especially for those programmes taught in Hungarian (e.g. in Cluj-Napoca and Oradea). Also, some of the teaching staff were able to participate in various exchange programmes to learn more about social work education in more developed countries. Some of the new social work graduates (especially those enrolling into doctoral studies) were attracted as teaching staff within these universities.

Admission was possible after a written exam, and for a few years (until 1994) a vocational evaluation focusing on suitability for social work studies was also in place. Some special (subsidised) places were available for students coming from the Roma ethnic group, under a positive discrimination/affirmative action policy (this practice continues and was expanded to other domains and universities). Courses were rather generalist (coming from sociology, psychology, social psychology, political science, philosophy, (social) medicine, economics), with only some specific social work content (e.g. on social work theories and methods or practice placements). Since 1994 doctoral studies have been possible in sociology (with a social work topic). Donations of books for faculty libraries allowed the creation of a documentary collection for students in the first years after 1990. During the transition period many private universities were established and some also offered social work training/education, although the majority of social work programmes were at public universities. Practice placements were included in the curricula throughout each academic year (during each semester and at the end of each year), but the general approach of the social work programmes was academic, not vocational. After 2000 the Ministry of Education started to promote a higher degree of uniformity (i.e. criteria) of higher education programmes. As a result, social work schools (too) were encouraged to fulfil specific requirements in terms of core, secondary, optional and elective courses.

In 2003 distance learning/part-time programmes in social work were introduced at the University of Bucharest, Babes-Bolyai University, Alba Iulia University, Alexandru Ioan Cuza University of Iaşi, and West University of Timişoara, whilst at the University of Bucharest between 1999 and 2005 (2008 graduation year) a 3-year College of Community Social Work (Cozărescu 2012) was organised and designed for those with some social work practice background (created with a Swiss NGO and the Pestalozzi Foundation and with some social pedagogy influence/courses).

Since 2005, as a result of the adoption of the Bologna Charter, the duration of study was reduced from 4 to 3 years, although with some resistance from the teaching staff, who saw some of their courses disappear from the curriculum. In 2008, two generations of students graduated – those with 3 and those with 4 years of study – with a very large cohort of graduates. Master's programmes increased from three to four semesters of study, whilst doctoral studies were reduced from 5 (up to 7) to no more than 3 years. No professional doctorate (in sociology) is possible, doctoral studies being research-based.[1]

To respond to this new situation and inspired by the success of the College of Community Social Work programme, at the University of Bucharest, for instance, modules of specialisation comprising blocks of specific courses (approx. five to seven courses) were available to students from the third semester (apart from elective courses), initially in areas such as social work with children and families, community social work, social policy and administration and probation and victim protection. Since the 2008–2009 academic year the modules have been offered only in the last two semesters and included counselling in social work, social work with groups at risk and probation and victim protection.

Since 2003, as in other countries aligned with the Bologna Process, the length of study has been 3 years with a minimum of 180 European Credit Transfer and Accumulation System (ECTS) points for undergraduate studies leading to a Licence in Social Work. The final exam comprises one written exam, one 'licence paper' and a defence of the licence paper/oral exam. The licence paper usually includes research or a social work intervention or at least proposals for an intervention. The master's programmes take 2 years, four semesters, with a total of 120 ECTS points. The final

---

[1] In Romania, professional doctorates are possible only in some arts and humanities areas.

exam is a master's thesis, usually a research-based paper or a policy analysis, presented/defended in an oral exam.

The National Quality Standards in Higher Education proposed by the Commission on Social and Political Sciences, updated in 2019 (ARACIS 2019: 30–34), categorised undergraduate courses into fundamental courses (general), courses of the domain (together representing up to 25–30% of total courses), specialty courses (minimum 60%) and complementary courses (10–15%) (Tables 1, 2, 3, and 4). Using the criteria of mandatory, elective (students can choose from a list) and optional (additional to the other courses), at least 70% of courses must be mandatory and up to 30% must be elective; a programme can also include optional courses. Practice is proposed to constitute a minimum of 90 h (either during the fourth semester or at the end of the year, for 3 weeks) and must represent at least 10% of specialty courses. Also, practice must be carried out under the supervision of a social worker. The specific courses in each category represent a guideline, each university being free to decide the order and content of each course (as is the case with practice). Each course lasts one semester and ends with an evaluation (continuous evaluation is encouraged) and a final/written evaluation rather than multiple-choice tests. In master's programmes, practice must cover at least 10% of the curriculum (60 h or at least 3 weeks per year).

3.1 Suggested Courses for Social Work Domain – Undergraduate Studies (2016) by Structure and Type

Despite university autonomy, centralised educational structures leave little room for variation in curricula among the social work education programmes existing at 23 universities (in 2011). Social work framework curricula evolved from a rather generalist one focused on theories and policies in the early post-communist period to more specialised core courses adapted to changing social realities as new generations of social work educators (i.e. social work graduates) emerged within

Table 1 Fundamental (general) courses (ARACIS 2019: 30)

No.	Course	Type of course
1.	Introduction to sociology	Mandatory
2.	Diagnosis and resolution of social problems	Elective
3.	Introduction to psychology	Mandatory
4.	Human development	Mandatory
5.	Research methodology in social sciences	Mandatory
6.	Law and social work legislation	Mandatory
7.	Public policies	Elective
8	Critical thinking	Elective

Table 2 Courses of the domain (ARACIS 2019: 31)

No.	Course	Type of course
1.	Introduction to social work/bases of social work	Mandatory
2.	Theories and intervention methods in social work (person/individual and family)	Mandatory
3.	Theories and intervention methods in social work (group and community)	Mandatory
4.	Social policies	Mandatory
5.	Social work system	Mandatory
6.	Professional deontology	Mandatory

Table 3 Specialty courses (ARACIS 2019: 31)

No.	Course
1.	Evidence-based social work
2.	Counselling in social work
3.	Communication techniques in social work
4.	Human rights and anti-discriminatory strategies
5.	Social inclusion policies
6.	Social work in the European Union
7.	Family social work
8.	Child protection services
9.	Adoption and foster care
10.	Abuse and domestic violence. Support services
11.	Organisation and management of social work services
12.	Demography and family planning
13.	Social work with elderly people
14.	Social work with disabilities
15.	Social work with unemployed. Integration services for vulnerable people on labour market
16.	Social work in school
17.	Social work in probation system
18.	Social work with offenders
19.	Social work with people with chronic and terminal illnesses
20.	Prevention and rehabilitation of people with a substance addiction
19.	Quality-of-life and anti-poverty policies
20.	Case management
21.	Management and evaluation of social work programmes
22.	Social work supervision
23.	Statistical data analysis

No.	Course
Table 4 Complementary courses (ARACIS 2019, 32)	
1.	Human resource management
2.	Social informatics
3.	Applied social psychology
4.	Psychopathology and psychotherapy
5.	Crisis intervention
6.	Special psycho-pedagogy and educational inclusion
7.	Foreign language
8.	Physical education
9.	Academic techniques and skills
10	Introduction to economics
11	Ethics

universities. Eighteen years after the first social work students graduated in 2012, the first positions of full professor were occupied by former social work students who also earned the right to supervise doctoral theses (in sociology).

In terms of curricula, from our analysis of the available ones in the National Register of Qualifications in Higher Education (RNCIS/NRQHE), in 2019 there were 22 social work programmes, of which 5 are part-time/distance learning programmes. To these may be added 7 Orthodox theology-social work and 3 other theology-social work programmes (2 Roman Catholic and 1 Baptist). The decision of the Minister of Education, which lists the specialisations approved to have admission exams in 2019–2020, mentioned 38 programmes at 21 universities (Hotărârea nr. 326/2019), which includes also those taught in Hungarian at the Babeş-Bolyai University of Cluj and in German at the Lucian Blaga University of Sibiu. The total number of available spots was 2950 (which, at public universities, include subsidised and fee-paying spots, usually about a third being subsidised). Of these spots, about 1080 are in theology-social work faculties/departments, 305 are for part-time studies/distance learning at 5 universities, and a similar figure (295) applies at all 5 private universities. The number of actual students each year varies and is not available in a centralised database. We estimate that about half of the schooling/enrolment capacity is filled, and based on an average drop-out rate of 35% according to a study of the National Association of Student Organisations in Romania/ANOSR cited in the media (Bechir 2017) at least 800–1000 undergraduate students complete their social work studies every year. Educational and demographic statistics show a decrease in the student population since 2008 as a result of a sharply declining birth rate after 1989. With the exception of larger universities, where in recent years the number of students has been relatively stable (or even increased, for instance at Bucharest University), universities are having difficulties keeping the programmes running (e.g. since 2011, one university cancelled admission to social work schools: Universitatea "George Bacovia" din Bacău, while Universitatea "Avram Iancu" din

Cluj-Napoca started to offer only postgraduate education, but no more in social work).

Law 466 on the status of social workers was passed in 2004, which led to the creation in 2005 of the National College of Social Workers of Romania (NCSWR) as a regulatory body. The law determined that only those with a university education in social work are entitled to be called social workers and be registered in the National Register of Social Workers. Those carrying out social work activities without a university degree in social work had 5 years to attend or start undergraduate studies in social work. Since there were no penalties for employers or employees not respecting the provision, social work activities are still often carried out by people without a social work qualification/university education.

For graduates of theology-social work programmes, in order to be registered with the NCSWR, at least 70% of all ECTS points/transferable credits received during their studies should be in social work. The theology-social work programmes were replaced with programmes in social theology for a few years (Cojocaru et al. 2011). Research on the profile of registered social workers revealed that about 20% graduated from faculties of theology-social work (Lazăr 2015a). At the end of 2019 about 9200 social workers were registered with the NCSWR and about 100 had opened private practices (NCSWR 2019).

In 2010 a National Association of Schools of Social Work was created by the leaders of the four main schools (Bucharest, Cluj, Iaşi and Timişoara). There are no official statistics on the overall number of graduates from social work programmes, but Doru Buzducea, president of NCSWR and dean of the Faculty of Sociology and Social Work at the University of Bucharest, estimated that since 1994 at least 40,000 have graduated from all social work programmes.[2]

To facilitate the registration of new graduates, since 2012, NCSWR has signed agreements with all universities having schools of social work, to register free of charge social work graduates and pass the information and files/requests to the professional organisation.

The collaboration between social work schools, practitioners and NCSWR is strengthened by the involvement of many social workers as associated practice supervisors as well as social work schools' staff in local branches of NCSWR. In 2016 a Social Work Research Commission was officially established within NCSWR (it functioned informally from 2014 to 2015), its members being social work graduates who were also academics in Bucharest, Cluj and Timişoara. The research carried out includes one on the profile of social workers (Lazăr 2015a), on the human resources from local social work services (Lazăr 2015b), a workforce study (Lazăr et al. 2016), a study on the working conditions of social workers (Lazăr et al. 2017, unpublished) and a study on the image of social workers in mass media

---

[2] See Doru Buzducea's presentation in November 2018: https://dorubuzducea.ro/conferinta-internationala-strengthening-the-social-work-and-social-service-workforce-in-europe-central-asia-investing-in-our-childrens-future/ . This figure is based on statistical data from the National Institute of Statistics on the number of students enrolled each year (since 1999) in social work programmes minus about 30% considered average drop-out rate.

(Lazăr et al. 2018). Another study on the competencies acquired by social workers and the barriers in everyday practice is under way, whilst the NCSWR Strategy for 2018–2022 is proposing a research project every year (e.g. on evidence-based practice, on self-care practices and a repetition of the workforce study). These studies aimed to provide evidence for the advocacy efforts of NCSWR among decision-makers, to improve the working conditions of social workers as well as the quality of services provided.

There are virtually no service users involved in teaching activities in Romanian social work schools, at least not permanently/continuously, but rather as guests with little interaction with students during courses. However, all programmes provide practice placements in social work public institutions or NGOs, usually under the supervision of a qualified social worker. Students begin practice placement from the first year of their studies (first or second semester) to the last year (usually 1 day/week of school – 28 weeks/academic year) and at the end of each academic year a daily practice (usually 2 weeks, 56–60 h). As a general evaluation based on our analysis of the curricula of all social work programmes in Romania, the number of hours of practice placements during the 3 years of undergraduate studies varies between 400 and 700 (some universities have 4 h/week, others 6 h/week, some have fewer hours of summer practice, whilst others have also reflective/mentoring labs on practice).

In an analysis of curricula in three Romanian social work schools (University of Bucharest, Babes-Bolyai University of Cluj and Alexandru Ioan Cuza University of Iaşi), Roman et al. (2015) determined that about 60% of courses can be described as being part of the social work core courses, 23% as sociology courses and another almost 17% as a category of complementary courses (e.g. foreign language, social informatics, physical education, practice). On average, an undergraduate programme in social work at the three aforementioned universities comprised 42 courses (about 7 courses per semester). Practice placement hours represent between 15% and 28% of all teaching hours during the 3 years of undergraduate studies in social work (6 semesters × 14 weeks × 28 h + practice hours, outside semesters weeks).

An analysis of master's programmes carried out by Roman et al. (2015) revealed that on average for each undergraduate programme there are 3.5 master's programmes in social work (5 in Bucharest, 6 in Romanian and 2 in Hungarian in Cluj and 4 in Iaşi). Regarding the current educational offer of the aforementioned schools (as of July 2019), we discover that some of the master's programmes are focused on a specific area of practice (children's rights, probation, gerontology, prevention of illegal drug use, clinical social work and counselling, supervision, social economy, social work for mental health – in Hungarian), whilst other are more general (high-risk groups and social support services, management of social (and health) services). If we expand our analysis to other schools of social work we discover more general programmes (e.g. European social policies, social work services, assistance and community development, values-centred social work practice), some specific (social work for the elderly and people with disabilities), but also some offered by religious-type schools[3] (e.g. social assistance of the Church, Christian contemporary family, pastoral counselling and psycho-social assistance). A general overview of master's programmes reveals the emphasis placed on specific areas of practice (for instance, at the Babes-Bolyai University of Cluj, master's programmes are included in the category of professional masters), especially in children and family, management of social services, counselling (clinical social work) and probation and legal areas. New areas of specialisation (in Romania) at the master's level (such as social economy, high-risk groups) are also available, demonstrating how social work schools have tried to adjust their educational offerings to respond to new social problems.

In December 2018, nine academics from the University of Bucharest (3), the West University of Timişoara (3), the Alexandru Ioan Cuza University of Iaşi (2) and the Babeş-Bolyai University of Cluj (1) defended their *habilitation*[4] thesis in social work (newly approved domain for doctoral studies). Later on, requests to approve the establishment of social work doctoral schools were sent to the Ministry of Education by the Universities of Bucharest and Timişoara (the only ones fulfilling the requirement to have at least three approved doctoral supervisors in social work), but no response was received by the time of this writing. Official recognition of social work as a field of doctoral study and the establishment of doctoral schools of social work are further steps in the academisation process. Furthermore, research in social work is vital for building the evidence base of practice and gaining scientific recognition for the field.

4   Critical Analysis and Paths Forward

In this section we discuss the current and medium-term challenges of social work and social work education in Romania at various levels. At the educational system level, probably the most important challenge is the shrinking student population, which is the result of low fertility rates following the fall of communism combined with high levels of emigration (Preda 2009; Ministry of Education 2018). Due to this demographic contraction, in the coming years, small universities will find it harder to attract students, a trend already in place (e.g. since 2011, three universities have ended their social work education programmes). The alternatives are either to attract foreign students to compensate for the foreseeable loss in the number of students (e.g. maybe from the neighbouring Republic of Moldova or from lower-income countries) or to merge and create consortia of universities (from the same

---

[3] The master's programmes offered by religious/theology faculties are not included in the social work field of study, but in theology.

[4] *Habilitation* was introduced in 2011 by the new education law as a way of recognising the right to supervise doctoral students. The process itself requires that the candidate fulfil the criteria (mainly scientometric criteria) to be full professor/scientific researcher I. Although the candidate does not need to hold this position, he/she should at least be a lecturer.

city or region). Some wider structural/social and political factors can also play a role in the shaping of the future education system, such as financing, competition for resources or short-term priorities. The reform of the educational system carried out with the introduction of the new law (Law No. 1/2011 on education) introduced mainly quantitative/scientometric measures of academic performance.

To enter/open themselves up to the global education market, social work schools from Romanian universities need to join existing networks (e.g. EASSW, IASSW, ESWRA), offer more opportunities (undergraduate, master's level, postgraduate) for international students (e.g. programmes taught in English) and extend collaboration with international partners/other schools.

At the local level, already some faculties have launched more recruitment drives by visiting high schools, using social media networks to attract new students, promoting the social work profession and student life and diversifying course offering and teaching methods. Also, the expansion of postgraduate (online, part-time) courses/modules is another possible means of both addressing the needs of social workers for lifelong learning and keeping up with labour market changes. Renewal of the teaching staff and of their academic performances will need to continue (this is also strengthened by the current regulations on advancing/entering an academic career). Inclusion in the education process, at least for practice supervision, of experienced social workers needs to expand to other schools of social work, as does the involvement of service users, which is currently (almost) absent. Collaboration between practitioners and researchers/academics must be enhanced in order to extend the level of usage of evidence-based practice (Iovu and Runcan 2012), as well as to increase the adequacy of research to practice needs. Combined with the actual establishment of the first social work doctoral schools in the coming years, all these factors are likely to further the academisation of the area of study.

From the profession/practice perspective, social workers have expressed the need for more correspondence between education and practice needs (Lazăr et al. 2016). If we look at the total estimated number of graduates (40,000) and at the same time consider that those registered in the National Register of Social Workers also practice in the field (about 8500), we discover that only about one in five social work graduates continue their career in the field. Taking into consideration the current deficit of social workers in rural areas and in small cities (Lazăr 2015b; Tesliuc et al. 2015), schools of social work need to pay more attention to preparing students for work at the community level and in rural areas (Sorescu 2015). Some accompanying policy measures are also needed to encourage graduates to work in remote or rural areas (e.g. incentives to cover transport and accommodation costs). Although in the last 2 years wages of social workers in public institutions have increased, there remain pay inequities between counties and institutions which need to be addressed in order to increase retention in the field of newly qualified as well as experienced social workers. Considering the need for supervision expressed by social workers (Lazăr et al. 2016), schools of social work could decide to take an active role in offering more educational opportunities in this area.

References

Adascalitei, D. (2012). Welfare state development in Central and Eastern Europe: A state of the art literature review. *Studies of Transition States and Societies, 4*(4), 59–70.

Agenţia Română de Asigurare a Calităţii în Învăţământul Superior – ARACIS [Romanian Agency for Quality Assurance in Higher Education]. (2019). *Standarde specifice privind evaluarea externă a calităţii academice la programele de studii din domeniile de licenţă şi master aferente Comisiei de specialitate nr. 4 Stiinţe sociale, politice si ale comunicării* [Specific standards for external evaluation of academic quality of undergraduate and master study programmes in the areas of the Specialty Commission no. 4 Social, political and communication sciences].

Bechir, M. (2017). *Abandonul în universităţi: Mai mult de unul din trei studenţi nu ajunge la licenţă* [Drop-out in universities: More than one in third students does not reach graduation]. Retrieved online from: https://cursdeguvernare.ro/abandonul-in-universitati-mai-mult-de-unul-din-trei-studenti-nu-ajunge-la-licenta.html. Accessed 25 Aug 2020.

Bucur, M. (1994). In praise of wellborn mothers: On the development of eugenicist gender roles in interwar Romania. *East European Politics and Societies, 9*(1), 123–142.

Bucur, M., & Miroiu, M. (2018). *Birth of democratic citizenship: Women and power in modern Romania.* Bloomington: Indiana University Press.

Buzducea, D. (2009). *Sisteme moderne de asistenţă socială: Tendinţe globale şi practici locale* [Modern social work systems. Global trends and local practices]. Iaşi: Polirom.

Buzducea, D. (2018). Evolution of social work as a profession in Romania: Past and present challenges. Paper presented at the international conference *"Strengthening the social work and social service workforce in Europe and Central Asia: Investing in our children's future"*, 21–23 November 2018, Bucharest, organised by UNICEF Regional Office for Europe and Eastern Asia, Ministry of Labour and Social Justice National Authority for the Protection of Children's Rights and Adoption. Retrieved from: https://dorubuzducea.ro/conferinta-internationala-strengthening-the-social-work-and-social-service-workforce-in-europe-central-asia-investing-in-our-childrens-future/. Accessed 25 Aug 2020.

Cojocaru, Ş., & Cojocaru, D. (2008). *Managementul de caz în protecţia copilului: evaluarea serviciilor şi practicilor din România* [Case management in child protection: Evaluation of services and practices in Romania]. Iaşi: Polirom.

Cojocaru, D., Cojocaru, S., & Sandu, A. (2011). The role of religion in the system of social and medical services in post-communism Romania. *Journal for the Study of Religions and Ideologies, 10*(28), 65–83.

Cozărescu, M. (2012). *Pedagogia socială de la teorie la practică* [Social pedagogy – From theory to practice]. Bucharest: Editura Universităţii din Bucureşti.

Dale, G., & Fabry, A. (2018). Neoliberalism in Eastern Europe and the Former Soviet Union. In D. Cahill, M. Cooper, M. Konings, & D. Primrose (Eds.), *The SAGE handbook of neoliberalism* (pp. 234–247). London: SAGE Publications Ltd.

Deacon, B. (1993). Developments in east European social policy. In C. Jones (Ed.), *New perspectives on the welfare state in Europe* (pp. 177–197). London: Routledge.

Deacon, B. (2000). Eastern European welfare states: The impact of the politics of globalization. *Journal of European Social Policy, 10*(2), 146–161.

Dickens, J., & Serghi, C. (2000). Attitudes to child care reform in Romania: Findings from a survey of Romanian social workers. *European Journal of Social Work, 3*(3), 247–260.

Esping-Andersen, G. (1990). *The three worlds of welfare capitalism.* Princeton: Princeton University Press.

Eurostat. (2019a). *People at risk of poverty or social exclusion by age and sex*, ilc_peps01.

Eurostat. (2019b). *Income poverty statistics.* Retrieved from: https://ec.europa.eu/eurostat/statistics-explained/index.php?title=Income_poverty_statisticsandoldid=440992. Accessed 25 Aug 2020.

Fenger, H. (2007). Welfare regimes in Central and Eastern Europe: Incorporating post-communist countries in a welfare regime typology. *Contemporary Issues and Ideas in Social Sciences, 3*(2), 1–30.

Ferrera, M. (1996). The 'Southern model' of welfare in social Europe. *Journal of European Social Policy, 6*(1), 17–37.

Goian, C. (2013). The success of the social work apparatus in the Banat region. *Analele Ştiinţifice ale Universităţii "Alexandru Ioan Cuza" din Iaşi. Sociologie şi Asistenţă Socială, 6*(2), 31–39.

Haggard, S., & Kaufman, R. R. (2008). *Development, democracy, and welfare states: Latin America, East Asia, and eastern Europe.* Princeton: Princeton University Press.

Hotărârea nr. 326/2019 privind aprobarea Nomenclatorului domeniilor şi al specializărilor/programelor de studii universitare şi a structurii instituţiilor de Învăţământ superior pentru anul universitar 2019-2020 [Decision no.326/2019 for the approval of Nomenclature of domains and specialisation/university education programmes and the structure of higher education institutions for the academic year 2019-2020]. Publicat În Monitorul Oficial, Partea I nr. 467 din 10 iunie 2019. Formă aplicabilă la 13 iunie 2019.

Iovu, M. B., & Runcan, P. (2012). Evidence-based practice: Knowledge, attitudes, and beliefs of social workers in Romania. *Revista de cercetare si interventie sociala, 38*, 54–70.

Law no. 466/2004 on the statute of social workers.

Lazăr, F. (2000). Statul bunăstării din Romania in căutarea identităţii [Romanian welfare state looking for an identity]. *Calitatea Vieţii, 1–4*, 7–37.

Lazăr, F. (2009). Persoanele cu handicap [People with disabilities]. In M. Preda (Ed.), *Riscuri si inechităti sociale în România. Raportul Comisiei Prezidentiale pentru Analiza Riscurilor Sociale si Demografice* [Social risks and inequities in Romania. Report of the presidential commission for analysis of social and demographic risks] (pp. 206–226). Iaşi: Polirom.

Lazăr, F. (2015a). *Profilul asistenţilor sociali din România* [The profile of social workers from Romania]. Timişoara: Editura de Vest.

Lazăr, F. (2015b). *Patimile asistentei sociale din Romania* [The sufferings of Romanian social work]. Bucharest: Tritonic.

Lazăr, F. (2015c). Social work and welfare policy in Romania: History and current challenges. *Quaderni del Csal, Numero speciale di Visioni LatinoAmericane, Anno VII, Numero 13, Luglio,* 65–82.

Lazăr, F., Degi, C. L., & Iovu, M. B. (2016). *Renaşterea unei profesii sau despre cum este să fii asistent social în România* [Rebirth of a profession or what is like to be a social worker in Romania]. Bucharest: Tritonic.

Lazăr, F., Mihai, A., Gaba, D., Rentea, G., Ciocanel, A., & Munch, S. (2017). *Social workers in Romania: Who, what, where, how?* Unpublished report.

Lazăr, F., Marinescu, V., & Branea, S. (2018). *Dincolo de senzaţional. Imaginea asistenţilor sociali din România în mass-media: 2010–2016* [Beyond sensational. The image of social workers from Romania in mass-media]. Bucharest: Tritonic.

Leibfried, S. (1993). Towards a European welfare state? On integrating poverty regimes into the European community. In C. Jones (Ed.), *New perspectives on the welfare state in Europe* (pp. 133–153). London: Routledge.

Mănoiu, F., & Epureanu, V. (1996). *Asistenţa socială în România* [Social work in Romania]. Bucharest: All.

Mănuilă, V. (1936). Asistenta sociala ca factor de politică socială [Social work as a social policy factor]. ARHIVA PENTRU ŞTIINTA ŞI REFORMA SOCIALA *Omagiu Profesorului D. GUSTI: II. XXV de ani de Invatamant Universitar (1910–1935),* Anul XIV, 960–963.

Ministerul Educatiei Nationale [Ministry of Education]. (2018). *Raport privind starea Învăţământului superior din România 2017–2018* [Report on the state of higher education in Romania 2017–2018]. Retrieved from: https://www.edu.ro/sites/default/files/Raport%20privind%20starea%20învăţământului%20superior%20din%20România_%202017%20-2018.pdf. Accessed 25 Aug 2020.

Ministry of Labour, Family, Social Protection and Elderly. (2015). *National strategy on social inclusion and poverty reduction 2015–2020*. Retrieved from http://www.mmuncii.ro/j33/ images/Documente/Familie/2016/StrategyVol1EN_web.pdf. Accessed 25 Aug 2020.

National College of Social Workers. (2019). *Hotărârea Biroului Executiv nr. 147 din 13 decembrie 2019 privind aprobarea Registrului Naţional al Asistenţilor Sociali din România* [Executive Office Decision no. 147/13 December 2019 to approve the National Register of social workers in Romania]. Retrieved online from: http://www.cnasr.ro/module/registru-cnasr/unu/1. Accessed 25 Aug 2020.

National Institute of Statistics. (2013). *Recensământul populaţiei şi locuinţelor, 2011* [Population and housing census, 2011]. Retrieved from: http://www.insse.ro. Accessed 25 Aug 2020.

Nelson, C. A., Zeanah, C. H., Fox, N. A., Marshall, P. J., Smyke, A. T., & Guthrie, D. (2007). Cognitive recovery in socially deprived young children: The Bucharest early intervention project. *Science, 318*(5858), 1937–1940.

Ordin Nr. 393/630/4236/2017 din 13 martie 2017 pentru aprobarea Protocolului de colaborare În vederea implementării serviciilor comunitare integrate necesare prevenirii excluziunii sociale şi combaterii sărăciei [Order to approve the protocol of collaboration to implement the integrated community services to prevent social exclusion and fight poverty].

Ordinul Nr. 288/2006 pentru aprobarea Standardelor minime obligatorii privind managementul de caz În domeniul protecţiei drepturilor copilului [Order no.288/2996 to approve the Minimum standards for case management in child protection].

Pop, L. M. (2002). *Dicţionar de politici sociale* [Dictionary of social policies]. Bucharest: Expert.

Preda, M. (2002). *Politica socială românească între sărăcie si globalizare* [Romanian social policy, between poverty and globalisation]. Iaşi: Polirom.

Preda, M. (Ed.). (2009). *Riscuri si inechităţi sociale in Romania* [Social risks and inequities in Romania]. Iaşi: Polirom.

Roman, A., Oşvat, C., & Marc, C. (2015). Programele de Asistenţă Socială (nivel licenţă) [Social work programmes (undegraduate level)]. In A. Hatos (Ed.), *Ghid orientativ: Sociologie şi Asistenţă socială pe piaţa muncii* [Guide: Sociology and social work on the labour market] (pp. 35–54). Cluj-Napoca: Presa Universitară Clujeană.

Sorescu, E. M. (2015). Social work in the rural area from Dolj County, Romania. *European Scientific Journal, ESJ, 11*(10), 367–379.

Tesliuc, E., Grigoras, V., & Stanculescu, M. (2015). *Background study for the national strategy on social inclusion and poverty reduction, 2015–2020*. Bucharest: World Bank.

Văcărescu, T. E. (2011). Coopter et écarter. Les femmes dans la recherche sociologique et l'intervention sociale dans la Roumanie de l'entre-deux-guerres. *Les études sociales, 153–154*(1), 109–142.

Văcărescu, T. E. (2014). Contexte de gen: roluri, drepturi şi mişcări ale femeilor din România la sfârşitul secolului al XIX-lea şi la începutul secolului XX [Gender contexts: Roles, rights and movements of women from Romania at the end of XIX century and beginning of XX century]. *Sociologie Românească, 1–2*, 92–118.

Walsh, T., Griffiths, W. H., McColgan, M., & Ross, J. (2005). Trans-national curriculum development: Reflecting on experiences in Romania. *Social Work Education, 24*(1), 19–36.

Zamfir, C. (1999). *Politici sociale în România: 1990–1998* [Social policies in Romania: 1990–1998]. Bucharest: Editura Expert.

Zamfir, E., & Zamfir, C. (coord.) (1995). *Politici sociale: România În context european* [Social policies: Romania in a European context]. Bucharest: Editura Alternative.

Social Work Education in the United Kingdom

Steven Lucas and Hakan Acar

1 Introduction and Historical Background

In this chapter we provide a general overview of arrangements for the education of social workers in the United Kingdom and offer a summary of the regulatory regime which not only protects the professional status of social workers but also informs the standards and benchmarks set for education and continuing professional development (CPD). In doing so we reflect on the costs and benefits of this close regulatory relationship with the national government and offer some analysis of the challenges this has presented, and continues to present, to the future identity and autonomy of UK social work.

Whilst the English region is the largest area of the UK population and is governed directly by the UK parliament, recent decades have seen a process of devolution of national statutory powers to the regions of Scotland, Northern Ireland and Wales. While each of the four regions has had a devolved parliament since 1998, the historical trajectory in each case has been distinct. Equally, while the range of reserved powers retained by the UK parliament varies from region to region, for historical reasons each of the devolved regions exercises control over health and social services.

For example, Scotland has had a separate legal system which pre-dates the establishment of a United Kingdom and has required a distinct legislative programme for social work prior to devolution in 1998. Northern Ireland has developed a unique trajectory in social work due to the political instability and paramilitary history of the twentieth century. In 2016 the Welsh National Assembly's Social Services and Wellbeing Act (2014) came into force and reflects both a distinctly Welsh approach and wider global trends in uniting child and family and adult social work in a single,

S. Lucas · H. Acar (✉)
School of Social Science, Liverpool Hope University, Liverpool, UK
e-mail: lucass1@hope.ac.uk; acarh@hope.ac.uk

© Springer Nature Switzerland AG 2021
M. Laging, N. Žganec (eds.), *Social Work Education in Europe*,
European Social Work Education and Practice,
https://doi.org/10.1007/978-3-030-69701-3_11

outcome-focused, statutory framework. England itself currently has the most complex regulatory arrangements in the UK and has driven a strong neoliberal privatisation agenda. Here the engagement of the private sector in so-called fast-track postgraduate qualifying programmes and a post-qualifying accreditation test for child and family social workers has proved controversial and is discussed further in what follows.

But before taking a closer look at regional differences, we discuss the historical roots of social work and social work education more generally in the UK.

1.1 Historical Roots (1800–1920)

In the UK, the origins of social work are most frequently attributed to two distinct ideological strands, from three areas of early social work activity. The industrial wealth of nineteenth-century philanthropists funded the Charity Organisation Society (COS), associated with a moralising and disciplinary approach to the poor and vulnerable in society. In contrast, an important social action strand is represented in the work of settlements and of individual pioneers who championed the need for welfare programmes, including public health measures and decent housing and education. The settlements championed and provided direct provision for particular vulnerable groups, such as children. Together with the 'statutory' strand emerging from the centralising of Poor Law provisions, these two strands were harbingers of the contemporary statutorily focused casework tradition representing the standard UK model of professional social work. Within this contemporary social work model we find the same polarities of individual moral discipline or solidarity and social justice within its canon, procedure, and practice (Walton 1975, cited in Lyons 2018: 1).

By the early twentieth century, the need to 'educate' of 'social workers' was recognised in Britain (beyond the training of volunteers already provided through COS), and courses were developed at universities such as London (LSE 1903/1912) and Birmingham (1908) (Lyons 2018: 1). During this early period the education and training of social workers emerged from a variety of independent initiatives across the health and welfare sector.

It was not until the major transformations of the 1970s that there was a step-change in the bringing together of practitioners and educational pathways into a unified and regulated national system.

1.2 A Unified Profession (1970–1990)

It would not be until 1970, following the influential Seebohm Report of 1968 (Seebohm 1968), that the Local Authority Social Services Act (LASSA 1970) created unified social service departments in the local state. And not until then were there attempts to create a unified social work with a professional identity in the UK. An umbrella organisation for various professional associations had been established in 1963, known as the Standing Conference of Organisations of Social Work. The eight member groups were the Association of Social Workers, the Association of Family Caseworkers, the Association of Moral Welfare Workers ('moral welfare' was in large part work with unmarried mothers), the Association of Child Care Officers, the Society of Mental Welfare Officers, the Association of Psychiatric Social Workers, the Institute of Medical Social Workers and the National Association of Probation Officers. Despite tensions among them, the various professional associations formed a unified body in 1970, the British Association of Social Workers (BASW) (McDougall 1970, cited in Dickens 2011). The only member group of the Standing Conference that did not join was the National Association of Probation Officers. However, probation remained a social work profession, and probation officers continued to be trained in social work courses until the 1990s despite remaining a separate service throughout the UK. The exception here is Scotland, where criminal justice work was absorbed into local state generic social work teams until the increased moves towards specialisation that accompanied the marketisation of state services in the 1990s (Dickens 2011: 29). Although probation officers in Northern Ireland have a separate regulatory body, a degree in social work is compulsory for working as a probation officer in Northern Ireland (PBNI 2019).

Linked with the goals of having generic social work departments in the local state and a unified profession, the third limb of the reforms concerned social work training. Five bodies provided or approved qualifying-level social work courses (Seebohm 1968, Appendix M). The Council for Training in Social Work approved non-university courses, leading to the certificate in social work, which was the principal qualification for social workers in the health and welfare departments; the Central Training Council in Child Care approved courses in universities and other institutions and awarded a letter of recognition to successful graduates; the Advisory Council for Probation and Aftercare approved university-based and other probation courses; the Institute of Medical Social Workers ran a 1-year course itself and approved other university programmes; and the Association of Psychiatric Social Workers approved a number of university-based courses. Seebohm observed that, although most social work courses claimed to provide a generic education, nearly all students were recruited for, and funded by, a specific service, and Seebohm considered this 'an impediment' to genuinely common training (Seebohm 1968: 165; Dickens 2011: 25).

As for social work education, the LASSA Act (1970) created the Central Council for Education and Training in Social Work (CCETSW), which came into being in 1971. It incorporated the three national councils and the training functions of the two professional associations and launched the generic Certificate of Qualification in Social Work (CQSW) in 1972. This qualification was awarded to graduates of approved courses, which could be at the master's, bachelor's or sub-degree level. (It was replaced by the Diploma in Social Work in 1989 and by the social work degree in 2003. CCETSW was replaced by the General Social Care Council in 2001) (Dickens 2011: 28).

The Seebohm (1968) vision of social work shared with the Scottish Kilbrandon Report (The Scottish Government 1964) was a local community-orientated vision promoting ideals around localism and co-production, engaging service users and professionals within a responsive local state planning apparatus. However, the impending economic crisis of the 1970s impinged greatly on the ambitions of Seebohm and led to the introduction of cost restraints and rationing that, for all intents and purposes, put paid to the advancement of a community development social work role. The highly state-regulated casework model of social work in the UK was established across the regions of the UK during this period.

1.3 Neoliberal Modernisation 1990s

Esping-Andersen (1990) categorises the United Kingdom as a 'liberal' regime of welfare. Liberal welfare regimes would tend towards lower levels of state intervention, leaving market forces to establish a level of social security to which the state makes modest reallocations (Isakjee 2017: 5–6). Similarly, Aspalter (2001: 8) claims that "The United Kingdom developed a unique form of welfare capitalism that is mainly based on flat rate universal social security programmes." Aspalter argued that "Tony Blair's New Labour Party of the 1990's, in essence, pursues the same set of Conservative social policies as did the Conservative Governments before. Not extensive redistributive programs but work incentives and less welfare dependency have become core arguments of the New Labour."

In parallel with the shift in welfare policies, the 1990s saw social work in the UK having to respond to watershed legislation and policy change in each of the main branches of its activity – children and families, community care and criminal justice. Primed as it was by the arrival of a neoliberal economic and political context of the 1980s, it moved – enthusiastically for some, with resistance from others – into the managerial culture of the 1990s. This was an era marked by the introduction of marketisation, privatisation and the prevailing negative assessment of highly unionised state service provision. The social work role and labour process was transformed through the introduction of the purchaser provider split and the care manager role bringing a steady retreat from direct work towards ever more technically aided assessment functions and the mantra of consumer choice as a means to drive a modernisation process (Harris 2009; Garrett 2009; Jones 2001). Social work across the UK struggled with a social context that included rising crime coupled with rising unemployment and a strong emphasis on managing 'outcomes' – a word never before connected with welfare services and swiftly adopted by the 'new managers' (Cowen 1999, cited in Gregory and Holloway 2005: 46). Government and political opposition offered a neoliberal consensus marked by decreasing focus on underlying structural causes accompanied instead by a corresponding increase in the public scapegoating of vulnerable groups such as the unemployed, youth and single mothers (Pilcher and Wagg 1996).

The New Labour government explicitly promoted this general orientation in social services as part of its modernising agenda (Webb 2001). Many common contemporary ideas were developed in this period, including notions of partnership between public and private and citizen and state. Citizenship in social policy was offered as a renewed contract of responsibility rather than the entitlement of the Welfare State (Clarke and Newman 1997). Corporate, targeted, outcome-led strategic planning and evidence-based practice especially suit a privatised and competitive market for services.

The concept of case or care management spread from the UK to virtually all European countries, giving rise to new courses and qualifications, with Germany (Wendt 1997, cited in Lorenz 2008: 16) and Italy (Paladino and Cerizza Tosoni 2000, cited in Lorenz 2008: 16) taking up the concept especially eagerly. In the UK the competence approach to social work education was introduced, and we discuss this development further in what follows.

At this stage we pause the UK-wide narrative to look at the regions of the UK and contemporary and historical developments found there.

2   The Four Nations

Before setting out the regional arrangements for education, we offer a brief profile of social work in the four countries composing the United Kingdom.

Northern Ireland

Social workers in Northern Ireland, both in practice and in the academy, are still reconsidering their roles in social service provision and addressing the post-conflict legacies of poverty, inequality and social exclusion (Heenan 2004, cited in Moore 2018: 386). The issues of sectarianism and the period of 'the Troubles' have had a particular impact on the development of professional social work in Northern Ireland (Houston 2008; Pinkerton and Campbell 2002, cited in Das O'Neill and Pinkerton 2016: 199). For example, Pinkerton and Campbell (2002, cited in Ramon et al. 2006: 436) suggest that during the conflict in Northern Ireland, social workers were very unlikely to challenge the causes and manifestations of sectarian violence because it was safer to adapt a 'technocratic' neutral stance.

During this very difficult period, many social workers in Northern Ireland attempted to provide services in a 'non-sectarian' manner, which focused on delivering services and largely ignored the issues of sectarianism (Houston 2008; Pinkerton and Campbell 2002). This strategy enabled social workers to reach clients as well as protect themselves while working in a deeply divided context. However, this also resulted in a delay in the development of anti-sectarian approaches. This de-politicisation of social work through withdrawal from community and emphasis on 'client'-based work (Houston 2008) meant that social work in Northern Ireland disengaged from an analysis of politics and power and had little capacity to develop a social justice agenda. (Houston 2008; Pinkerton and Campbell 2002, cited in Das O'Neill and Pinkerton 2016: 199).

Professionalism, adherence to a medical model of clinical detachment, and the notion of 'rising above' sectarianism classified practice during the conflict. Smyth and Campbell (1996, cited in Moore 2018: 386) argued that sectarianism actually provided a rationalisation for the removal of local service provision to non-sectarian government bodies. Despite being created to eradicate biases and prejudice from practice, it resulted in a social service sector that was removed from clients and from tackling discrimination in Northern Ireland, creating a practice culture that discouraged an open discussion of sectarianism and its influence on social work practice. Social workers, for example, often had to collaborate with paramilitary forces in certain neighbourhoods in order to gain access to communities and individuals. Additionally, certain policies, such as child-care provision in child welfare, saw services split down sectarian lines, similarly to the educational system, which is still organised by religion, with only 5% of the schools in Northern Ireland desegregated to this day (Houston 2008, cited in Moore 2018: 386).

Wales

The Care Council for Wales exercises regulatory power over professional social work education and practice throughout the sector in Wales since granted through the Care Standards Act 2000. Social workers need to register with the Care Council, although successful completion of a professional course accepted by other regulatory bodies in the UK is accepted as sufficient by the Care and Social Services Inspectorate for Wales (CSSIW).

In 2004, reflecting developments across the UK, new degree courses set up a minimum degree-level qualification for social work. The framework established through the Care Council for Wales looks much like that in other UK devolved regions, including a set of National Occupational Standards (NOS) for professional practice, quality assurance and subject benchmark statements for social work higher education institutions (HEIs) to meet as a requirement for courses (QAA 2019). One additional condition of the Welsh NOS and Quality Assurance Agency (QAA) benchmarks is the explicit requirement to integrate measures under the Welsh Language Act 1993 and the Welsh Language Measure 2011. This duty requires that social workers understand and promote in practice the desirability of assessing need and providing services in a service user's and carer's preferred language. Welsh is widely spoken as the first language of choice in many parts of Wales.

Wales has legislated for its own statutory social work framework and the Social Services and Wellbeing Act 2014 came into force in April 2016. The act is a distinctive departure from some of the language and emphasis of the UK acts it largely replaces, not least because it combines adult and child services into one act using a similar language of eligibility for care and support. However, it also reflects wider trends in service delivery and policy frameworks developed in England and other UK regions. The fundamental principles of the 2014 act include the following:

- Voice and control for service users
- Prevention and early intervention

- Well-being
- Co-production between professionals and service user organisations

Scotland

Social work in Scotland reflects many of the themes apparent in social work throughout the UK, though it has some distinctive features. The distinct judiciary and legal system of Scotland has existed since before the union of parliaments with England in 1707. While there is a Supreme Court in England, the distinct Scottish legal system also means that legislation in Scotland, although it may reflect themes similar to those in English legislation, is subject to the devolved parliament which has sat in Edinburgh since 2001.

Social work graduates in Scotland can register with the UK Social Work England (SWE) body or the Scottish Social Services Council (SSSC), which was set up in 2001 by the Regulation of Care Act (Scotland) 2001. Standards for social work education in Scotland are defined by the framework of Standards in Social Work Education (SiSWE) derived from previous UK NOS. They were set up with a degree programme in 2006 and are currently under review as part of a wider evaluation of social work education in Scotland being undertaken by the Scottish government and the Convention of Scottish Local Authorities (COSLA).

In addition, within Scotland there is another requirement for students to meet 'key capabilities in child care and protection' aligned with the SiSWE generic document (Scottish Executive 2006).

The main distinctive features of Scottish social work's institutional and legal arrangements within the UK relate to children's social work and criminal justice. During the 1960s when the generic local authority social work teams were formed across the UK, the influential Kilbrandon Report (The Scottish Government 1964) promoted a welfare-oriented view of youth justice in response to concerns over youth crime. The foundational Social Work (Scotland) Act (1968) established the Children's Hearing System, which engages a panel of trained lay people to hear cases and approve and review care plans where grounds of referral are established, either with reference to a higher court proof hearing, if need be, or through an acceptance of grounds by young persons and their parents or carers. Grounds may include either offences against a child or committed by a child.

Another distinctive feature of the Scottish social work system is that probation work with adult offenders is also a part of the local authority's social work responsibility, albeit a specialised service, unlike in England, Wales and Northern Ireland, where there is a separate, centrally managed National Probation Service.

In many respects the devolved parliament has sheltered Scotland from the worst of the ravages of austerity south of the border, and Scotland has deservedly gained recognition for rendering more generous support to vulnerable people with free prescriptions, free travel on registered local and long-distance buses, a greater financial commitment to provide free personal care services for the elderly, and no fees for university students. In addition, in Scotland social workers and social work education have largely escaped the kind of public humiliation and scrutiny meted out in England under the close regulatory supervision of the national UK parliament and main media conglomerates. However, as Smith and Cree (2018) note, there has been no significant challenge to the market-orientated, managerial paradigm dominating the statutory domain.

3 Contemporary Social Work Education Prospectus Across UK

Social work regulation is organised through four different regulators across the UK. The newly established SWE is only responsible for social worker regulation in England, while the SSSC operates in Scotland, the Northern Ireland Social Care Council (NISCC) in Northern Ireland and Social Care Wales in Wales. The degree in social work is the recognised professional qualification for social workers throughout the UK, as well as for probation officers and education officers in Northern Ireland and criminal justice social workers in Scotland.

Social work education takes 3 (three) years (full-time bachelor's degree) in England, Northern Ireland and Wales. However, the standard undergraduate degree is 4 (four) years in Scotland. UK tuition fees vary depending on the home country. English universities can charge up to a maximum of £9250 per year for an undergraduate degree. Institutions in Wales can charge up to £9000 for home students, and universities in Northern Ireland can charge up to £4275 per year. There are different fee policies for international students as well (UKCISA 2019). In Scotland students do not have to pay tuition to the university. Instead, they can apply for government funding to pay fees whether they choose to study in Scotland or elsewhere in the UK (Scottish Government 2019). There are bursaries available for UK resident social work students in the four regions of the UK.

It is worth noting that qualifying social workers in the different regions can apply for registration throughout the UK due to a memorandum of understanding between the four countries to allow the movement of social workers. This enables social workers to register in the different parts of the UK. This applies to social work degree holders from all generic social work programmes. However, in Wales, Scotland and Northern Ireland, the position with respect to specialist fast-track, non-generic programmes, such as Frontline, Step Up or any other specialist fast-track programmes, is that they are 'entitling' qualifications that will require additional compensatory measures to meet standards for generic training set by the regional authorities. If applicants have a degree in a different subject, they may apply for a fast-track programme. Step-Up to Social Work is a funded 14-month intensive training programme, Frontline is a funded 2-year training course, and Think Ahead is a graduate programme for those who wish to become mental health social workers.

Practice education (placements) in social work education differs slightly in the four regions of the UK. Students are required to spend 170 days for practice education in England plus 30 additional so-called skills days, this number is 180 days in

Wales. In Scotland students must spend 200 days in practice learning, of which at least 160 must be spent in supervised direct practice in service delivery settings. Up to 60 days of the supervised direct practice element can be subject to credit from prior experiential learning (Scottish Executive 2003). In Northern Ireland students are required to undertake a total of 225 days of practice learning, of which 25 days must be spent in preparation for direct work with service users, 185 days must be in direct supervised practice, 85 days at level 2 and 100 days at level 3, and 15 days are to be used for individual practice development (NISCC 2019).

All four regulatory bodies have professional development policies for registered, practising social workers. The regulatory bodies have structured policies on practice education, CPD, educational routes and financial support which shape social work education across the UK. Many of these educational policies in social work have commonalities as well as differences which reflect regional characteristics.

In England, registered social workers must meet five CPD standards, as follows:

1. Maintain a continuous, up-to-date and accurate record of CPD activities.
2. Demonstrate that CPD activities are a mixture of learning activities relevant to current or future practice.
3. Seek to ensure that CPD has contributed to the quality of practice and service delivery.
4. Seek to ensure that CPD benefits service users.
5. Upon request, present a written profile (which must be their own work and supported by evidence) explaining how they have met the standards for CPD (HCPC 2019). The English regulatory body, HCPC, indicates that 'CPD ensures that you continue to develop new skills throughout your career, meaning you can practice safely. If a registrant cannot prove they have kept up their CPD, they may be removed from the Register' (ibid).

In Scotland, every registered social worker must undertake post-registration training and learning consisting of study, training, courses, seminars, reading, teaching or other activities which could reasonably be expected to advance the social worker's professional development or contribute to the development of the profession as a whole. The SSSC stipulates annually 24 days (144 h) of training and learning for newly qualified social workers and 15 days (90 h) for experienced social workers (Scottish Executive 2003).

In Wales, there are post-registration training and learning (PRTL) requirements of 15 days or 90 h of learning every 3 years. This programme must be completed to fulfil a mandatory requirement for continuing registration for practice as a social worker in Wales.

In Northern Ireland, the Professionals in Practice (PiP) programme lays out the requirements for social workers (PiP 2019). The PiP programme offers social workers two routes. The first route is referred to as 'credit accumulation', which offers post-registration training and learning and recognises all CPD activity. The programme defines the second route as an 'individual assessment route', which offers potential for self-directed learning to be assessed in fulfilment of PiP requirements or awards (NISCC 2016).

3.1 Employment Across the UK

Across the UK qualified social workers are mostly employed in the local authority statutory sector. Available figures from England, Scotland and Wales stand close to 80% as an approximate percentage (Department for Education 2020; Skills for Care 2017; Care Council for Wales 2014). This includes employment in Child and Family Teams and Adult Social Work Teams largely in fieldwork roles involving casework with service users and their families. Workforce statistics are not uniformly available, however. According to data collection sources in England and supported by data from Scotland and Wales, the voluntary sector, while offering a growing range of direct service provision to a range of adult- and child-based service user groups, offers a minority of openings for qualified professional social work employment (Department for Education 2020; UK Civil Society NCVO 2019; Skills for Care 2017; Local Government Data Unit – Wales 2019). In England the turnover rate of staff is around 16%, with a consistent need for new qualified staff in child and adult sectors. There is also an increasing trend towards agency staff largely filling vacant posts. The overall vacancy rate across England has tended recently to vary substantially from region to region but averages around 16%. Social workers in England tend to be more ethnically diverse than the rest of the local authority workforce, and 21% are from black and minority ethnic (BAME) backgrounds.

The residential social work sector across the UK, for both children and adults, has historically been considered to be relatively undertrained and heavily dependent on agency staff who are not qualified as social workers (Narey 2016). Scotland is unique in developing a distinct degree-level programme for residential care staff in child-care services (SSSC 2015). The Scottish aspiration is to eventually establish a regulatory framework for a professional qualification in residential child care.

The health sector has specialised mental health social roles with a prescribed statutory role in dealing with mental health assessments, where secure orders are considered by health professionals. These Approved Mental Health Professionals (AMHPs) tend to be experienced social workers with several years of experience in social work practice (Skills for Care 2019). Generally across the UK, health services are funded by devolved government through the National Health Service (NHS), and social care services are funded through local authorities. The integration of health and social care has become a political and practical problem for service providers. Currently social workers tend to be employed by local authorities in adult community teams or through social work units based in hospital settings (Parkin 2019). Management and funding of social work posts in integrated health settings across the UK are part of the complex arrangements forming a small but growing part of the social worker workforce (ADASS 2018). In August 2019 NHS England announced plans to directly employ up to 600 social workers as part of a strategic plan for mental health services for adults and children (NHS England 2019).

4   Challenges of Education and Regulation in UK

In this section of the chapter we look at some of the major themes in contemporary UK social work education. Earlier we introduced historical developments in social work at least since the key institutional and regulatory developments in the mid-twentieth century. These are the developments which brought unified generic social work and social service departments within the local state into being and began a process of professional social work education and, eventually, a regulatory framework by the beginning of the twenty-first century. These have been modified over time through the global political and social developments of the neoliberal period (Garrett 2010; Cleary 2017; Parker 2019; Bamford 2015; Murphy 2016; Ferguson 2016; Dominelli 2007). Here we consider only some of the themes as they have impacted social work education in the contemporary situation in terms of challenge and opportunity to social work both in practice and in the academy.

4.1   *Academisation*

We have already shown how the educational frameworks for social work education were brought to a university-level degree structure across the UK seated firmly within universities. One element of this process is the development of an academic body of research within the academy itself. Moriarty et al. (2015) surveyed 249 social work academics across the UK regions and found that 70% were active in research. Forty-three percent of respondents had a PhD. Their respondents, however, also gave a clear account of the challenges faced where the demands of teaching and administering a professional programme of practice learning represent a significant drain on resources of time and energy for pursuing research. On average, some 25% of the time of the respondent academics was devoted to research activity, while administration was closer to 31% of the available time. Marsh and Fisher (2005) underlined the poverty of available research funding devoted to social work and social care, and resource issues have posed a challenge to the growth and development of social work research in the UK. If there is a paradigmatic approach to research in the UK, it might be said to have strong themes of qualitative and emancipatory methodologies (Shaw and Lorenz 2016).

The establishment of a degree programme has brought with it the promotion of a research-minded element to the curriculum. The benchmarking QAA statement for social work and the regulatory frameworks have also included the teaching and practice of research methodologies within the curriculum (QAA 2019). Regulated master's and bachelor's social work programmes across UK regions must include a research component, which will commonly include a dissertation assessment, although this is not mandatory for a social work practitioner qualification at the diploma level.

Having completed our overview of the social work academy, we now explore some challenges to the social work academy in the UK which have accompanied the professional regulation of social work as a practice with a statutory role.

4.2   Professional Regulation

Over the decades since the 1960s and 1970s, when the foundations for a government social work service were laid down, one could see this process as one filled with tension and often a struggle between models of social work both as idea and practice. Firstly, there is a model of an outward looking profession with an eye towards the establishment of a global social work identity and solidarity aligned with the international agenda for human rights (Higgins 2015; Dominelli 2007). This is a politically independent and confident voice engaging service users' knowledge and linking domestic agendas to global ones of social rights from housing, poverty and anti-racism to standpoint identity social movements, community politics and sustainable futures. This includes more informal social work often cited as part of an early radical and more political tradition (Jones and Lavalette 2014).

The other model is the professionalism of the statutory agent of the state, which reflects some of the former but is wedded to statutory protocol and an increased professional distance from service users, reflecting more of the care and control agenda of the state. This idea of social work could be said to institutionalise the instincts of the former and both modify and codify the politics through training, regulation and statutory guidance. This is largely the employer and government version of social work. Higgins (2016) contrasts these as a double curriculum in social work education which seeks to serve both perspectives.

The development of the social work degree in the UK in 2003, in line with the European Bologna Process, promoted and enabled the compatibility of professional social work qualifications throughout Europe. The regulation and protected title also support a developing professional identity. However, Welbourne (2011) draws attention to the ongoing paradox of a state policy agenda explicitly based around the idea of empowerment and greater professionalisation but characterised by an undermining of that professional autonomy through a close and often disciplinary relationship of governance in the regulatory framework.

In the aftermath of serious case reviews, public inquiries and government-commissioned reports, social work in the UK has at the same time faced seemingly relentless attacks on the proficiency and professional credibility of social workers and social work education. These attacks have actively sought to silence critiques from within the profession highlighting the growing evidence of the effects of fiscal austerity, poverty and child welfare inequalities resulting from the predominant risk-focused social policy in place (Bywaters et al. 2014; Bilson and Martin 2017). The resulting friction between the profession, government and employers is increasingly fraught in the era of privatisation and marketised responses to social need in the post-2008 austerity United Kingdom (Cleary 2017; Bamford 2015; Jones 2001, 2018).

The new social work degree in England was only allowed a brief honeymoon before the death of Peter Connolly (Baby P) in 2007 triggered a bout of horse trading between governments and media giants that pre-empted any measured evaluation of professional social work education under the new degree (Jones 2015, 2018; Moriarty and Manthorpe 2013, 2014). After a round of public sackings and humiliation of social workers, the New Labour government, now 12 years in office, set up the Social Work Task Force (2009) which, following consultation, acknowledged serious employer reservations about the quality of social work education. Moriarty and Manthorpe (2013) noted submissions expressing reservations under five themes: skills and knowledge graduates should acquire during their qualifying education, assessment methods, systems for accrediting university courses, curriculum content, and procedures for selecting suitable candidates for educational programmes. Moriarty and Manthorpe's (ibid) review of available evidence as part of an evaluation of the degree programme found little to either confirm or disprove these concerns.

4.3   From Competence to Capability

The Social Work Reform Board and in turn the College of Social Work carried on the work to develop a professional developmental agenda for social work in England. After creating the Professional Capability Framework (PCF) for education and CPD from student through to senior social work management the Social Work College was dropped and became financially insolvent in 2015 when the Conservative and Liberal Democrat coalition government awarded the contract for the future accreditation of child and family social workers to a private company and withdrew financial backing for the college. The PCF, however, was passed on to BASW to maintain.

The difference between the competence and capability approaches, as advanced by the PCF, has generated some discussion and a fair amount of hope for the significant evolution of professional education and CPD of social work in England (Higgins 2016; Bamford 2015; Jasper and Field 2016). The earlier competence-based system for practice assessment drew some criticism for its limited scope as a basic tool to tick boxes and assess what students could and could not do using inventories of practical task-focused indicators (Dominelli 2007). The capability framework sets out to encompass a wider remit, which is more holistic, and make it possible to track progress on a developmental pathway (Taylor and Bogo 2013; Higgins 2016). Recently revised in 2018 by BASW, it includes nine domains: professionalism, values and ethics, equality and diversity, rights justice and economic well-being, knowledge, critical reflection and analysis, skills and interventions, context and organisations, and professional leadership (BASW 2019). Each is reflected in developmental parameters at nine levels: from acceptance into a qualifying course as a student, through readiness for fieldwork placements, to a supported year of employment (ASYE) for newly qualified social workers, and on to include more advanced practitioners and senior managers in the field. While the PCF has offered a framework attracting significant support from the profession, it occupies an insecure position in the developing apparatus of regulation at this point following the demise of the Social Work College and its transfer to the professional association of social workers (BASW). The new regulator, SWE (since December 2019), may well inaugurate a new chapter of change. The new regulator has meanwhile appointed a board with one currently registered social worker only and is chaired by a former social worker, Lord Patel, now no longer registered. Other questions from the academy, aside from the issue of a representative voice from frontline social work, relate to the extent to which the new body will be independent of the government of the day and reflect the perspectives of the professional body of social workers and educators (Haynes 2018).

Two reviews of social work education in England were commissioned, reporting in 2014, and they offered alternative perspectives reflecting the disputed double curriculum evident with regard to social work education. The Narey Report, anecdotal and polemical in style, reflects the technical approach, challenging the social justice perspective and finding favour with the government of the day. This report strongly disapproved a perceived over-emphasis on educating social work students on politics, ideology and social justice whilst advocating a specialist training for child social work (Narey 2014; Bamford 2015). The Narey Report was commissioned by Michael Gove, then Education Secretary in the Cameron government, who suggested on the 12 November 2013 that social work education 'involves idealistic students being told that the individuals with whom they will work have been disempowered by society…This analysis is, sadly, as widespread as it is pernicious' (Gove 2013: no pagination).

The other report, by Croisdale-Appleby (2014), a more rigorously evidence-based report, offered a more generous or expansive professional ideal of the social worker as a practitioner, a professional and a social scientist. Whilst both reports discussed a more rigorous approach to recruitment, including by raising academic requirements for applicants at the degree level, Narey recommended a move towards specialisation within training, and Croisdale-Appleby supported continuing the generic degree approach. These reports have kept the focus on the education and training of social workers, and in particular child and family social workers. Though the generic degree has remained fundamental in the other regions in England, it has not been very secure.

A brief statement of government intentions for further social work reform followed the Narey and Croisdale-Appleby reports (Department for Education 2016). Subsequently, the government produced two specialised Knowledge and Skills (KSS) statements, one for children and families, in 2014, and another for adults in 2015, which provide a set of specialised standards for social workers after 1 year in statutory practice. Altogether, there are now three points of reference to guide professional social workers in England. Further, for child and family social workers, an accreditation scheme (NAAS) being piloted and scheduled for general introduction in England will introduce a test of proficiency without which social workers will not be approved for statutory child and family work. This additional accreditation process has been met with statements ranging from reluctance to forthright opposition from across the social work sector, including a recommendation from the main social workers union to boycott the scheme. Private-sector piloting arrangements were scaled back, and now a general roll-out of the scheme is expected in 2020.

4.4   Teaching Partnerships

Another plank of the government regulation and reform process has been a teaching partnership scheme drawing higher education institutions (HEIs) into closer engagement with employers. Teaching partnerships were piloted in 2015 and have been supported with further funding following an evaluation in 2016 (Berry-Lound et al. 2016). The teaching partnerships bring groups of HEIs and employers into strategic partnership with mutually agreed arrangements for student recruitment and training. The rationale for the partnerships is to raise standards in social education through co-production, including service users and employers, from recruitment, improvement in statutory placement opportunities, better recruitment practice for students, and closer collaboration between partners over teaching curriculum to support of CPD, the child and family social worker national assessment and accreditation system (NAAS) and other government regulatory initiatives.

4.5   Fast-Track Social Work Education

The introduction of so-called fast-track social work courses in the mental health and child and family social work fields in England has been a controversial move which has challenged the academy and threatens university master's programmes while placing further pressure on the generic social work education approach. The first such scheme, Step Up to Social Work, was initiated in 2009 as a government initiative to address the issues of recruitment and retention of child and family social workers in England. A Department for Education commissioned evaluation was favourable in 2018 (Smith et al. 2018). While the Step Up to Social Work programme and the mental social work programme, Think Ahead, are offered through university teaching partnerships, Frontline has developed as a private business initiative and has cut its initial partnership link with Bedfordshire University to challenge the academic route to social work in a more fundamental way. These postgraduate programmes require a 2:1 degree for entry and offer a guaranteed salaried position in a local authority upon qualifying. With a bursary that far exceeds university courses, these courses are attractive to postgraduate applicants, and government funding has expanded their availability. Frontline recently received a £45 million grant from the government to expand its programme to a target of 900 applicants. Analyses from academia, particularly in the social work professional press, have been scathing in their criticisms of the lack of formal academic input, the lack of reference to social justice, and the basic premise of government funding for an expensive privatised elite route into social work (Gupta and SocialWhatNow 2018; Jones 2018; Murphy 2016). Frontline participants, in year one, work 206 days with one employer in a small supervised group with two other Frontline participants. They receive 46 days of teaching and a government bursary. In the second year they become a fully salaried and registered social worker and can complete their ASYE year as a newly qualified social worker at the postgraduate diploma level. They may but are not obliged to work towards their master's degree by submitting a dissertation. Fast-track courses face challenges, however, with respect to their recognition further afield, and this has been cast in doubt by the Scottish and other care councils who require a generic qualification, as do European Association of Schools of Social Work (EASSW) affiliated programmes throughout Europe. Some master's-level university courses are already facing closure at universities in England, and the future impact of fast-track schemes on university master's programmes is causing widespread concern in the university sector. The growth of an array of apprenticeship and post-qualifying master's and advanced practitioner courses is increasingly becoming a viable option for universities as they turn to opportunities for CPD.

This privatisation agenda in social work education and service delivery has effectively undermined some of the oppositional potential to these challenges facing the university sector. A substantial and powerful lobby now exists, drawing on government funding, for the various projects of the privatised and marketing process; particularly significant have been the fast-track social work courses and arrangements for the accreditation of child and family social workers (Jones 2018).

5   Concluding Discussion

This chapter has offered a general overview of the history and development of social work education in the UK, offering details on devolved regional disparities and central governance from the national government. National arrangements throughout the regions of England, Scotland, Northern Ireland and Wales reflect similar features of development as they have a shared history and overarching structural similarity with respect to professional regulation and educational arrangements. However, with the development of devolved powers and legislative independence in matters of social work, there are significant divergences, which were summarised with an acknowledged central focus on contemporary developments in the context of the English region and the national parliament. We have highlighted professional regulation as a central theme which has conditioned developments in social work education as in practice. Global themes of neoliberal economic policies, managerialism and marketised growth within the sector are representative of international challenges being faced by the field throughout Europe.

While we note the seemingly strong position of a professionally regulated and protected professional title, we find that the very closeness with government this relationship entails serves as a constant and enduring challenge to the social justice perspective and to social work as a self-confident and politically aware profession. We have also noted the central challenges to the academy in universities, including the struggle against the divisions sowed by the establishment of privatised markets in social work provision and in the context of neoliberal state-sponsored pathways for fast-track educational development and accreditation.

Equally, the recovery, if it does come, from the years of austerity and unsustainable environmental catastrophe will require a profession ready to re-invigorate the latent community development and neighbourhood social work part of the vision of social work that emerged in the early years of the 1960s and 1970s in the UK.

References

ADASS (Directors of Adult Social Services). (2018). *AMHPs, Mental Health Act assessments and the mental health social care workforce*. Available from: https://www.adass.org.uk/media/6428/nhsbn-and-adass-social-care-national-report.pdf. Accessed 8 Apr 2020.

Aspalter, C. (2001). *Different worlds of welfare capitalism: Australia, the United States, the United Kingdom, Sweden, Germany, Italy, Hong Kong and Singapore*. Discussion paper no. 80. Available from: https://pdfs.semanticscholar.org/1e50/cf413e77883e1fed48ba5e898f9c944eab83.pdf?_ga=2.207282960.2065742173.1586293547-1894886558.1577661264. Accessed 7 April 2020.

Bamford, T. (2015). *A contemporary history of social work*. Bristol: Policy Press.

Berry-Lound, D., Tate, S., & Greatbatch, D. (2016). *Social work teaching partnership programme pilots: Evaluation: Final Research Report*. Available from https://www.gov.uk/government/publications/social-work-teaching-partnerships-programme-pilots-evaluation. Accessed 12th March 2021.

Bilson, A., & Martin, K. E. C. (2017). Referrals and child protection in England: One in five children referred to children's services and one in nineteen investigated before the age of five. *British Journal of Social Work, 47*(3), 793–811. https://doi.org/10.1093/bjsw/bcw054.

British Association of Social Workers (BASW). (2019). *The professional capability framework*. Retrieved from: https://www.basw.co.uk/professional-development/professional-capabilities-framework-pcf. Accessed 4 June 2019.

Bywaters, P., Brady, G., Sparks, T., & Bos, E. (2014). Inequalities in child welfare intervention rates: The intersection of deprivation and identity. *Child & Family Social Work, 21*(4), 452–463. https://doi.org/10.1111/cfs.12161.

Care Council for Wales. (2014). *Register of social care workers June 2014*. Available from: https://socialcare.wales/cms_assets/file-uploads/The-Profile-of-Social-Workers-in-Wales-2014.pdf. Accessed 2 Apr 2020.

Clarke, J., & Newman, J. (1997). *The managerial state: Power, politics and ideology in the remaking of social welfare*. London: Sage.

Cleary, T. (2017). Social work education and the marketisation of UK universities. *The British Journal of Social Work, 48*(8), 1–19.

Cowen, H. (1999). Community care, ideology and social policy. In M. Gregory, & M. Holloway (2005). Language and shaping the social work. *British Journal of Social Work, 35*(1), 37–53.

Croisdale-Appleby, D. (2014). *Re-visioning social work education: An independent review of social work education*. London: Department of Health.

Department for Education. (2016). *Children's social care reform. A vision for change*. Available from, https://www.gov.uk/government/publications/childrenssocial-care-reform-a-vision-for-change. Accessed 12th March 2021.

Department for Education. (2020). *Official statistics: Children and family social work workforce in England, year ending 30 September 2019*. Available from: https://assets.publishing.service. gov.uk/government/uploads/system/uploads/attachment_data/file/868384/CSWW_2018-19_ Text.pdf. Accessed 30 Mar 2020.

Dickens, J. (2011). Social work in England at a watershed—As always: From the Seebohm report to the social work task force. *British Journal of Social Work, 41*(1), 22–39.

Dominelli, L. (2007). Contemporary challenges to social work education in the United Kingdom. *Australian Social Work, 60*(1), 29–45.

Esping-Andersen, G. (1990). *The three worlds of welfare capitalism*. Princeton: Princeton University Press.

Ferguson, I. (2016). Hope over fear: Social work education towards 2025. *European Journal of Social Work, 20*(3), 322–332.

Garrett, P. M. (2009). *Transforming children's services?* Maidenhead: Open University Press.

Garrett, P. M. (2010). Examining the "conservative revolution": Neoliberalism and social work education. *Social Work Education, 29*(4), 340–355.

Gove, M. (2013). *Gove speech to the NSPCC: Getting it right for children in need*. Retrieved from: https://www.gov.uk/government/speeches/getting-it-right-for-children-in-need-speech-to-the-nspcc. Accessed 4 June 2019.

Gregory, M., & Holloway, M. (2005). Language and shaping the social work. *British Journal of Social Work, 35*(1), 37–53.

Gupta, A., & SocialWhatNow. (2018). Frontline training scheme poses a threat to social work education. *The Guardian*. 16th October. Available from: https://www.theguardian.com/ society/2018/oct/16/frontline-training-scheme-threat-social-work-education. Accessed 4 June 2019.

Harris, J. (2009). Customer-citizenship in modernised social work. In J. Harris & V. White (Eds.), *Modernising social work*. Bristol: Policy Press.

Haynes, L. (2018). *Lack of registered social workers on Social Work England board criticised*. Community Care. Available at: https://www.communitycare.co.uk/2019/04/18/social-work-englands-failure-appoint-registrants-board-criticised-sector/?utm_content=Story%20of%20 the%20week&utm_campaign=CC%20Snapshot%2018-04-19&utm_source=Community%20 Care&utm_medium=adestra_email&utm_term=https%3A%2F%2Fwww.communitycare. co.uk%2F2019%2F04%2F18%2Fsocial-work-englands-failure-appoint-registrants-board-criticised-sector%2F. Accessed 4 June 2019.

HCPC (Health and Care Professions Council). (2019). *Standards of continuing professional development*. Available from: https://www.hcpc-uk.org/standards/standards-of-continuing-professional-development/. Accessed 4 June 2019.

Heenan, D. (2004). Learning lessons from the past or re-visiting old mistakes: Social work and community development in Northern Ireland. *British Journal of Social Work 34*(6), 793–809. In M. W. Moore (2018). Social work practitioners in post-conflict Northern Ireland: Lessons from a critical ethnography. *International Social Work, 61*(3), 383–394.

Higgins, M. (2015). The struggle for the soul of social work in England. *Social Work Education, 34*(1), 4–16.

Higgins, M. (2016). How has the professional capabilities framework changed social work education and practice in England? *British Journal of Social Work, 46*(7), 1981–1996.

Houston, S. (2008). Transcending ethno-religious identities: Social work's role in the struggle for recognition in Northern Ireland. *Australian Social Work, 61*(1), 25–41. https://doi. org/10.1080/03124070701818716. In C. Das, M. O'Neill, & J. Pinkerton (2016). Re-engaging with community work as a method of practice in social work: A view from Northern Ireland. *Journal of Social Work, 16*(2), 196–215.

Isakjee, A. (2017). *Welfare state regimes: A literature review* (IRiS working paper series, no. 18/2017 (UPWEB working paper series, no. 5/2017)). Birmingham: Institute for Research into Superdiversity.

Jasper, C., & Field, P. (2016). An active conversation each week in supervision: Practice educator experiences of the professional capabilities framework and holistic assessment. *British Journal of Social Work, 46*(6), 1636–1653.

Jones, C. (2001). Voices from the front line: State social workers and new labour. *British Journal of Social Work, 31*(4), 547–562.

Jones, R. (2015). The end game: The marketisation and privatisation of children's social work and child protection. *Critical Social Policy, 35*(4), 447–469.

Jones, R. (2018). *In whose interest? The privatisation of child protection and social work.* Bristol: Policy Press.

Jones, C., & Lavalette, M. (2014). The two souls of social work: Exploring the roots of "popular social work" – Popular or radical social work? *Critical and Radical Social Work, 2*(3), 381–383.

Local Authority Social Services Act. (1970). Retrieved from: https://www.legislation.gov.uk/ukpga/1970/42. Accessed 6 Apr 2020.

Local Government Data Unit – Wales. (2019). *Social worker's workforce planning 2017-18.* A National Report on the Social Worker Workforce in Wales. Available from https://social-care.wales/cms_assets/file-uploads/Social_Worker_Workforce_Planning_2017_18_eng.pdf. Accessed 12th March 2021.

Lorenz, W. (2008). Towards a European model of social work. *Australian Social Work, 61*(1), 7–24.

Lyons, K. H. (2018). Social work education in Europe: A retrospective view (accepted version). *Practice: Social Work in Action, 31*(1), 5–19. Available from: http://repository.londonmet.ac.uk/4572/. Accessed 4 Apr 2020.

Marsh, P., & Fisher, M. (2005). *Developing the evidence base for social work and social care practice.* London: Social Care Institute for Excellence.

McDougall, K. (1970). A chairman's eye view. *Social Work Today, 1*(1), 5–10. In J. Dickens (2011). Social work in England at a watershed—as always: From the Seebohm Report to the Social Work Task Force. *British Journal of Social Work, 41*(1), 22–39.

Moriarty, J., & Manthorpe, J. (2013). Shared expectations? Reforming the social work qualifying curriculum in England. *Social Work Education, 32*(7), 841–853.

Moriarty, J., & Manthorpe, J. (2014). Controversy in the curriculum: What do we know about the content of the social work qualifying curriculum in England? *Social Work Education, 33*(1), 77–90.

Moriarty, J., Manthorpe, J., Stevens, M., & Hussein, S. (2015). Educators or researchers? Barriers and facilitators to undertaking research among UK social work academics. *British Journal of Social Work, 45*(6), 1659–1677.

Murphy, T. (2016). The frontline programme: Conservative ideology and the creation of a social work officer class. *Critical and Radical Social Work, 4*(2), 279–287.

Narey, S. M. (2014). *Making the education of social workers consistently effective: Report of Sir Martin Narey's independent review of the education of children's social workers.* Department for Education. Available from: https://www.gov.uk/government/publications/making-the-education-of-social-workers-consistently-effective. Accessed 7 Apr 2020.

Narey, S. M. (2016). *Residential care in England report of Sir Martin Narey's independent review of children's residential care.* Department for Education. Available from: https://www.gov.uk/government/publications/childrens-residential-care-in-england. Accessed 3 Apr 2020.

NCVO. (2019). *UK Civil Society Almanac 2019.* Available from: https://data.ncvo.org.uk/workforce/. Accessed 4 Apr 2020.

NHS (National Health Services). (2019). *Mental health implementation plan 2019/20 – 2023/24.* Available from: https://www.longtermplan.nhs.uk/wp-content/uploads/2019/07/nhs-mental-health-implementation-plan-2019-20-2023-24.pdf. Accessed 9 Apr 2020.

NISCC (Northern Ireland Social Care Council). (2016). *Professional in practice: The CPD framework for social work.* Accessed from: https://learningzone.niscc.info/files/pip_flip_leaflet.pdf. Accessed 4 June 2019.

NISCC (Northern Ireland Social Care Council). (2019). *(NISCC) Degree in social work*. Available from: https://niscc.info/degree-in-social-work. Accessed 4 June 2019.

Paladino, M., & Cerizza Tosoni, T. (2000). Il case management nella realtà socio-sanitaria Italiana. In W. Lorenz (2008). Towards a European model of social work. *Australian Social Work*, 61(1), 7–24.

Parker, J. (2019). Descent or dissent? A future of social work education in the UK post-Brexit. *European Journal of Social Work*, 23(5), 837–848. Available at: https://www.tandfonline.com/doi/full/10.1080/13691457.2019.1578733

Parkin, E. (2019). *Health and social care integration*. Briefing paper. Number 7902. House of Commons Library. Available from:https://commonslibrary.parliament.uk/research-briefings/cbp-7902/. Accessed 5 Apr 2020.

PBNI (Probation Board Northern Ireland). (2019). Retrieved from: https://www.pbni.org.uk/recruitment/work-experience/. Accessed 1 June 2019.

Pilcher, J., & Wagg, S. (1996). *Thatcher's children? Politics, childhood and society in the 1980s and 1990s*. London: Falmer Press.

Pinkerton, J., & Campbell, J. (2002). Social work and social justice in Northern Ireland: Towards a new occupational space. *British Journal of Social Work*, 32(6), 723–737. https://doi.org/10.1093/bjsw/32.6.723. In C. Das, M. O'Neill, & J. Pinkerton (2016). Re-engaging with community work as a method of practice in social work: A view from Northern Ireland. *Journal of Social Work*, 16(2), 196–215.

PiP Programme (Professionals in Practice). Further info: https://niscc.info/storage/resources/20160416_pip_cpd_booklet.pdf. Accessed 20 May 2019.

QAA (The Quality Assurance Agency for Higher Education). (2016). *Social work: Subject benchmark statement*. Gloucester: QAAHE.

QAA (The Quality Assurance Agency for Higher Education). (2019). *Social work: Subject benchmark statement*. Gloucester: QAAHE.

Ramon, S., Campbell, J., Lindsay, J., McCrystal, P., & Baidou, N. (2006). The impact of political conflict on social work: Experiences from Northern Ireland, Israel and Palestine. *British Journal of Social Work*, 36(3), 435–450. https://doi.org/10.1093/bjsw/bcl009. In C. Das, M. O'Neill, & J. Pinkerton (2016). Re-engaging with community work as a method of practice in social work: A view from Northern Ireland. *Journal of Social Work*, 16(2), 196–215.

Seebohm Report of the Interdepartmental Committee on Local Authority and Allied Personal Social Services. (1968). Accessed from: http://filestore.nationalarchives.gov.uk/pdfs/small/cab-129-138-c-88.pdf. Accessed 7 Apr 2020.

Scottish Executive. (2003). *Framework for social work education*. Retrieved from: https://www.gov.scot/publications/framework-social-work-education-scotland/pages/1/. Accessed 4 June 2019.

Scottish Executive. (2006). *Key capabilities in child care*. Edinburgh: Scottish Executive.

Shaw, I., & Lorenz, W. (2016). Editorial-special issue: Private troubles or public issues? Challenges for social work research. *European Journal of Social Work*, 19(3–4), 305–309. https://doi.org/10.1080/13691457.2016.1168081.

Skills for Care. (2017). *Headline social worker statistics*. Retrieved from: https://www.skillsforcare.org.uk/Documents/NMDS-SC-and-intelligence/NMDS-SC/Social-Worker-headline-data.pdf. Accessed 2 Apr 2020.

Skills for Care. (2019). *Approved mental health professional (AMHP) workforce*. Available from: https://www.skillsforcare.org.uk/adult-social-care-workforce-data/Workforce-intelligence/publications/Topics/Social-work/Approved-Mental-Health-Professional-workforce.aspx. Accessed 3 Apr 2020.

Smith, M., & Cree, V. (2018). Introduction. In M. Smith & V. Cree (Eds.), *Social work in a changing Scotland*. London: Routledge.

Smith, R., Stepanova, E., Venn, L., Carpenter, J., & Patsios, D. (2018). *Evaluation of step up to social work, Cohorts 1 and 2: 3-years and 5-years on, research report*. Department for Education. Available from: https://assets.publishing.service.gov.uk/government/uploads/system/uploads/attachment_data/file/707085/Step_Up_to_Social_Work_evaluation-3_and_5_years_on.pdf. Accessed 1 Apr 2020.

Smyth, M., & Campbell, J. (1996). Social work, sectarianism and anti-sectarian practice in Northern Ireland. *British Journal of Social Work*, 26, 77–92. In M. W. Moore (2018). Social work practitioners in post-conflict Northern Ireland: Lessons from a critical ethnography. *International Social Work*, *61*(3), 383–394.

Social Services and Well-Being Act. (2014). Retrieved from: https://www.legislation.gov.uk/anaw/2014/4/contents. Accessed 7 Apr 2020.

Social Work (Scotland) Act. (1968). Retrieved from: https://www.legislation.gov.uk/ukpga/1968/49/contents. Accessed 7 Apr 2020.

Social Work Task Force. (2009). *Building a safe, confident future*. Available at: http://webarchive.nationalarchives.gov.uk/20130401151715/https://www.education.gov.uk/publications/standard/publicationdetail/page1/dcsf-01114-2009. Accessed 7 Apr 2020.

SSSC (Scottish Social Services Council). (2015). *The standard for residential child care in Scotland*. Retrieved from https://www.sssc.uk.com/_entity/annotation/a1bdfcf4-a050-872c-bb2c-df648e72dfeb. Accessed 12 March 2021.

Taylor, I., & Bogo, M. (2013). Perfect opportunity perfect storm? Raising the standards of social work education in England. *British Journal of Social Work*, *44*(6), 1402–1418.

The Scottish Government. (1964). *The Kilbrandon report*. Retrieved from: https://www.gov.scot/publications/kilbrandon-report/pages/4/accessed. Accessed 7 Apr 2020.

The Scottish Government. (2019). *Tuition fees for university*. Retrieved from: https://www.mygov.scot/tuition-fees/. Accessed 4 June 2019.

UKCISA (UK Council for International Student Affairs). (2019). Retrieved from: https://www.ukcisa.org.uk. Accessed 4 June 2019.

Walton, R. (1975). Women in social work. In K. H. Lyons (2018). Social work education in Europe: A retrospective view (accepted version). *Practice: Social Work in Action*, *31*(1), 5–19. Available from: http://repository.londonmet.ac.uk/4572/. Accessed 4 Apr 2020.

Webb, S. A. (2001). Some considerations on the validity of evidence-based practice in social work. *British Journal of Social Work*, *31*(1), 57–59.

Welbourne, P. (2011). Twenty-first century social work: The influence of political context on public service provision in social work education and service delivery. *European Journal of Social Work*, *14*(3), 403–420.

Wendt, W. R. (1997). Case-management im Sozial- und Gesundheitswesen: Eine Einfuhrung. In W. Lorenz (2008). Towards a European model of social work. *Australian Social Work*, *61*(1), 7–24.

Correction to: Social Work and Social Work Education in Germany: Development and Challenges in a Scientific and Practice-Based Profession and Its Education

Marion Laging, Peter Schäfer, and Miriam Lorenz

Correction to:
Chapter 5 in: M. Laging, N. Žganec (eds.), *Social Work Education in Europe,* **European Social Work Education and Practice, https://doi.org/10.1007/978-3-030-69701-3_5**

Owing to an oversight on the part of Springer, an incorrect URL was placed in the references section of the chapter which has been corrected. The correct URL has been given below.

Correct URL:
https://www.fbts-ev.de/qualifikationsrahmen-soziale-arbeit

The updated version of this chapter can be found at
https://doi.org/10.1007/978-3-030-69701-3_5

© Springer Nature Switzerland AG 2021   C1
M. Laging, N. Žganec (eds.), *Social Work Education in Europe,*
European Social Work Education and Practice,
https://doi.org/10.1007/978-3-030-69701-3_12